Car Crime

Crime and Society Series

Series editor: Hazel Croall

Published titles
Sex Crime, by Terry Thomas
Burglary, by R. I. Mawby
Armed Robbery, by Roger Matthews
Car Crime, by Claire Corbett

Car Crime

Claire Corbett

WILLAN
PUBLISHING

Published by

Willan Publishing
Culmcott House
Mill Street, Uffculme
Cullompton, Devon
EX15 3AT, UK
Tel: +44(0)1884 840337
Fax: +44(0)1884 840251
e-mail: info@willanpublishing.co.uk
website: www.willanpublishing.co.uk

Published simultaneously in the USA and Canada by

Willan Publishing
c/o ISBS, 5824 N.E. Hassalo St,
Portland, Oregon 97213-3644, USA
Tel: +001(0)503 287 3093
Fax: +001(0)503 280 8832
e-mail: info@isbs.com
website: www.isbs.com

First published 2003

ISBN 1-84392-025-5 (cased)
ISBN 1-84392-024-7 (paper)

British Library Cataloguing-in-Publication Data

A catalogue record for this book is available from the British Library

Project management by Deer Park Productions
Typeset by GCS, Leighton Buzzard, Beds
Printed and bound by T.J. International, Padstow, Cornwall

Contents

Table of cases		*ix*
List of tables		*xi*
Preface		*xiii*

1 Car culture and the construction of car crime **1**
Our embeddedness within car culture 1
Why a book on car crime? 3
What is car crime? 4
Theoretical perspectives on car crime 8
Key themes of the book and chapter outline 11
Summary of main points 13

2 The car in historical context **15**
Introduction 15
A privilege of the elite 16
Increasing accessibility and road casualties 18
Towards the millennium and the challenges ahead 20
Summary of main points 23

3 Not real crime? **25**
Introduction 25
Illustrations of the low perceived seriousness of road
  traffic offending 25
Explanations for the low seriousness accorded road
  traffic offending 28
Concluding comments 34
Summary of main points 34

4 'Car crime' as theft of and from a vehicle 37
  Car crime as theft 37
  Historical and legal context of car theft 39
  The extent and trends of vehicle theft 40
  Vehicle theft for contents and parts 48
  Vehicle theft for temporary use: joyriding 50
  Vehicle theft for permanent deprivation: professional theft 59
  Crime control efforts 62
  Concluding comments 68
  Summary of main points 70

5 Impaired driving: alcohol, drugs and fatigue 72
  Introduction 72
  Historical and legal context of impaired driving offences 75
  Alcohol-impaired driving 78
  Drug-impaired driving: illegal drugs 86
  Drug-impaired driving: legal drugs 88
  Fatigue-impaired driving 91
  Crime control efforts 94
  Concluding comments 101
  Summary of main points 102

6 Speeding 104
  Introduction 104
  Historical and legal context of speeding 107
  Extent and trends in speeding 109
  Female and male drivers compared 118
  Crime control efforts 120
  Concluding comments 125
  Summary of main points 126

7 Bad driving: dangerous and careless offences 128
  Introduction 128
  Historical and legal context of bad driving 131
  Extent and trends in bad driving offences 133
  Road rage 141
  Mobile phones and other in-vehicle distractions 143
  Police vehicle accidents (PVAs) 147
  The perspectives of victims and the bereaved 149
  Crime control efforts 154
  Concluding comments 157
  Summary of main points 159

8 Unlicensed driving   **161**
Introduction   161
Historical and legal context of unlicensed driving   163
Extent and trends in unlicensed driving   164
Crime control efforts   170
Abandoned and untaxed vehicles (AUVs)   172
Concluding comments   175
Summary of main points   176

9 Car crime in wider society   **177**
Introduction   177
The power of motor manufacturers   179
Work-related road risk   184
Concluding comments   188
Summary of main points   189

10 Past, present and future directions   **190**
Introduction   190
Legacy of the past   191
Concerns and dilemmas of the present   193
Future prospects   196
Back to the centre   201

References   202
Index   225

Table of cases

Beresford (Harold) Re [1952] 36 Cr App R1 149
Davis [2002] 1 Cr App R (S) 579 103
R *v.* Adomako [1994] 3 All ER 79 131
R *v.* Simmonds [1999] 2 Cr App R18 130
Rylands *v.* Fletcher [1866] WL 8245 35
Smith *v.* DPP [1999] 96(34) LSG 34 160
State of Indiana *v.* Ford Motor Co. (1979) 180

Tables

4.1 Comparison of recorded and BCS vehicle-related thefts in
    2001–2   42
4.2 Attrition rates estimated from British Crime Survey for
    theft-related offences (2001–2)   43
4.3 Comparison of recorded and BCS vehicle-related trends:
    percentage decline between 1991 and 2001–2   44
4.4 Prevalence of involvement of young people in car theft in
    England and Wales in 1992   52
5.1 Estimates of all GB road accident casualties where illegal
    alcohol levels were found among drivers and riders,
    adjusted for under-reporting   79
5.2 Drivers and riders screened in roadside breath tests:
    England and Wales   79
5.3 'Over the last month how often did you drink and drive
    when you may have been over the legal limit for drinking
    and driving?'   81
6.1 Proportions of cars travelling in excess of speed limits in
    2000 (%)   109
6.2 Proportions of cars exceeding posted limits on different
    road types, 1996–2000 (%)   110
6.3 Numbers of speed limit offences prosecuted in 1997 and
    2000   111
6.4 Proportions of European drivers who reported speeding
    at least 'often' on different kinds of roads, and percentage
    change between 1992 and 1997: selected countries   112
6.5 Penalty points on driving licence by sex and age (%)   119

7.1 Trends in bad driving offences since 1961: England
and Wales (thousands of offences)   133
7.2 Outcomes of bad driving offences dealt with by official
action in 2000: England and Wales (%)   134
7.3 Initial and final outcomes of a sample of fatal accident cases
occurring between 1989 and 1995 in England and Wales (%)   135
7.4 Profile of offenders convicted of bad driving offences 2000:
England and Wales   137
8.1 Driving licence offences proceeded against and findings of
guilt – England and Wales 2000   164
8.2 Prevalence of previous convictions among disqualified
drivers and mainstream offenders (%)   168

Preface

The idea for this book had been germinating for a while in view of the interdisciplinary nature of my earlier research and, when approached by Hazel Croall, the editor of this series, I agreed with some trepidation to try to put 'car crime' on the map for criminologists. What I had in mind was that car crime should be viewed as more than 'theft of and from vehicles', which tends to be the traditional conception, and that it was heavily intertwined with car culture and comprised other things.

Yet what I thought would be a fairly easy and quick book to write turned out to be the opposite. My underestimation of the complexity of the task was compounded by a growth in interest and research in many topics related to car crime during the period spent working on the text, with the consequence that my conceptualisation of the essence of the book continued to evolve until the final stages. The end result is somewhat different from what I had originally imagined, and not all will agree with my thesis. Nevertheless, I hope it will stimulate criminological interest in this still under-researched field and will encourage others to explore further. Pursuit of knowledge into car crime of all kinds is highly worth while and ultimately should benefit all of us.

I am very grateful for the help of many people in supplying information when requested, without which it would have been a far more difficult task. I am particularly appreciative of the encouragement given by my parents and the 'newspaper cuttings service' provided by my mum. I am also indebted to the great help and moral support given by Andy Ward when needed, and I thank Brian Solomons for reading early drafts, Kevin Stenson for encouragement and Maureen Purbrook for being there. Thanks are due to Brunel University for providing a few months' study leave, though much of this was completed in my 'spare' time. For this latter reason I acknowledge the forbearance of my daughter, Phoebe, and warm thanks are also due to Tony Aylett, for being a real friend. Finally, as often said at this point, any errors are all mine and apologies are sent.

Claire Corbett

Chapter 1

Car culture and the construction of car crime

Our embeddedness within car culture

The last century saw everyday lives, global economies and national infrastructures constructed around motor cars and the culture they have spawned. Growing dependence on the car is fast enveloping most countries. In 1997 in Europe four-fifths of all land travel was undertaken by car,[1] and almost one private car was owned for every two citizens.[2] In 1998, over half (54 per cent) of the European population held driving licences.[3] World traffic volumes are forecast to quadruple between 1990 and 2050 with the largest increases in developing countries (Red Cross and Red Crescent Societies 1998). The world's embeddedness in car culture looks certain. This has positive aspects, but negative ones are swiftly accumulating with alarming future global consequences.

The door-to-door convenience, ease of mobility, freedom and the supposed saving of time are generally seen as the greatest benefits of car usage (RAC 2000). Cars have been rated the second most popular item on people's wish list of possessions[4] and almost half of car-less young people want to own one more than anything else.[5] Other surveys reinforce the chilling extent of our emotional dependence on private motorised transport. The British Crime Survey 2000 (Kershaw *et al.*, 2000)[6] found that more car-theft victims were 'very much' affected than people who reported a violent incident, and most car owners believe that having a car was essential to their lives and being without would be disastrous (Lex 1999: 16–17). Cars for some are also linked with enhancing fun, thrills, excitement, status and image; hence the ceaseless interest in luxury, sports and performance cars which if not to own are to admire via glossy magazines or by watching Formula One races which can each attract 350 million global viewers (Hotten 1999).

Aside from their multiple positive uses, cars add considerably to levels of environmental pollution. According to the Department of Health (1998), air pollution contributes to the early death of up to 24,000 Britons per year, and exhaust emissions are strongly linked with lung cancer, heart disease, bronchitis and asthma.[7, 8] Traffic congestion causes huge financial loss to the national economy and great personal loss to drivers (RAC 2000), and lack of exercise, frustration and stress from driving, and back pain caused by poorly fitting car seats, deplete drivers' health (e.g. Porter 1999).

Perhaps the most disquieting product of car culture, however, is the huge worldwide crash death toll. In 1999, almost 46,000 were killed in road collisions in Europe, around 42,000 in the USA and 10,000 in Japan (DTLR 2001c: Table 8.7); global fatalities were estimated to have reached 880,000 and were set to rise, with 85 per cent of these occurring in developing countries where few own vehicles (Jacobs *et al.* 2000). Moreover, up to 34 million worldwide are estimated to be injured in road collisions annually costing in excess of US$500 billion (ibid.), and it has been calculated that road deaths will constitute the world's third biggest killer by 2020. They are currently the main cause of death for 15–24-year-olds (Red Cross and Red Crescent Societies 1998).

The challenge for international governments is how best to harmonise the competing interests of car culture – meeting the demands for more roads to facilitate safe, smooth and swift vehicle movement while simultaneously reducing the negative environmental consequences. Governments must appease polarised lobbying groups, road safety organisations, motor manufacturing groups, pedestrian and cycling associations and the driving public – and retain the electorate's support. Accommodating the opposing interests of all constituencies has so far proved elusive, and the formulation of comprehensive and coherent policies to encompass the demands and products of car usage looks set to be an ongoing dilemma.

The other long-standing challenge of car culture is deciding how best to regulate road usage and control car-related behaviours to minimise the likelihood of harmful consequences while maximising the benefits associated with car use. The problem is that road users rarely comply with the raft of laws designed to determine the boundaries between acceptable and unacceptable behaviour – so much 'car crime' occurs.

While, as we shall see, definitions of what constitutes car crime are far from straightforward, if the term encompasses road traffic offending – as will be argued here – it would be unwise to dismiss such crime as unimportant. Some road traffic offences are associated with crash involvement (e.g. Forsyth and Silcock 1987; Junger 1994; Junger *et al.* 2001), and with mainstream crime (e.g. Tillman and Hobbs 1949; Willett 1964; Sorenson 1994; Rose 2000; Soothill *et al.* 2002). Indeed, such correlations have led to suggestions of a common aetiology between crash involvement and offending on and off the road; this may have implications for the co-ordination of future health, road safety and crime control policies as some of the same individuals could be the focus of each policy (Junger *et al.* 1995). These connections underline the importance of exploring further the nature of 'car crime' which forms one impetus for this text. Others follow.

Why a book on car crime?

Few texts bring together the breadth of car-related offending covered in this book. Driving is one of the most common and frequent behaviours undertaken by adults in motorised societies, and a significant proportion of it is illegal since few drivers in Britain deny ever breaching traffic laws (Corbett and Simon 1992a), and at least most admit to exceeding speed limits (e.g. Lex, 1997). Many offending behaviours are easily observable, and the lack of stigma attached increases their transparency, and yet relatively little has been written about them by criminologists. Most such offences have national and international applicability; for instance, theft of and from a vehicle are two of the most common forms of global theft (Barclay *et al.* 2001: Tables 1.3., 1.4, 1.5). Moreover, car-related offending is highly topical in view of society's increasing reliance on this means of transport, and a mushrooming media focus indicates that the public is increasingly receptive to debates on car usage, car crime and car culture. Indeed, in view of the high volume of prosecutions for offences connected with road traffic law, people are more likely to come to the attention of police in relation to road traffic matters than in any other way (Department of Transport and Home Office 1988: 30).

Despite offences connected with the car and driving causing tremendous harm, it is particularly interesting that vehicle-related offences generally, and many illegal driving actions specifically, appear not to have been taken seriously by governments aside from occasional rhetoric to the contrary, and neither are they accorded much gravity by society and individual drivers. In fact, in many respects vehicle-related crime is hardly treated as 'real' crime.

Criminologists outside the establishment have largely shied away from an exploration of car crime, and most research has been internally or externally commissioned by the Home Office and the Department for Transport (DfT), which was formerly the DTLR (Department for Transport, Local Government and the Regions), the DETR (Department of the Environment, Transport and the Regions), and the DoT (Department of Transport). Not surprisingly Home Office focus has tended to centre on aspects of vehicle theft offences (e.g. Webb and Laycock 1992), although a few critical contributions on this topic have been ventured by other criminologists (e.g. Groombridge 1994, 1998). Interestingly, Bottoms (1999) thought we might look back on the twentieth century and wonder why car crime was so roundly eschewed by the criminological fraternity which, given the centrality of cars in our lives and a sharpening media focus on car-related matters, is indeed surprising. Perhaps apathy has arisen either because the concerns of car crime are perceived as too distinct and different from mainstream crime, or because it is not generally seen as true crime by criminologists, or because of the influence of powerful vested interests, as Mannheim (1960) ventured.[9] Contributions to a disparate literature have come from other disciplines – from psychologists, geographers, economists and transport scientists – and these will be drawn upon as appropriate. Use too will be made of news media reportage as a prime channel of communication about car crime to the public.

The context here is largely British. However, many issues will be recognised outside the UK, where similar debates are unfolding, and nearly all offences involving the car are worldwide occurrences. Moreover, the range of research studies discussed will have an international flavour as British criminological research into car-related offences is limited.

What is car crime?

The term 'car crime' is in common usage but is rarely followed by a description or definition of what is meant, a shared understanding of the term being assumed although this is not necessarily the case. The category most likely to conjure up the image of 'car crime' is almost certainly when vehicles, their contents or parts become the subject of theft. Such offences are subsumed under the theft laws and together constitute almost one fifth of both officially recorded and self-reported crimes (see Chapter 4). Yet offences involving vehicles and driving cover a far wider terrain. Vehicles are used in the commission of crimes like drug trafficking, smuggling, abduction, burglary and robbery (as 'getaway cars'). In a peripheral sense at least, such offences could be deemed car crimes, as could be cases of 'motor manslaughter', prosecuted under criminal law, where vehicles are used as weapons of assault.

Probably the main expansion to an understanding of car crime would be to encompass all those offences that relate to road traffic law. The number of these created by statute in Britain is vast and including those hidden away in subordinate legislation of regulations and orders – much of which has been amended and extended – probably runs to thousands (Gibson 1994). Road traffic law governs road usage and the operation and enforcement of legislation by police and courts, and offences are of several kinds. The main group relates to standards of driving which fall short of the minimum demanded by law, and others include the construction and use of vehicles such as braking, tyre, weight and lighting requirements, and vehicle document and driver licensing offences.

Strictly speaking all offences under road traffic law are crimes as this is an integral though separate part of the criminal law. Yet despite overlapping features of criminal and road traffic law, the perception persists that traffic crime is qualitatively different (e.g. Department of Transport and Home Office 1988: 20). Certainly acts associated with driving and vehicle use that have the *potential* to cause harm but which do not do so on each occasion are defined as crime under road traffic law which is not often the case under general criminal law, and in general the former aims to avoid collisions rather than to embody moral principle (ibid.). In addition, many 'crimes' on the road comprise a failure to act as or when expected, or are the result of momentary inattention, and some people think this reduces their seriousness, irrespective of the consequences, and means that they are not real crimes. This discourse is bound up with the complex legal principle of intention which is considered in Chapter 3.

Whatever the legal arguments, it would be short-sighted to accept that crimes on or off the road are simply what the law says they are, and criminologists and lawyers are well versed in the competing definitions of what crime is and how it is social constructed, such that only some acts become labelled as crime while other equally or more heinous acts fail to be so defined (e.g. Croall 1998a; Muncie and McLaughlin 2001). For instance, emphasis in the compilation of criminal statistics on 'street' crimes at the expense of 'suite' crimes is frequently critiqued in criminological texts to illustrate how the elite have used constructions of the law to serve their best interests. Thus de Haan (1991: 207) claims that crime is ideologically constructed and 'serves to maintain political power relations, justifies inequality and serves to distract public attention from more serious problems and injustices'.

Such views are often discussed in relation to corporate crime and crimes of the elite where it is pointed out (e.g. Croall 1998a: 270) that dubious business activities are rarely defined as criminal offences and instead tend to be cast as 'problems', 'wrongdoings', 'violations' or 'breaches'. Such 'irregularities' tend not to be enforced by the police but by other agencies whose role may be to encourage compliance with regulations or to provide advice, and prosecution is seen very much as a last resort (ibid.), which if successful tends to attract lenient treatment (ibid.: 272). So 'regulation' rather than recourse to the criminal law has been the dominant model for business crime. Similar arguments can be made with respect to questionable commercial activities linked with vehicle usage, such as discussed in Croall (1998b, 2001).

Critical criminologists commonly highlight the practices of *rulemakers* (institutions and corporations wielding power and influence) rather than individual *rulebreakers* (e.g. Scraton and Chadwick 1991: 161–87). In this regard, the activities of motor manufacturers, businesses using fleet cars, government departments, government agencies and politicians are worth scrutiny when considering behaviours under the broad heading of car crime (see Chapter 9). As examples, in 2000 a thirty-year cover-up of vehicle defects such as dangerous brake fittings was admitted by a prominent motor manufacturer (*Guardian* 30.8.00: 26); in the same year a parliamentary report blamed the Office of Fair Trading (OFT) for failing to deal adequately with unscrupulous car dealers who sell unroadworthy vehicles.[10] These vehicles were described in another official report as 'coffins on wheels' that could be a factor in up to 360 deaths annually (Allen 1999).

Other behaviours that might be perceived as car crime are problematic to measure. For instance, knowingly driving while very tired is common (see Chapter 5) and might be thought of as foolhardy and irresponsible given the raised risk of falling asleep and causing a crash, yet at present legislation would be impractical as well as impossible. Crashes with tiredness as a principal cause can be prosecuted under the catch-all categories of careless or dangerous driving laws, but therein lose their reference to the physical condition of the driver. Eyesight is measurable and usually worsens with age and up to 1 in 10 'would fail the standard driving test if retaken today' (Eyecare Trust 2002; HSA 2002). While the legally required standard of eyesight applies throughout one's driving career, most drivers – excluding lorry-drivers and bus-drivers – are tested only during their practical driving test. For the majority it is largely a perceptual and moral matter to decide if their eyesight is 'sufficiently good' for safe driving and whether they will take remedial steps. Whether it is a 'crime' to drive with sub-standard eyesight may be debatable, but as prevention is limited to self-regulation and compliance with the *Highway code* (rule 81) – that more than two thirds of drivers fail to consult after taking their driving test (RAC Foundation 2001) – it would seem that the danger presented by drivers who cannot see properly to drive is not currently considered important by lawmakers.

Driving without due care and attention covers a catch-all selection of undesired behaviours that are not specifically identified as criminal offences under road traffic law. The law inevitably trails behind the emergence or identification of unacceptable actions because it can be difficult either to draft appropriate legislation or to prosecute a particular behaviour. Mobile phone usage is an example (discussed in Chapter 7).

In actuality, then, no correct way exists of defining what should be deemed 'criminal' or 'crime' in a motoring sphere, but for present purposes the boundaries will be broadly drawn in line with Sutherland's (1949: 31) view that crimes are acts causing social harms or injuries. Sutherland's definition intended to widen out existing conceptions of crime to include infractions of administrative and regulatory codes connected with commerce, and in view of the focus on commercial links to car crime in Chapter 9, this definition will suit well. Certainly the criterion of 'social harm' resulting from car culture would qualify many offences associated with the car as crime, since each road fatality is estimated to cost society over £1.1 million.[11] However, such an interpretation of car crime is unlikely to bring concordance. Indeed, it is partly the lack of societal consensus in agreeing which actions should be treated as criminal that makes the regulation of driving and car usage so difficult to control and sanction. How the offences to be discussed in these chapters get socially constructed as 'crime', 'not crime' or 'not real crime' is an issue we shall revisit. However, an underpinning theme is that constructions of 'car crime' centring on crimes to the car such as vehicle theft are too narrow and should be widened to encompass crimes by drivers and by the vehicle industry; some might argue that in particular instances delay and inaction by the state should be included. In what follows, a broad definition of 'car crime' applies unless otherwise stated.

Theoretical perspectives on car crime

In view of criminological myopia, attempts to theorise car crime have largely been limited to 'theft of and from vehicles'. However, it is possible to apply a range of mainstream criminological theories to other kinds of car crime, even where research does not yet exist.

To set the scene, a sample of factors and theories that may be relevant will be considered here. More detail of how theory has *actually* been applied to car crime research will then follow in the 'explanation' section of each empirical chapter. Inevitably, it will seem that uneven theoretical coverage is given to different offences but this is merely a consequence of limited and patchy research to date. In general, a broad theoretical exposition to advance development and synthesis of car crime is outside the scope of this book and invites attention from others.

Most factors and theories naturally divide into (1) those with an individual focus and (2) those with a social or structural focus. Others combine the influence of all levels and their positioning below is somewhat arbitrary.

Individual-level theories

Deterrence theories
These classically based theories, on which much of the criminal justice penalty system is anchored, say that people will be deterred from offending to the extent they fear the perceived likely penalty multiplied by their fear of receiving it (detection and prosecution). Swiftness in receiving the penalty, the social stigma involved and moral commitment to the law are other factors sometimes included in deterrence equations. Deterrence is of two kinds: that intended to deter potential offenders through the threat of future punishment (general deterrence) and that to deter convicted offenders through the impact of the last penalty (specific deterrence). Deterrence theorists explain the scale and prevalence of all car crime (whether involving individuals, businesses or corporations) by inadequate levels of deterrence. Results of deterrence policies applied to mainstream and car crime tend to be mixed.

Rational choice perspective
This explanation arose from Home Office interest in situational measures to prevent crime. It is linked with the neoclassical perspective of offenders as rational beings, weighing up the opportunities, costs and benefits of committing a particular criminal act (Clarke and Cornish 1985). This perspective emphasises that because crimes differ in the

needs they serve and in the demands they make of potential offenders, rational choice is crime-specific and can be applied to any kind of offence (car-associated or mainstream). For each offence type, several different models are required to understand the factors involved in (1) decisions to start offending; (2) event decisions (e.g. why this car and not that one?); (3) decisions to continue; and (4) decisions to desist from offending. The underlying premise is that people typically make decisions based on limited rationality – cutting corners or using rules of thumb – to evaluate the anticipated costs against the anticipated opportunities, benefits and the needs served. Some criminologists reject rational choice because of its ideological links, and Pease (2001: 236) has critiqued the perspective for its circular reasoning.

Social control theories
Hirschi (1969) proposed that the extent of an individual's bonds to society serve to restrain the human tendency to act in self-interest; hence, the key question is not why people engage in crime but why they do not. Four connected elements were proposed to comprise the social bond – attachment, commitment, involvement and beliefs – and these have been tested in various researches. In general, it is predicted that the stronger the social bond the lower will be the risk of offending, and there is some evidence from mainstream crime to support this theory. It might also help explain some kinds of car crime though research has been limited (see Junger *et al.* 1995).

The general theory of crime
Hirschi later collaborated with Gottfredson (1990) in a general theory of crime, proposing that the extent of self-control, which is learnt through the socialisation process, is the key mechanism that inhibits or promotes crime and is stable throughout life once learnt in childhood. Low self-control is thought the result of ineffective parenting, and is typified by the desire for immediate gratification without much effort and a lack of concern for long-term consequences of behaviour. So those with low self-control are predicted to engage in more risky behaviours if relevant opportunities exist, while high self-control individuals will defer from such activities. Broad categories of criminal behaviour are therefore inter-related and are linked with crime-analogous behaviours such as promiscuity, smoking and heavy drinking. This theory posits an individual-level explanation for all mainstream and other crime, including car crime, with no specific theory required for any particular offence.

Despite the general theory's superficial attraction, many criminologists point out shortcomings. For instance, according to the theory, *all* crime is unsystematic, unplanned, of no real advantage to the offender and is part of a general pattern of irresponsibility. These criteria might apply to many risky illicit mainstream and driving behaviours, but they are hardly relevant to corporate fraud and white-collar crime, with Hopkins Burke (2001: 212) commenting that low self-control is incompatible with the discipline and effort normally required to climb the corporate ladder to high office. Further, because lifelong stability is claimed for the degree of self-control learnt in childhood the need for longitudinal studies is discounted, which fails to explain why and how criminal involvement generally diminishes with age (e.g. Jones 1998: 257).

Strain theory

This proposes that when gaps occur between aspirations and opportunities, as when access to a desired outcome is denied through using legitimate channels, some people may circumvent blocked avenues to achieve their objectives and goals by illicit means (e.g. Merton 1938; Agnew 1992). The theory could particularly find resonance with marginalised and excluded groups. It has not been specifically tested with car crime offenders, but could account for joyriding and other car theft (see Chapter 4) and for documentation offences like having no vehicle tax, insurance, MOT, registration document or driving licence (see Chapter 8).

Social and structural-level theories

Juvenile drift into offending, techniques of neutralisation and normalisation

A common theme of offender-based studies is the gradual slide into unlawful behaviour as part of the drift into and out of delinquency (Sykes and Matza 1957). The notion of drift posits that few young people make conscious decisions to get involved in delinquent activities, but are drawn into the excitement by peers and siblings until the motivation to continue requires little input from others. Repeated offending may then be reinforced through 'techniques of neutralisation' whereby offenders downplay the immorality or wrongfulness associated with offending by justifications that excuse feelings of guilt, such as views that everyone is doing it (ibid.).

Further, the everyday, routine nature of much car theft and other 'minor' car crime has been noted in research (e.g. Sutton 1998) – i.e. most offenders know others entangled in shady dealings, including family and friends, and personal involvement is thought unsurprising. Thus offending within such social networks is normalised. These theoretical models could also fit involvement in offences like drink-driving, licence and other documentation breaches.

Gender-based theories

The roots of gender division are deeply embedded in social, cultural and power relations, though together they may help account for the preponderance of male car crime of all kinds. In response to feminist inquiry into gender concerns, renewed interest has surfaced in regard to masculinity issues, and various efforts to understand different forms of male crime from a sociocultural gendered perspective have been made (e.g. Messerschmidt 1993; Stanko and Newburn 1994). In regard to car crime these include psychoanalytic approaches, those emphasising the search for an appropriate masculine identity among vulnerable groups, and those exploring a shared masculine culture where risky behaviour is admired by others and affords a sense of self-worth. Such frameworks have mostly been applied to car theft and occasionally to drink-driving and speeding but their application could embrace any type of car crime that enhances male status. But criminologists have made few attempts to account theoretically for female car crime, or indeed for female offending generally.

A critical approach

This has already been raised in relation to the construction of car crime and will be developed and drawn upon as appropriate throughout. Focusing on the state's evolving response to the escalation of car culture could lend insight into the commonly perceived minor nature and prevalence of car crime, and insight into the discourse which views 'accidents' as blameless, haphazard occurrences that could equally happen to anyone. This perspective could also highlight the elitism and hegemony which ensure the enduring sentiment that 'the car is king'.

Key themes of the book and chapter outline

This book endeavours to explore the contours of key kinds of car crime, considering it as a coherent whole despite its varied and disparate nature. It will do this by working through the concept of car culture, which provides the context in which car crime manifests. Recurring themes include: a lack of seriousness that characterises driving offences, their perception and treatment; how car crime is itself constructed; how ultimate legal responsibility is placed with individual drivers (which turns attention from the responsibilities of society and the state); and the fact that much car crime is male car crime.

Chapter 2 will set the scene by tracing the social history of the motor car through the last century in Britain, showing how car ownership began as a privilege of the elite and spread to the masses, courting hostility and conflict along the way. Chapter 3 illustrates how driving offences are rarely treated as 'real crime' or as serious by the criminal justice system, explanations for which include legal arguments concerning moral culpability and a critical criminological analysis.

Chapters 4–8 focus on specific kinds of car crime and the general format for each offence type is similar. An introduction will set out some of the key issues, then the extent and nature of the different offences will ensue before consideration is given to who commits them and any theoretical explanations that have been offered linked with research conducted. Current efforts at crime control will be reviewed, followed by concluding comments highlighting priority issues. A summary of the main points ends each chapter.

Chapter 4 explores the stereotypical representation of car crime – 'theft of and from vehicles' – showing how changes in reporting or recording habits could heavily impact crime reduction targets. It considers how situational measures are best placed to reduce crime given that motivations for vehicle theft are unlikely to disappear amid society's immersion in car culture. Chapter 5 addresses impaired driving, looking in detail at drink-driving, drug-driving (comprising impairment through legal and illegal drugs) and fatigued-driving, and considers the question of just how fit society requires drivers to be. Chapter 6 examines 'speeding', showing how this offence is treated as a minor crime but causes extensive harm, and continues to present difficulties for control given the perceptions of drivers and the consensual nature of the offence. A section comparing the proclivities of female and male drivers to exceed speed limits and commit other driving offences is included.

Chapter 7 focuses on bad driving, encompassing behaviours that comprise dangerous and careless offences, and shows how inconsistencies in their treatment by the criminal justice system and the tension between consequences and culpability continue to cause concern to all. Other important dimensions of bad driving include the extent, nature and causes of 'road rage', the consequences of mobile phone usage when driving and a consideration of the perspectives of victims of bad driving and their bereaved. A brief examination of crashes involving police vehicles is made though such incidents may not necessarily involve bad driving.

Chapter 8 assesses the serious problems posed by unlicensed driving that may unfold within a broad subculture of unregulated vehicle use, and notes the links between unlicensed driving, crash risk, mainstream offending and other serious traffic offending. The matter of abandoned, untaxed vehicles is also included. Car crime in wider society is the subject of Chapter 9, which broadens discussion from offending by individuals to delay, inaction, poor standards and a lack of safety culture involving the commercial sector, whose 'shortcomings' are rarely constructed as crime and may involve the state. Chapter 10 draws the main themes together within the context of the car's sociopolitical history and car culture, and highlights continuing and pressing concerns for the control of car crime and its future prospects.

Summary of main points

- Internationally, people are becoming practically and emotionally dependent on the car.
- Embeddedness in car culture is not painfree: associated problems are of massive scale – death and injury crashes and health impairment through pollution.
- Determining boundaries between legally acceptable and unacceptable standards of driver behaviour is a continuing and vexed global concern.
- A consensus on the parameters of what 'car crime' comprises is unlikely.
- Despite the extensive harm caused by cars, criminological interest in car-related offences and offenders has been limited.
- Car crime has been minimally theorised by criminologists, though a range of individual, social and structural level theories might be applied.

Notes

1 *Transport in Figures*, Table 3.5.2, europa.eu.int/en/comm/dg07.
2 Ibid.: Table 3.3.12.
3 Automobile Association (1999: 19) citing *Guide on driver licensing 1998*, Commission Internationale des Examens de Conduite Automobile.
4 Mintel survey reported in *The Times* (9.2.00).
5 Industrial Society survey reported in *The Independent* (19.11.97).
6 Extrapolated from Tables A5.17 and A6.14.
7 Kunzli and colleagues (2000) showed that 3 per cent of annual deaths in

France, Austria and Switzerland were attributable to air pollution caused by traffic fumes, accounting for over 25,000 new cases of chronic bronchitis and over 500,000 asthma attacks each year.

8 Thurston and Krewski (2002) showed that more Americans are killed by cancer-producing particulate emissions from industrial chimneys and car exhausts than by homicide or drink-driving.

9 Cited by Willett (1964).

10 *Guardian*, (30.8.00: 8), referring to Select Committee on Public Accounts 37th report: *The Office of Fair Trading: protecting the consumer from unfair trading practice.*

11 *Highway Economics Note 1: 2000* (DTLR, 2001). This valuation is based on human costs, reflecting pain, grief and suffering to the casualty and bereaved, and on direct economic costs reflecting lost output, and medical and police costs. See www.roads.dft.gov.uk/roadsafety/hen2000/index.htm.

Chapter 2

The car in historical context

Introduction

This chapter considers the meteoric rise of the motor car, and marks key steps in legislation designed to control car usage and abusage. It suggests that what began as a luxury and novelty for the elite inspired traffic laws with minimal sanctions for breaches because the lawmakers were among the car-owning minority. The initial ethos, which down-played the potential and actual danger and harm caused by cars, seems to have changed little since. Indeed, now that car owners comprise a sizeable proportion of adults in industrialised countries, changes to laws and enforcement policies must satisfy the views of this burgeoning proportion of the electorate.

This chapter briefly charts how the initially strong resistance of the car-less gradually gave way to resigned acceptance as car ownership increased, but feuds between groups with polarised concerns are far from over. In particular, motorists' relationships with police, fuelled by newspaper editorials and mediated somewhat by governments of the day, have often been acrimonious, as 'good' citizens have fallen foul of traffic laws and been cast as criminals.

The focus is on Britain although the first motorised vehicles were produced elsewhere and several other European countries and the USA have a similar length history of car culture and efforts to control its consequences.

A privilege of the elite

It is widely known that the first 'horseless carriage' comprised a petrol-driven internal combustion engine bolted on under a three-wheeled wagonette with the horse's shafts removed (e.g. Marshall 1986: 3), and was credited to Karl Benz of Mannheim, Germany, who received a patent on 29 January 1886. Two months later, Gottleib Daimler unveiled his four-wheeled motor vehicle in Stuttgart (Montagu 1986: 14). Initially, the car was seen as 'a passing fad of the rich' which would never depose the horse (Pettifer 1986: 27), yet as an indication of their later widespread social significance cars were given as expensive presents at Edwardian society weddings (*Illustrated London News Supplement* 1986: 6–7). Manufacturers producing Lancaster and Wolseley petrol-motor cars were established in Britain within a decade, and already competition from foreign manufacturers was marked by Daimlers starting production in Manchester under licence (Montagu 1986).

The researches of Professor Clive Emsley, the eminent historian, are gratefully acknowledged in this section. His work on the social and regulatory aspects of the enforcement of early traffic laws is particularly relevant in charting the rise of the motor car. As Emsley notes (1997: 78–9), the regulation and supervision of traffic had usually been dealt with under local by-law regulations in the first half of the nineteenth century, and it was not until 1861 that national legislation was instituted in the guise of the Locomotive Act that *inter alia* introduced a 12 mph speed limit (5 mph in towns) for traction engines. The better known Locomotive Act 1865 established the requirement for a man to walk in front carrying a red flag and reduced the speed limit to 4 mph (2 mph in towns), which was not superseded until 1896 when the Locomotive and Highways Act allowed self-propelled motorised vehicles to proceed without the man in front. As a result of lobbying by the Self-propelled Traffic Association, led by Sir David Salamans, Parliament acceded to this pressure and the speed limit was raised to 12 mph under the new Act, which was followed by the first of many London to Brighton Runs to celebrate the 'emancipation' (Gibson 1994).

Even before petrol-engined vehicles were established in Britain traffic congestion and problems caused by the poor driving standards of cyclists and drivers of carts and steam-engined vehicles kept police patrols increasingly busy (Emsley 1993: 361). Reckless driving, drunk-driving, driving without due care and attention, overloaded vehicles, and impeding traffic by 'loitering' required the police to act (ibid.), and excessive speed associated with the arrival of the motor car generated debates in newspaper columns, journals and Parliament which culminated in the Motor Car Act 1903 (ibid.: 362). That Act introduced disqualification from driving, registration of vehicles by number plates, the offence of reckless driving and the requirement to stop after a road traffic accident. Initially wealthy car drivers found their vehicles stoned upon or shot at (ibid.: 362–5) and clashes with horseriders, drivers of horse-drawn vehicles and victims of the car were common (Pettifer 1986: 26). Conflicts between opposing interest groups are therefore well established.

Issues of environmental pollution have also accompanied the rise of the automobile. Opposition to the noise and smell of the motor vehicle, first raised by those favouring the retention of horse-drawn vehicles, gave way partly because of the considerable smell, health and congestion hazards of mountains of horse manure that characterised town and city streets in the early 1900s (ibid.: 28)! Some of our now familiar discourses of car culture clearly surfaced during parliamentary debates of the Motor Car Bill in 1902, when the economic interests of those keen to nurture the nascent motor industry collided with the environmental concerns of agricultural communities angry with the dust and fumes thrown up by cars (Emsley 1993: 366). Nevertheless, despite increasing pressure to regulate the speed and other actions of motorists, the Motor Car Act 1903 raised the national speed limit to 20 mph. It also increased fines and provided for imprisonment in serious and repeated cases of dangerous driving, and with several renewals this Act remained in force until 1930. Enforcement was encharged to the police and licensing encharged to local government, and the first formal attempt to regulate drivers came in 1904 with the introduction of driving licences.

Motor car ownership had begun as a privilege of the wealthy, and reports suggested that they were not deterred from excessive speed by the seemingly paltry fines (ibid.). Indeed, motoring often brought the well-to-do into brushes with the police for the first time, and besides encouragement by offenders for the police to 'use their discretion', police were also subject to harassment, bribery attempts and verbal abuse by 'respectable' motorists angry at attempts to criminalise them. 'Road-hogs' were seen as other drivers, often 'foreign-born chauffeurs' (ibid.: 369), and resentment against the 'speed trap' enforcement activities of the police led to the formation of the Automobile Association in 1905, and a legal defence service for its growing number of members the following year (ibid.: 369–71). The new association thus helped establish both the hegemony of the motor car lobby and the notion of the 'poor oppressed motorist' (see Chapter 10).

Increasing accessibility and road casualties

In 1904, around 8,000 passenger cars were in use in Great Britain, and this soon grew to 139,000 in 1915 (Emsley 1997: 78). Growing familiarity with the motor car and the tarring of roads from 1909 to alleviate the problem of dust were factors in assuaging anti-car feeling (Emsley 1993: 371), but falling production and petrol costs also tempted would-be car owners in Britain. The trend for smaller and cheaper cars started in 1923 when the tiny Austin Seven appeared and soon became a familiar sight on the roads (Montagu 1986: 20). The decade to 1925 saw a 335 per cent increase in car usage, the highest yet recorded (Emsley 1997: 78), which was partly the result of enthusiasm for the car among demobbed women who had been taught to drive or maintain vehicles during First World War military service (Montagu 1986: 16).

A similar expansion in car usage occurred in the USA, facilitated by the introduction of Henry Ford's Model T car in 1908. Dubbed the car of the century (*The Sunday Times* 26.12.99), the low-priced, easy-to-drive 'Tin Lizzie' (as it was popularly known) symbolised the 'American Dream' and brought motoring to the masses. Ford sold more than 15 million by 1927 (Montagu 1986: 16) yet the century's bestseller became the rear-engined Volkswagen Beetle (*The Sunday Times* 26.12.99) which is still in production. The Beetle accumulated more than 22 million sales and was developed in Germany under Hitler, who was also responsible for sponsoring the fastest road-racing cars of the day (Montagu 1986: 20).

In fact, attaining faster speeds and racing cars have always under-pinned much of the interest shown in car production and design since the first model hit the roads, and the inherent danger in such enterprise has always accompanied it, exemplified, for example, by the Paris to Madrid international road race of 1903 during which 10 people were killed (*Illustrated London News Supplement* 1986: 19). Despite increasing casualties from everyday driving, the quest for higher speeds continued, facilitated by the construction of race circuits, and speeds of 100 mph were achieved by 1907 (Montagu 1986: 14).

In Britain, by the late 1920s antipathy towards the enforcement activities of traffic police resurfaced, with growing numbers of car drivers finding themselves on the wrong side of the law for the first time.[1] Even the Home Secretary stepped in to ask chief constables not to treat motorists who might be 'persons of the utmost respectability of character and position' as 'possible criminals'.[2] The move towards decriminalisation of speeding gathered pace and found support from magistrates,[3] the Automobile Association[4] and the National Safety-first Association.[5] In 1930, on grounds of reduced congestion, increased driver responsibility and therefore fewer crashes (Emsley 1993: 25), the Road Traffic Act abolished the speed limit for all but heavy commercial vehicles. This Act also established the offences of careless driving and driving a vehicle while unfit through drink or drugs – these offences have remained largely unchanged – and introduced a system of compulsory third-party insurance. Yet optimism soon foundered as road casualties continued to rise.[6] A higher urban speed limit of 30 mph was introduced in 1934 under the Road Transport Act and driving tests were made compulsory in 1935.

The escalation of car ownership not only had concentrated minds on the enforcement of crimes by drivers, but attention also turned to the growing problem of crime to cars, notably, theft of them. Though theft offences for temporary use – commonly referred to as 'joyriding' – had been noted in the criminal sense since 1909 (Partridge 1984), early legislation had not recognised such incidents, offenders most commonly being charged with the theft of the petrol that had been used (Light *et al.*, 1993: Appendix 1). It was not until car ownership grew markedly in the 1920s along with an accelerating theft rate – because of poor security like the use of push-button starter motors (Webb and Laycock 1992) – that acknowledgement was also made of the inadequate protection provided by the law against joyriders. According to Taylor (1999), the lack of protection for car owners should be set in the broader sociopolitical context of the 1920s and the competing interests of the police, government and car owners. He noted that the owners' need for better theft protection neatly paralleled the police's need to justify rising numbers of officers tasked with traffic duties that included the investigation of car theft, and both needs culminated in s. 28 of the Road Traffic Act 1930. That Act also reconsidered some earlier offences and made provision for new ones, and became the cornerstone of road traffic law for several decades.

By the start of the Second World War, Italy, Germany, France and the USA had built vast stretches of 'motorway', but the first motorway section in Britain, the M1, did not open until 2 November 1959 and was accompanied by the breakdown of more than 100 vehicles (*Guardian* 19.10.99). The roadworthiness of cars was not subject to testing until 1962 when 10-year-old cars were required to pass the Ministry of Transport test (later altered to cover three-year-old cars). Yet even mechanically sound vehicles in the 1950s were replete with safety hazards. The Mini Minor, introduced in 1959 by Sir Alec Issigonis, had a door latch that sprung open at the slightest pressure (Faith 1998: 66–7). Despite this early 'problem', the Mini went on to sell five million and be voted into second place as the 'car of the century' (*The Sunday Times* 26.12.99).

The growing accessibility of the car saw the proportion of households with 'regular use of a car' grow from 14 per cent in 1951 to 52 per cent in 1971 (DTLR 2001c: Table 9.4), and the road toll rise from 5,250 to 7,699 over the same period, fatalities peaking in 1966 with 7,985 dead, 46 per cent being pedestrians or cyclists (ibid.: Table 9.10). To counter the upward trend in road casualties, the Labour government of the day introduced a raft of safety measures in the Road Safety Act 1967, prompted by Transport Minister, Barbara Castle. This act required *inter alia* seat belts to be fitted in all new cars, a 70 mph speed limit for all previously unrestricted roads and new drink-driving regulations. Drivers suspected of committing a moving traffic offence, and crash-involved drivers, would be liable to a breath test and prosecuted if driving with over 80 mg of alcohol per 100 ml of blood (still unchanged in Britain).

While careless offences have remained largely unchanged since they were created under the Road Traffic Act 1930, more serious instances of bad driving have been revisited several times undergoing various modifications since 1956, following the early introduction of reckless driving in 1903. An oft-recurring awkward issue was to determine the driver's mental state when committing the offence which necessarily involved subjective interpretation of the evidence. This was supposedly resolved by the Road Traffic Act 1991 that required an objective assessment on how far the observed driving behaviour deviated from what a careful and competent driver would do, and on whether it would be obvious to a careful and competent driver that the behaviour was dangerous. Ironically, subjective interpretation of the quality of driving still seems essential and this is developed in Chapter 7.

Towards the millennium and the challenges ahead

Despite Road Traffic Acts in 1956 and 1972 that introduced and then modified specific offences to deal with bad driving, continuing dissatisfaction led to the setting up in 1985 of the Road Traffic Law Review (Department of Transport and Home Office 1988). Under its terms of reference it reviewed the structure and penalties for a range of offences, including causing death by reckless driving, reckless driving and careless driving, and considered new means of enforcement for other offences (ibid.: 7–8). The review body took evidence from around 150 organisations, including local authorities, police groups, driving instructors, the judiciary and a range of campaigning pressure groups. It commissioned its own survey research and produced wide-reaching recommendations in its 1988 'North report'. Many of these recommend-ations were enshrined in the subsequent Road Traffic Act 1991, most notably a new dangerous driving offence based on an objective test, requirements to retake the driving test for those convicted of very serious offences or those disqualified for more than 12 months, and the introduction of automatic camera devices to detect red light and speeding offences.

Car ownership has expanded at a far faster rate than ever envisaged by civil servants,[7] and was encouraged latterly by Mrs Thatcher's pivotal role in promoting private transport. The resulting congestion on the roads has become commonplace despite considerable expansion through road-building programmes. The quest of how to get people out of their cars on to less-than-perfect public transport to ease congestion and environmental pollution greeted the Labour Party in 1997 after 17 years out of office, and was taken up as a core aim in its integrated transport policy.[8] Yet the Labour government was also required to deal with the campaigns of new-age eco-warriors against further road building, the growing voices of pressure groups – such as Sustrans representing cycling groups (e.g. Sustrans 1997) and RoadPeace (e.g. RoadPeace 1996) comprising mainly bereaved relatives of crash victims – the lobbying of road hauliers and motor manufacturers, and driver groups vociferously represented by the media angry at drivers' perceived criminalisation (e.g. *Daily Mail* 15.9.99). Mid-term survey results in 1999 showed that transport was the government's weakest link (*Guardian* 13.7.99), illustrating its tardiness in realising that matters linked with car culture were dear to the hearts and minds of a substantial proportion of the electorate. This had not been helped by the ownership of two Jaguar cars by the then Minister for Transport, John Prescott, which earned him the media sobriquet of 'Two Jags' and brought forth comments of his personal contribution to congestion rather than his easing of it (*The Times* 13.12.99). There followed a package of measures designed to appease the disgruntled.

These attempts to show Labour did care about the motorist included a well publicised U-turn in transport policy as revealed in the Transport Bill 1999, which indicated abandonment of plans to reduce traffic levels on Britain's roads, and announced that the proposed schemes for congestion charging and the taxing of work car-parking spaces would take up to four years to realise (*Guardian* 2.12.99). Instead, a new reliance would be placed on solving the pollution problem through technology rather than a reduction of car numbers (*The Independent* 28.11.99), and within a few weeks the government was encouraging the car-less to become car owners (*Daily Mail* 18.12.99), marking a striking reversal of

Labour's earlier core policy aimed at getting people out of their cars (*Guardian* 21.12.99). The publication of the government's road safety strategy for the next ten years (DETR 2000a) and a speed policy review (DETR 2000b) followed. While the road safety strategy drew few comments in the press, the Speed Policy Review brought swift criticism from road safety campaigners claiming that the government had caved in to the motoring lobbying by failing to cut speed limits against expectations (*Daily Mail* 27.11.99), and failing to increase speeding penalties and to provide more money for safety schemes (*Guardian* 2.3.00).

There was an ongoing debate between police and government about enforcement of speed limits and the margin of tolerance that would be allowed, a debate which echoed the discussions of 1903, the late 1920s and the like. An announcement by senior officials that '30 mph would mean 30 mph'[9] prompted furious headlines and editorials in newspapers about the government's 'war on the motorist' (*Daily Mail* 18.11.99). The intention to clamp down on speeding motorists was soon countered by police saying this was unrealistic given their limited resources (*Guardian*, 5.2.00). This in turn was seized upon by Transport 2000, a road safety pressure group which was given leave to start high court proceedings against the police for failing to enforce the law (*Guardian* 25.7.00). The upshot was an out-of court compromise whereby police agreed to use their discretion to enforce the speed limits allowing no latitude in many situations but some tolerance in others (*Daily Express* 24.7.00).

The detection soon after of a police vehicle carrying the Home Secretary, a supporter of 'zero tolerance' for speed limits, at more than 100 mph on a 70 mph motorway, and angry reactions from road safety campaigners for the decision not to prosecute the police driver (*The Times* 25.11.00) merely added to the government's discomfort on its speed policy and how to keep all constituencies 'on side'.

Moreover, rising petrol prices led to a swift and dramatic crisis for government when it was called upon to resolve 'The Great Petrol Revolt of 2000' (e.g. *The Sun* 12.9.00) orchestrated by angry drivers. This rapidly brought the country to the verge of a standstill as pickets blockaded refineries discouraging oil tankers from leaving, and left the Prime Minister defending his reputation (e.g. *The Independent* 17.9.00). Thus conflicts that started over 100 years earlier were rehearsed throughout the last century. Reconciliation between driver groups, some sections of the media, road safety groups, eco-warriors, motor manufacturers and the government seems no nearer.

That said, as part of Labour's millennium package, recognition was eventually given to the anomalies surrounding driving offences that resulted in death or serious injury and the penalties that were awarded, and in 2000 a Traffic Penalty Review consultation was set up to consider any modifications needed in these and other road traffic laws (Home Office 2000b). The *Road Traffic Law Review report* (Department of Transport and Home Office 1988: 21) had earlier noted the strength and scale of public concern about the perceived failure of the criminal justice system to mark the seriousness of offences leading to road deaths and injuries, and road safety groups had long campaigned for less disparity in sentences for deaths caused on the road as off it (e.g. RoadPeace 1996). Academics too have noted the relatively lenient sentences given for road traffic offences generally. While the government's response to the Traffic Penalty Review (Home Office 2002a) indicated its intention to introduce higher maxima sentences for several bad driving offences including those leading to death, the low gravity accorded to the censure and control of car crime in general is a key theme underpinning this text, and the next chapter will amplify this.

Summary of main points

- Motor car ownership began as a privilege of the elite in industrialised countries, and has spread to the masses a century later.
- Self-interest of the elite probably coloured the construction of original road traffic laws to downplay dangerous driving actions, their 'accidental' consequences and sanctions for breaches.
- Hostility and conflict between opposing groups have accompanied the passage of private motorised transport and are well rehearsed (e.g. enforcement of speed limits).
- Appeasing polarised groups is still problematic for British government with little resolved, despite continuing attempts.

Notes

1 *Report of the Royal Commission on Police Powers and Procedure*, Cmd 3297, 1929: 81, in Emsley (1993: 374).
2 *Staffordshire Constabulary Archives Chief Constable's memo book 1926–1931*, fol. 62, Memo (All Stations) 27.9.29, reproducing memos of December 1927 and 11.6.28, in Emsley (1993: 374).
3 Justice of the Peace, LXXXIX, 1925: 452, in Emsley (1993: 374).
4 Barty-King (1980: 42) in Emsley (1993: 376).
5 Packard, J. 'Some developments in street accident prevention'. Chief

Constables' Association: *Report of general conference*, 19.6.30, and *Special general conference*, 20.6.30, 49–62, in Emsley, (1993: 376).

6 Road crash and casualty statistics are reliant on the vagaries of reporting and recording practices as much as criminal statistics are. Discretion may be exercised in the reporting or recording of serious injuries as slight or of slight injury as non-injury crashes, and in whether a death sometime later is perceived as a direct result of a collision. In this regard, Taylor (1999) concluded that the apparent uniform increases in road crash casualties between 1930 and 1934 and the longer period of 1918–34 were subject to police manipulation.

7 For example, Pettifer (1986: 30), although the 1963 'Buchanan report' showed foresight of future traffic volumes.

8 *A new deal for transport: better for everyone*. White paper on the future of transport (1998), London: DETR.

9 On the *Today* programme, BBC Radio 4 (14.9.99).

Chapter 3

Not real crime?

Introduction

This chapter picks up some themes already foreshadowed and develops them further. It contends that car crime in broad terms and road traffic offences specifically seem not to be taken as seriously as other crime, a prevailing ethos shaped by the car's particular history. Several examples are given of how car crime is usually perceived and treated as minor crime, and then various theoretical explanations are offered, some of which draw upon the car's sociopolitical heritage.

It bears repeating that all offences under road traffic law are crimes. They comprise a separate part of criminal law, though like off-road offences they are enforced by the police, prosecuted by the Crown Prosecution Service in Britain and handled by criminal courts. The same procedures, standard of proof and rules of evidence are required as for conventional crime. The perception of traffic offences as different from other crime probably arises from a legal discourse where terms like premeditation and deliberation are more often associated with mainstream criminal acts. This legal argument will preface the second section of this chapter.

Illustrations of the low perceived seriousness of road traffic offending

In Britain, most offences that are breaches of road traffic law are heard in magistrates' courts in separate sessions convened as 'motor courts', immediately setting them apart from other crime. Yet under the Magistrates' Court Act 1980, s. 12, drivers in England and Wales in receipt of court summonses for summary offences do not have to attend court unless a sentence of imprisonment or detention is being considered. Drivers may plead guilty by post. Although this practice was ostensibly instituted for the purpose of achieving greater court efficiency, it still suggests that such offences are conceived as administrative infractions rather than 'real' crime. Echoing the debates of earlier decades, research by Hood (1972) in the late 1960s confirmed the concern to separate the 'errant' and respectable driver from the 'wicked' one. The stigma of appearing in a criminal court was removed for well-to-do motorists who did not fit the criminal stereotypes.

The fact that errant drivers can be prosecuted for various road traffic offences, such as speeding and failing to stop at red traffic signals, up to four times before accumulating sufficient penalty points for disqualification under the 'totting up' rules might also suggest low perceived seriousness by the courts. Also, discretionary rather than mandatory disqualification is currently applicable to many road traffic offences, including exceeding speed limits.

In recent times, a tougher attitude has been shown by the Lord Chancellor to magistrates convicted of motoring offences. So, for example, those convicted of drink-driving (and disqualified for 12 months or more) will be removed from office unless they resign, and those disqualified for other reasons could also be removed.[1] However, magistrates having two endorsements of three penalty points each for speeding within the last five years will usually be allowed to continue in office (LCD Circular AC (12) 2001). This might be thought surprising in view of speed's contributory causal role in around one third of fatal crashes (e.g. Taylor *et al.* 2000). This tolerance to speeding magistrates may also permeate through to juries. In 1999, a jury acquitted a driver of dangerous driving for doing 145 mph on a motorway (*The Times* 25.3.99), and, in 2000, a business driver who hit and killed a 73-year-old pedestrian at 183 mph was acquitted of dangerous driving but convicted instead of careless driving (*The Times* 16.6.00).

With respect to roads policing it might be thought that as the volume of vehicles has risen sharply (e.g. DTLR 2001c: Tables 3.3 and 4.7) so too would the proportion of officers on traffic policing duties, but this is not the case. In fact, in 1966 around 15–20 per cent of constable strength in England and Wales was deployed on traffic patrol duties but, as noted by Her Majesty's Inspector of Constabulary (HMIC), by 1998 this proportion had shrunk to around 5–7 per cent (HMIC 1998: 12). The decentralisation of many police forces in the 1980s may account for some reduction in specialist traffic officers, but another explanation is the continuing lack of a Home Office core objective for the police to investigate and reduce road offences. Indeed, HMIC (ibid.: 19) remarked with disappointment how roads policing had not received the attention it warranted from senior police, and that most forces saw road policing as a peripheral task with officers to be redirected to 'more important work'. Partly to avoid the risk of the marginalisation of traffic policing, HMIC rather limply recommended that police should take the opportunity offered under the Crime and Disorder Act 1998 to assess local road policing needs to increase public safety and reduce fear of crime as part of the community safety audits required (ibid.: 17). Tellingly, it was noted that police process departments tended to ration traffic prosecutions, especially when busy, to make way for 'crime' prosecutions (ibid.: 22), underlining the police's disparate perceptions of seriousness between offences occurring on and off the road. To some extent the notion that car crime is not 'real crime' might be supported by the perceived enjoyment and excitement inherent in police car chases of joyriders and other likely offenders that have often been noted by researchers (e.g. Holdaway 1983: 130–38; Smith and Gray 1985; see also Chapter 7). These chases reportedly serve to enliven routine police duties and reinforce a shared masculine culture of a desire for action and challenge.

Not all injuries and deaths on the road are caused by motorists breaching the laws, though studies have found that over a quarter of injury crashes do result in criminal prosecution (e.g. Forsyth and Silcock 1987) and, as noted above, excessive speed is implicated as a contributory cause in about one third of fatal crashes. This equates to at least 75,000 people in England and Wales being injured every year as a result of a driver breaking a law,[2] of whom around 1,100 are killed partly because of excessive speed. If this number of deaths arose from any other cause – the annual homicide total is around 800 (Simmons 2002: Table 3.04) – it would be of considerable concern to the Home Office (responsible *inter alia* for crime). Yet efforts to reduce speed-related fatalities have in the past been largely encharged to the government department responsible for transport (currently the DfT, formerly the DTLR, DETR and DoT), suggesting they have been seen more as a traffic rather than crime problem.

Breaches of road traffic laws seem not to be treated by the criminal justice system as seriously as breaches of general criminal laws, and traffic offences are not considered to be 'crime' in the sense that theft or robbery usually are. This certainly is the view of drivers themselves (Department of Transport and Home Office 1988: 20; Corbett and Simon

1992a: 37–42), and indications from traffic police, magistrates and approved driving instructors suggest they have similar perceptions about speeding (Corbett, *et al.* 1998: 37, 40, 45). Hood (1972: 99–101) also found that magistrates tended to perceive traffic offences as qualitatively different from other crime. Together, these examples indicate that offending on the road is not seen as 'real' crime in the wider socio-cultural sphere.

Explanations for the low seriousness accorded road traffic offending

The legal view

Various accounts of the marginalisation of car crime are possible and several theoretical frameworks are worth noting. First, however, many will point to an obvious legal explanation for the downgrading of traffic offences. For the most part, harmful consequences of legal or illegal driving actions are not intended or sought out by drivers, so transgressions of road traffic laws tend to be different from other criminal acts. Moreover, in contrast with other criminal law most road traffic offences are regarded as less morally reprehensible since dishonesty for personal gain is not intended, and there is rarely premeditation to cause harm. Indeed, negative consequences often arise from a fleeting carelessness or an oversight. At its extreme, the 'lack of intention' argument holds that there should be no greater liability or moral culpability where the consequence of a transgression is accidental, as, for example, when a pedestrian happens to be in the way of a careless driver. That is, the intent or state of mind of the driver is more important than the outcome, and the punishment should take this into account.

Unlike criminal law, a main purpose of road traffic law is the promotion of accident avoidance and the legal argument emphasises this difference. Because offences under the criminal law are underpinned by moral principle they are quite naturally regarded as 'crimes' and can be taken more seriously than those created under road traffic law where strict liability applies. This means that no mental or 'fault' element (*mens rea*) must be proved, and moral principles are largely superfluous. Instead, where harm results only the *actus reus* – evidence that the defendant's voluntary conduct caused the consequences – is required to be proved.

The trump card in the legal argument, however, is the convention whereby the risks involved in normal driving are usually found acceptable to the courts and are not thought unjustifiable in the circumstances (e.g. Heaton 1997; 53). In other words, the risk and likely seriousness of the harm that could ensue are set against the social utility of normal driving and its value to the community and this view is accepted by the courts as worth taking (ibid.). This tends to suggest an underlying discourse of the 'car as king', where the social mobility of the masses is considered more salient than the byproducts of harm to the unfortunate victims and their families.

Yet one might counter the legal argument by considering the extent to which some crashes are indeed fortuitous. Any semi-rational person would appreciate that a pedestrian hit at 40 mph will be more gravely injured than one hit at 20 mph, and that stopping distances will increase with speed, thus causing greater risk of harm as speed escalates. It might also be reasonably inferred that failing to observe red traffic lights, 'give way' signs or blood/alcohol limits will create more harmful consequences than adherence to these laws. In this view, therefore, if a death or injury results from deliberate breaches of the law, some blameworthiness attaches since the consequences can hardly be argued as entirely unforeseen.

Much revolves around the concept of 'normal driving', and what the courts consider reasonable. If the majority of British drivers exceed the 30 mph speed limit (DTLR 2001c: Table 4.13) this may constitute 'normal driving' even though there is more risk of death on impact. Of course, not all British drivers travel at top speeds, but as more than a third were recorded as at least 5 mph above the 30 mph limit (ibid.), and death is considerably more likely on impact at 35 mph than at 30 mph (e.g. Hobbs and Mills 1984), when does 'more risk' become the 'unjustifiable risk' associated with dangerous driving? This question is difficult to answer since while road deaths constitute one of the main causes of worldwide death, especially for young persons (Red Cross and Red Crescent Societies 1998), the kind of 'normal' acts that cause them, such as excessive speed or driving without due care and attention, only rarely end in harm. So as noted above, many driving actions are prosecuted for their potential to cause harm rather than the actual harm caused, and this is a key distinguishing feature between offences in motoring and criminal law. Nevertheless, risks of harm tend to increase through nonadherence to laws even if the harm fails to occur.

A critical criminological view

Although the legal argument helps explain why car crime tends to be marginalised, other explanations are needed. One of these is a critical

29

criminological framework that often has been applied to the neglected 'crimes of the elite' (e.g. Box 1983; Croall 1998a, 1998b; Tombs 1999). It could also apply to the construction of offences linked with cars and driving.

Until motorised vehicles became more affordable in the 1920s ownership was confined to the ruling classes and wealthy, including Members of Parliament responsible for shaping road traffic legislation and judges responsible for interpreting it. In the same way that Marxist ideology espouses that law is made and operated in the interests of the rich so that 'crimes' and dubious business activities of the capitalist elite are shielded from legislative scrutiny – or at least subject to regulatory rather than criminal law – so the leisure interests of the well-to-do could have impacted on the construction of crimes involving the car.

For example, the excitement provided by the car as a new form of personalised transport for the rich conferring (within small margins) a personal choice of speed, may have led to the discourse where the burden was, and arguably still is, on the pedestrian to avoid the car rather than the other way around (e.g. Davis 1992: 114–17; Gibson 1994).[3] Pursuit of this new leisure activity may also have caused the elite to overlook the dangers to others resulting from poor road infra-structure, poor vehicle road handling, defective brakes, raised speed limits (1903) and the repeal of speed limits (1930). Prior to 1956, when causing death through dangerous driving was criminalised, prosecutions were limited to manslaughter with juries notoriously reluctant to convict.

A critical view might explain why 'car crime' is traditionally seen as 'theft of and from a vehicle', and it explains the traditionally low penalties that are still awarded for exceeding speed limits and danger-ous driving. These traditions would be seen as outcomes of the early power of the elite to criminalise those seen as theatening to the social order (the poor who might wish to steal vehicles), and to deal sympathetically with the well-to-do who wished to indulge their new-found driving pleasures without fear of heavy penalties for 'slips' and 'errors'.

Critical analysts might also provide evidence of favours for the elite – government subsidies and tax breaks to car manufacturers to continue production in Britain, bolstering the country's dependence on motor manufacturers as major employers. The £3.3 billion 'sweetener' allocated to BMW in 1999 to save the Longbridge plant, which was sold to the rival Phoenix consortium a year later (*Guardian* 24.6.99), illustrates this. Other examples include the failure of successive administrations to discourage the production of high-performance vehicles that can reach highly illegal speeds, and a 'hands-off' approach that allows manufacturers a voluntary code of self-regulation in advertising standards. With little state opprobrium to fear, manufacturers are prepared to risk censure by the Advertising Standards Authority,[4] although Europe is getting tough with advertisers (see Chapter 9).

A critical framework might also be applied to explaining why fleet car and company drivers are obliged to exceed speed limits in order to meet tight scheduling arrangements. It could also conceive the aiding and abetting of company employees to exceed speed limits and endanger others for the good of the company profit motive as corporate crime.

Interestingly, the discourse of 'accidents' fits well with a critical explanation for the marginalisation of road traffic offending[5] and connects with the legal argument above, since the first road traffic legislators and legal interpreters included the car-owning elite. This discourse has helped to neutralise the dangers posed by moving vehicles in everyday conversation and in constructions of the law through the convenient social construction of collisions as blameless, hapless, unlucky, chance events with unknown causes which could happen equally to anyone.[6] Further, within an 'accident' discourse deliberate non-adherence to traffic laws tends to be overlooked, and the apportionment of blame tends to be superfluous (e.g. Green 1997; Howarth 1997). In turn, so-called 'accidents' have helped to determine the prevailing social context of car culture in which a 'thrills and spills' image has been allowed to flourish at the expense of the real pain and suffering that frequently transpire (e.g. Mitchell 1997b). Sidelining any serious harm wrought through the portrayal of collisions in this way would have suited the interests of the car-owning elite.

Almost a century on, arguably we are hardly aware of the elitism associated with the car, so embedded is it into the social fabric. Pedestrians stop for cars, rarely the other way round except at designated crossings – and even here they can get knocked down.[7] Gloomy underpasses aid traffic flow and promote pedestrians' safety from vehicles at the expense of fear of other crime. The gradual erosion of public transport services marginalises further the car-less and implicitly reinforces the superiority of car drivers. Indeed, the attitude of 'car is king' still prevails (e.g. Davis 1992) along with the widely perceived 'right to drive' (and to do so as one wishes), reinforced among some sections of the driving community by the derogation of motorists who keep to speed limits (e.g. Clarkson 2002a).

The role of gender

Issues of gender provide an associated theoretical lens through which to consider the downgrading of car-related offending, the primary one being that men were the main architects of road traffic laws, and that men have dominated car usage since then. On the roads, the proportion of male drivers overshadowed the proportion of females for much of last century and only now is the proportion of women licence holders catching up.[8] Other gender differences in car usage and offending will be considered later (especially Chapter 6), but it is pertinent to note that men express higher enjoyment of risk and thrill-seeking behaviours such as driving fast (Matthews *et al.* 1997), and admit to more traffic law breaches than women (e.g. Simon and Corbett, 1996; McKenna *et al.* 1998). In fact most 'car crime' of all types – including vehicle theft – is male car crime.

If the first legislators also warmed to thrill-seeking when driving their cars, it is quite possible that such enjoyment would have coloured the construction of those laws, with the danger implicit in breaching the new laws minimised through favourably low sanctions. Thus issues of masculinity may be linked with perceptions of low seriousness of illegal driving actions, as is evident in the macho subculture of some men who profess fitness to drive when well above the legal blood-alcohol limit (e.g. Gusfield *et al.* 1981; Corbett *et al.* 1991).

Neoliberalism and Mrs Thatcher

Another theoretical strand feeding in to the low importance of car-related offending could be a consequence of the neoliberal ethos promoted by Mrs Thatcher's years of stewardship in the 1980s. As part of this ideology and her thrust to 'roll back' the intervention of the state, the notions of freedom, self-determination, autonomy and self-responsibility were promulgated, connecting with her support of a car economy, and this fusion almost certainly facilitated the explosion of journeys made by private transport in that decade.[9] Assimilation of these ideas probably suited drivers' self-images, and would have strengthened drivers' often-heard wishes to decide for themselves the manner of their driving and to use laws such as speed limits and blood-alcohol limits as guidelines rather than absolutes (e.g. Corbett *et al.* 1991; Corbett and Simon 1992a: Ch. 4). A legacy of neoliberal ideology therefore could have reinforced failures to comply strictly with traffic laws, which would help explain the view of many drivers that 'more or less complying' with traffic laws is synonymous with being law-abiding.[10] In other words these watchwords of neoliberal thinking may have helped maintain perceptions of car-related offending as trivial.

The power of the electorate

It is also useful to consider the driving public's role in the low seriousness associated with car and driving offences. The majority of adults in Britain (and Europe) now hold driving licences,[11] and it is known that the bulk of licence holders break some laws of the road some of the time (e.g. Lex 1997). It is unlikely that the state and the criminal justice system could maintain the traditional low-key response to traffic offending without the tacit endorsement of most drivers. This is implied in the high volume of transgressions, such that parking offences and exceeding speed limits are arguably consensual activities which are legitimated by the majority. Attempts to get tough with motorists on speeding in 1999 were roundly criticised by newspapers, who exhorted the police to seek out the 'real' criminals rather than treat drivers as criminals (e.g. *Daily Mail*, 15.9.99). If this view has wider applicability – and anecdotal police evidence suggests it may be common among drivers – a major problem for crime control arises in light of the current popular strategy to target high-risk offending groups (Home Office 1998). If the driving public deny that their offending on the roads is crime, and the bulk engage in breaking some traffic rules, there is clearly great political danger in criminalising the majority.

Thus the driving public has became an electoral force to be reckoned with, and one difficult to stereotype and control since speeders and drink-drivers, *inter alia,* do not fit the traditional pictures of deviants, including as they do middle-class, middle-aged and 'average' citizens (e.g. Research Services Limited 1994; Stradling 2001). The power of the elite in setting the initial parameters for the regulation of driving actions has been more recently augmented and perhaps transformed by the power of the car-owning masses in influencing official responses to the control of traffic law breaches.

It is also worth emphasising the powerful role of the media in advancing not only the view of the ordinary motorist as 'victimised' and 'outraged' (often in tabloid newspapers), but also of the desirability and glamour of high-performance luxury cars and high speed (often in glossy laddish magazines). Given that media create as well as reflect public opinion (e.g. Reiner 2002), politicians must monitor all this when formulating changes to enforcement policies and laws lest public disaffection escalates.

Concluding comments

Critical debates on which kinds of acts get criminalised have some relevance for car-related offending. The elite's interest in neutralising dangerous driving actions, and the consequences of this in the development of road traffic laws may have been one reason for the low seriousness associated with road crime. This may have been enhanced by the discourse of accidents which has long underpinned the emerging car culture, and by legal arguments focusing on the lack of intention to cause harm when driving. Issues around masculinity, especially the greater appeal of risk-taking among men, could be a continuing influence in low seriousness perceptions, and Mrs Thatcher's neoliberal ideology, encouraging self-responsibilisation, autonomy and freedom to choose, has fitted well with images of car ownership. Lastly, the power of the driving public as a constituency to be courted rather than penalised underlines the state's need to tread carefully in sanctioning motorists for transgressions, especially given most drivers' emotional and practical dependence on the car (e.g. Lex 1999: 16–17).

In all, borrowing from a 'North Committee' view (Department of Transport and Home Office 1988: 22), road traffic offending and law are different in some respects from general criminal offending and law but should be regarded as just as important, and deaths and injuries arising in the motoring sphere should be treated with similar gravitas to those arising in other contexts. Which offences involving the car should be regarded as 'crime' will depend on an individual's perspective, and debates around how car crime should be defined – and debates concerning mainstream crime – will continue as a 'site of legal, political and moral contestation' (Muncie 2001: 63–4). Certainly, control of the car and reducing associated illegalities will remain a fraught area of policy-making for international democracies, especially as car ownership rapidly escalates. Whether or not we count ourselves among the car-dependent, the ideology of car culture touches all of us.

Summary of main points

- Driving offences are rarely treated as 'real' crime or as serious by criminal justice agencies, professional groups or drivers. Traffic policing and enforcement have not been accorded high priority.
- Road deaths have largely been seen as a traffic rather than crime problem.
- Legal arguments concerning lack of intention to cause harm have

downgraded the moral culpability and the perceived seriousness of road 'crime' and 'accidents'.

- A critical criminological analysis can help account for the marginalisation of car crime.
- Most car crime is 'male car crime', and the male propensity to take risks could be instrumental in downplaying the danger of some driving actions.
- Neoliberal ideology has reinforced and promoted car dependency and helped maintain low seriousness perceptions of car-related offending.
- There remains a political unwillingness to criminalise motorists.

Notes

1 Paragraphs 19.44–46, *Conduct and competence guidelines for magistrates*, Lord Chancellor's Department (2001).

2 In 2000, 320,283 road accident casualties, including 3,409 fatalities, were recorded in the *Transport statistics*, Table 4.15, DETR (2001c).

3 Also Emsley (1997: 83) notes that from the early twentieth century judges began shifting their reliance on the interpretation of a driver's strict liability, as in Rylands v. Fletcher [1866], to the view that a driver's negligence in causing any damage had to be proved.

4 For example, Jaguar was defiant on being reprimanded by the ASA for encouraging middle-aged men to recapture their youth by driving fast with the headline: 'Suddenly weekends are a blur again', and showing a blurry background set against a new shiny Jaguar (*The Times* 9.2.00).

5 See Tombs (1999) for more.

6 As Sorenson (1994: 113) points out, if accidents were a 'fortuitous happening', their frequency distribution would approximate a normal bell-shaped curve, but some people have higher accident rates that are stable over time, suggesting the causes lie deeper than in uncontrollable environmental circumstances.

7 STATS 19 figures for 2000 showed that the proportion of all pedestrian casualties killed or seriously injured at or within 50 m of a zebra or pelican crossing was 12.6 per cent, which equated to 6.4 per cent of all road casualties. Some pedestrian casualties may have stepped out without allowing sufficient time for vehicles to stop.

8 For example, in 1975-6, 29 per cent women and 69 per cent men held full driving licences in Britain, though by 1998–2000 the proportions had risen respectively to 60 per cent and 82 per cent, the female proportion doubling (DTLR 2001c: Table 3.15).

9 The increase in the miles travelled by private cars and taxis was greater in Britain in the 1980s than in any other decade of that century. See Table 9.4 (DTLR 2001c).

10 Many who admitted exceeding limits by up to 10 mph nevertheless perceived themselves as law-abiding in Corbett and Simon (1999).

11 In 1998–2000 in Britain, 71 per cent of all adults held full licences (DTLR 2001c: Table 3.15) and, in 1998, about 70 per cent of all European adults held driving licences (as cited in AA 1999: 16, from *Guide on driver licensing 1998*, Commission Internationale des Examens de Conduite Automobile).

Chapter 4

'Car crime' as theft of and from a vehicle

Car crime as theft

When 'car crime' in whatever context is discussed by politicians, the media, criminologists or the public, the traditional understanding is of 'car theft'. Though the text takes issue with this narrow definition of car crime as noted in Chapter 1, there is no doubting the importance and scale of the vehicle-theft problem. Three main subtypes of 'car crime' are recorded in the Criminal Statistics in England and Wales: theft of the contents and external parts of a vehicle, which includes cars and commercial vehicles; taking a vehicle without the owner's consent for temporary use; and theft of a vehicle for permanent deprivation. Together these categories constitute almost one fifth of officially recorded and self-reported crimes, and vehicle crime is the largest single category of recorded crime. The estimated cost of vehicle theft to the nation now tops £3.5 billion annually (e.g. Home Office 2000e: para. 4), and one survey estimated that proceeds from professional vehicle theft if legal would rank fifth in the earnings of the world's top companies (*The Times*, 17.02.97).

In 1999, theft of a vehicle (variously defined) constituted 12 per cent of recorded crime in Italy, 10 per cent in the USA and 32 per cent in Japan.[1] This offence is one of the world's most numerous crimes, with an aggregate of almost four million in 29 industrialised countries, and it is the third most frequently recorded offence type behind domestic burglary and violent crime in these countries overall.[2]

Victims of vehicle theft also suffer considerably (as shown in Chapter 1). Figures from the 2000 British Crime Survey (BCS) revealed that the impact was more severe on victims of vehicle theft than on all violence victims[3] (Kershaw *et al.* 2000: Tables A5.17 and A6.14), and another survey showed that more than two thirds of a representative sample of 1,297 car owners thought that being deprived of one would be 'disastrous' (Lex 1999: 16–17). These findings illustrate drivers' emotional and practical dependence on motorised transport (mainly cars).

In view of the scale of the theft problem which represents a threat to the values of a society deeply embedded in car culture, it is not surprising that moral panics of indignation and fear have at times been generated by hostile and alarmist media coverage encouraging spiralling social reaction and demands for greater social control of the perpetrators.

In this chapter, we shall consider the historical backdrop and the legal context in which car theft has rapidly escalated, and then the extent and patterns of the different kinds of vehicle crime. Next, car theft will be treated as three broad types of activity: (1) theft of contents and parts of vehicles; (2) 'joyriding' or theft for temporary use; and (3) theft for permanent deprivation. Categories (1) and (3) would most usually be theft for financial gain, and (2) and (3) together comprise the category of 'theft of a vehicle' in the Criminal Statistics. However, vehicle theft is a complex matter and individual incidents may not sit happily in any of these three categories. For instance, thieves stealing a car for temporary use to get home could then do any number of things – dump the vehicle, take valuables for personal use or remove the in-car entertainment system to sell among a network of friends or to a handler – which could qualify the incident for the (1) and (2) categories. Alternatively, if the car was set alight after its temporary theft usage this offence could be classified as arson. Moreover, several different kinds of theft activity could be grouped in the same category. Thus cars stolen for permanent retention, as in category (3), could be stripped or dismantled for their parts, or they could be driven by the owner to a breakers' yard in order to make a fraudulent insurance claim, or they could be kept for the thief's own use, or shipped abroad as part of a organised crime ring. Nevertheless, for ease of presentation we shall use the tripartite typology above and it should be borne in mind that several different offences can occur as part of the same incident and that several different theft activities can share the same purpose. It is also worth recognising that offenders themselves often progress from one form of theft activity to another as their offending careers lengthen, so there is often commonality between different kinds of car thieves.

Within the three-part framework key research studies conducted on vehicle theft will be addressed, noting that the majority of work has centred on joyriding, especially in terms of explanations for 'car crime'. As females appear largely disinterested in stealing cars or parts, theories linked with masculinity are provided as an alternative vantage point to explain the gender imbalance. Less research has been carried out on professional vehicle theft and fraud-related offences and, although this area is less well theorised, the nature of these crimes will be touched upon in view of their prevalence and importance.

The final section will focus on preventive efforts and, where undertaken, the research to evaluate these. The control of this kind of crime is ripe for opportunity reduction, and various efforts have been made to reduce theft by situational, technological and legislative means. These will be reviewed along with other strategies to reduce vehicle theft, such as cognitive behavioural programmes for offenders.

While the main intended referent in this chapter is 'car-related theft and its various aspects', a broader definition will necessarily be used when discussing the extent of car theft and its trends. This is because figures for car theft are not given separately in commonly available tables such as the Criminal Statistics, and the more generic 'vehicle theft' also includes thefts relating to mopeds, motorcycles, company cars and all vehicles used solely or partly for commercial purposes. Meanwhile the British Crime Survey's indices of vehicle theft excludes thefts of vehicles used solely for commercial purposes and lorries, but includes the other types listed here. As a consequence, the terms 'vehicle theft' and 'car theft' will be used advisedly as and where appropriate.

Historical and legal context of car theft

As noted in Chapter 2, it was not until 1930, under s. 28 of the Road Traffic Act, that 'theft of vehicle' offences were formally recognised in law. Before then, car thieves had usually been charged with stealing the petrol used. Henceforth for almost forty years 'theft of' offences (where the vehicle was recovered within 48 hours) were framed as 'taking and driving away any motor vehicle without having the consent of the owner thereof or other lawful authority', and the acronym 'TDA' has endured to this day.

The offence was amended in the Road Traffic Act 1962 so that a charge of TDA could include passengers allowing themselves to be transported in a stolen vehicle. Only in 1968, under the Theft Act, was a legal distinction drawn between 'theft for temporary use' and 'theft for permanent deprivation'. Under s. 1 of this Act, theft of property –

including vehicles, their contents and parts – is determined by the mental element of intention permanently to deprive; where it is not, as in the case of joyriding for temporary use only, an offence of 'TWOC' – taking a conveyance without the owner's consent or lawful authority – is provided for under s. 12(1) of the Act, and it refers to the same activity as TDA.

Under the Theft Act 1968, TWOC became a notifiable offence and could be heard in magistrates' or crown courts (as an 'either-way' offence), and was subject to a three-year maximum term of imprisonment. But in efforts to reduce workload, and consequently waiting times at crown court, the Criminal Justice Act 1988 reduced various offences to summary status only. Taking without consent was one such offence and subsequently this carried a maximum six-month term of imprisonment. According to Light and colleagues (1993), little notice was taken of this switch at the time yet when a sharp escalation in the frequency and seriousness of TWOC offences gained media attention in 1991, the six-month maximum was condemned as inadequate. Reports of ramraiding (using a stolen car to smash into commercial premises to steal goods), performance driving (driving a car to its limits using motor-sport techniques) and high-speed police chases became commonplace (see, for example, Campbell 1993), the former contributing to waves of moral panics created by the media warning of the threat posed.

In consequence, the Aggravated Vehicle-taking Act 1992 attempted to meet public concern about inadequate sanctions. This Act inserted a new s. 12(A) into the Theft Act 1968 and created an aggravated offence of taking without consent, committed if a stolen vehicle is driven dangerously, or results in an accident causing injury to any person or damage to any property or the vehicle itself. It is an either-way offence subject to two years' maximum imprisonment or five years where death results and/or an unlimited fine. Interestingly, the maximum for the either-way offence of theft of a vehicle is seven years' imprisonment and/or an unlimited fine, so in theory permanent deprivation of a vehicle could result in a more severe consequence than where a death results from temporary use of a stolen vehicle,[4] seemingly confirming that the value of a car is held to be greater than the value of a life.

The extent and trends of vehicle theft

Extent of vehicle theft

In the 2001–2 financial year (to end March 2002), over 983,000 'theft of and from vehicle' offences[5] were recorded by police in England and

Wales, comprising almost 18 per cent of the total volume of criminal offences recorded during that year and 43 per cent of all theft offences recorded (Simmons *et al.* 2002: Table 3.04). Two thirds of these vehicle thefts were of contents and parts (66.6 per cent), and a third (33.4 per cent) were of the vehicle itself (ibid.). However, these proportions are far from straightforward. Earlier returns have shown that between 10 per cent and 12 per cent of each kind of theft involved lorries and other sole-purpose commercial vehicles, and about 16 per cent of 'theft of' and 19 per cent of 'theft from' offences were attempted thefts (e.g. Kershaw *et al.* 2000: Appendix C).

Moreover, the picture is further complicated by two other notifiable offence categories which are *not* included in discourses of 'car crime' nor in the totals above. Since 1998, when new counting rules were introduced, an existing summary offence – vehicle interference and tampering – was included as part of the notifiable offences recorded by police, and nearly 81,000 were recorded in 2001–2. The other offence is criminal damage to a vehicle where, for example, a window is smashed but nothing taken, and almost 420,000 were recorded in the same year. The importance of these two offence categories is that they are not easily distinguishable from attempted thefts, yet are excluded from the government's vehicle crime reduction targets (Simmons 2002: 42). The upshot was a situation where the proportions of these different offences varied widely between police forces (ibid.: 41) as there was clearly some latitude for the police to record an incident under any of them,[6] the implication being that classifying attempted thefts as criminal damage or interference and tampering could help achieve the reduction targets. However, the introduction of the National Criminal Recording Standard in April 2002 was intended to facilitate clarity and consistency in offence classification, and the impact on the government's vehicle crime reduction targets (see below) remained to be seen.

The British Crime Survey (BCS) provides a more accurate appraisal of the extent of vehicle theft, relying as it does on self-reports by representative samples of the population of offences occurring during the previous 12 months which were reported or unreported to police and not just those recorded by police. During 2001–2, excluding thefts of and from vehicles used solely for commercial purposes, the BCS estimated that 2,597,000 offences occurred (Simmons 2002: Table 2.01). These comprised 60 per cent thefts from vehicles, 27 per cent attempted thefts of or from vehicles and 13 per cent thefts of vehicles. However, a further 1,579,000 vehicle vandalism (criminal damage) incidents were reported but as in the recorded Criminal Statistics, these are not counted as attempted thefts even though a proportion may be such.

A comparable subset of recorded offences is regularly produced from the Criminal Statistics to enable comparison with BCS offences. This irons out the differences between the two sets of figures. For example, recorded attempted thefts are amalgamated with recorded interference offences in one category to compare with BCS attempted thefts of and from, and theft-related offences involving sole-purpose commercial vehicles are excluded from the Criminal Statistics.

As seen in Table 4.1, when using the comparable subset, the BCS best estimate of 2,597,000 vehicle-related offences is almost three times as great as the adjusted comparison of 926,000 offences recorded in the year to end September 2001.

Because 'theft of vehicle' offences are more likely to be reported and recorded by police than the other categories, and because unreported crime is included in the BCS distribution, it is unsurprising that 'theft of' offences comprise a higher proportion of the recorded offence distribution than of the BCS. This is shown more clearly below.

Attrition rates in recorded offences

Table 4.2, derived from the 2001–2 BCS interviews, shows that in the comparable subset there was a high reporting rate for 'theft of vehicle' offences (94 per cent of BCS incidents were reported in 2001–2), though it was much lower for 'thefts from vehicles' and 'attempted thefts' (48 per cent and 40 per cent, respectively) (Simmons 2002: Table 2.01). There was a higher police recording rate for 'theft of' offences (71 per cent of those reported) than for 'theft from' but not for attempted thefts (64 per cent and 82 per cent, respectively). Based on BCS figures, this means that 67 per cent of theft of vehicle offences ended up as officially recorded,

Table 4.1: Comparison of recorded and BCS vehicle-related thefts in 2001–2

	Theft of vehicle		Theft from vehicle		Attempted theft of/from vehicle		Total number	
	%	n	%	n	%	n	%	n
BCS	13	330,000	60	1,560,000	27	707,000	100	2,597,000
Recorded offences*	24	221,000	51	476,000	25	229,000	100	926,000

*Recorded figures are for the year ended September 2001 and the proportions are derived from comparable subset figures shown in Simmons (2002: Table 2:01).

though only 31 per cent of thefts from a vehicle and 32 per cent of attempted thefts were logged in the Criminal Statistics. The higher reporting rate of thefts of vehicles is usually attributed to insurance requirements, the high value of vehicles and the reasonable likelihood of vehicle retrieval with police help. By contrast the lower reporting rates for thefts from vehicles and attempted thefts are usually credited to police inability to resolve these matters (ibid.: Table 3.07) and victims deciding that they may have more to lose than to gain by claiming on insurance for thefts of contents or parts of vehicles. Explanations for the shrinkage in the recording of reported offences centre on insufficient evidence to suggest a crime has been committed, a perceived mistaken or disingenuous report, or the offence is too trivial to warrant recording (Mirrlees-Black *et al.* 1998: 21).

Overall from BCS data an attrition rate of 64 per cent is derived corresponding with a loss of roughly 1,671,000 offences from official records, suggesting that just over a third (36 per cent) of all (non-commercial) vehicle-related theft offences committed end up in official figures as 'car crime'. If in some way owners were encouraged to report more thefts of contents and parts to police, or more of the offences reported were recorded by police, the nation's crime reduction target figures could be in jeopardy.

Trends in theft offences

According to the recorded Criminal Statistics for England and Wales, the incidence of theft-related offences increased markedly but fairly smoothly from 1934, when the first separate statistics for vehicle thefts

Table 4.2: Attrition rates estimated from British Crime Survey for theft-related offences (2001–2)

	Theft of of vehicle	*Theft from vehicle*	*Attempted theft*	*Total*
% reported	94	48	40	52
% recorded (of those reported)	71	64	82	69
% recorded (of all estimated BCS offences)	67	31	2	36 (*n* = 926,000)
Total % (*n*)	100 (330,000)	*100 (1,560,000)	*100 (707,000)	*100 (2,597,000)*

*Numbers and percentages have been rounded up to nearest thousand so are subject to slight error. Derived from Simmons (2002: Table 2.01).

were collected, to the late 1960s, roughly in line with growing numbers of registered vehicles (e.g. Webb and Laycock 1992: 4). Then the risk of theft rose sharply, with a sudden jump after the Theft Act 1968, when TDA offences were counted as notifiable offences and added to 'theft of vehicle' offences. The incidence of recorded theft continued to rise fast until a peak was reached in 1992. The trend since has been markedly downwards despite the escalating number of vehicles registered. Between 1991 and 2001–2, 44 per cent fewer 'theft of or unauthorised taking' offences and 28 per cent fewer 'thefts from vehicles' were recorded (derived from Simmons, 2002: Table 3.04). This yields an average drop in recorded vehicle crime of 34 per cent over the decade (see Table 4.3), though a small increase of around 1 per cent was estimated in the year to 2001–2.

The BCS, biennial since 1981, shows the highest number of vehicle-related thefts in 1993, since when the pattern has also been downward. Using the comparable subset figures from the BCS for greater accuracy, Table 4.3 shows an overall 32 per cent drop in all vehicle thefts that occurred between 1991 and 2001–2, comprising a 35 per cent fall in thefts from vehicles, a 36 per cent drop in thefts of vehicles, and a 21 per cent decrease in theft attempts of and from vehicles (Simmons 2002: Table 3.01). It also contrasts these reductions with those indicated in the recorded Crime Statistics over the same period, and highlights the similar nature of the decrease over the decade for these types of vehicle theft.

Interestingly, this pattern of declining vehicle theft rates is consistent with, though more marked than, that for property crime nationally (Kinshott 2001) and falling car theft 'of' and 'from' rates noted inter-nationally between 1992 and 1996 (Mayhew and van Dijk 1997: Tables 1–3). These figures seem to suggest that preventive efforts are reaping rewards, and capitalising on national downward trends, in 1998 the

Table 4.3: Comparison of recorded and BCS vehicle-related trends: percentage decline between 1991 and 2001–2*

	Theft of vehicle**	Theft from vehicle	Attempted theft of/from vehicle	Average drop
BCS	36	35	21	32
Recorded offences	44	28	n/a	34***

*   Figures derived from Tables 3.01 and 3.04 (Simmons 2002)
**   Includes aggravated vehicle-taking in 2001–2.
*** This figure is the average fall of 'theft of' and 'theft from' offences which includes attempts.

British government launched a campaign to reduce car crime by 30 per cent by 2004 from a baseline measured in the year to March 1999 (e.g. VCRAT 1999).

Proportions of temporary and permanent thefts

As recognised in the Theft Act 1968, vehicle thefts tend to be of two types: where temporary use is planned, as in 'joyriding' or TWOC, and the vehicle abandoned after use; and theft for permanent deprivation (often with the purpose of financial gain). Determining the proportions of each kind is impossible as the clear-up rate (where arrests are made) for theft of vehicle offences was only 13 per cent in 2001–2 (Simmons 2002: Table 8.04). Yet a rough approximation can be made by considering the recovery rate of stolen vehicles, since recovery is thought less likely in the case of professional theft (e.g. Tremblay *et al.* 1994). Criminal Statistics (at least since 1970) and British Crime Survey figures (at least since 1993) show a general downward trend in the proportion of stolen vehicles recovered, suggesting fewer opportunist thieves operating. In 1999, 58 per cent of stolen vehicles were recovered (Kinshott 2001) and, in 2000, up to two thirds of vehicle thefts were estimated as temporary use (amateur) ones, and around one third permanent (professional) ones. USA figures tend towards similar proportions (e.g. Clarke and Harris 1992: 3; NHTSA 1998).

Explanations for the probable fall in 'temporary use' theft include better car security measures which defeat the opportunist thief (e.g. Webb and Laycock 1992: 12–15), mounting traffic congestion preventing swift getaways and high-speed rides, and the notion that more would-be offenders have legitimate access to vehicles as registrations have increased. By contrast, though each new technological advance may prevent more temporary theft by amateurs, professional thieves seem thwarted only briefly and their slice of the market may be growing internationally.

Tremblay and colleagues (1994) examined changes in trends of unrecovered and recovered vehicles in Canada. They concluded that the rise or fall in each of these rates were not linked, and that the two sets of offenders operated in different worlds with different motivations and constraints and different explanatory processes were needed. Changes in rates of recovered stolen vehicles were sensitive to the available pool of motivated offenders (which depended on age, household ownership of cars, target vulnerability and the risks of arrest). By contrast, rates of unrecovered vehicles varied according to changes in market regulatory factors such as the control exerted by insurance companies to prevent overcharging practices in the repair industry, and government regulations on the resale of crashed vehicles. So when legitimate cars and parts became more expensive, demand for stolen cars and parts increased among individual consumers and repairers.

The apparent rise in professional theft in Canada has also been attributed to higher levels of vehicle ownership in developing countries fuelled by geo-social-political factors such as the dissolution of the USSR which created new democracies and led to massive road-building programmes, and the advent of the single European market (Maxwell 2000). Thus the dynamics of developing markets may have international knock-on effects regarding the volume of stolen vehicles set for foreign sale.

Risk of victimisation

The incidence of reported or recorded vehicle theft is often better appreciated in terms of risk of victimisation, and in 1999 an international comparison of victimisation rates (van Kesteren *et al.* 2001, cited in Barclay *et al.* 2001: Table 2) showed that of citizens in 17 EU and other industrialised countries, car owners in England and Wales were at the highest risk of vehicle theft (although variations in recording practices may reduce the reliability of this calculation). Australians and French citizens were next most vulnerable, and Japanese and Swiss vehicle owners were the least at risk.

More specifically, as revealed in the 2001–2 BCS in England and Wales, 1.7 per cent of owners had a vehicle stolen, 7.1 per cent were victims of theft from their vehicles and 3.3 per cent experienced an attempted theft of or from their vehicles. One in nine vehicle-owning households were victimised at least once in that year (Simmons 2002: Table 5.04).

Women car-owners were slightly more worried about the theft of their vehicle than men (18 per cent v. 16 per cent were 'very worried'), and young owners more than older ones (ibid.: Table 9.04). Interestingly, although women owners expressed more worry about kinds of physical attack than vehicle theft (e.g. 25 per cent 'very worried' about rape v. 18 per cent about theft of a car), men were more worried about vehicle theft (16 per cent 'very worried') than about physical attack (7 per cent) or burglary (13 per cent) (ibid.). These figures clearly indicate substantial concern among men and women about the possibility of their car being stolen, though the exact meaning of 'worry' in this context is unclear in view of the fear element being confounded with perceived likelihood of such an event occurring and actual level of exposure to risk.

Actual risk varies by other demographic characteristics, and the likelihood of any vehicle-related theft is greatest in areas of 'high physical disorder', in inner-city areas and where the head of household is aged 16–24 or lives in a flat/maisonette (ibid.: Table 5.04); it is lower in rural areas or where there are detached houses (ibid.). Ethnicity also has an impact with a slightly raised risk of vehicle-related theft among black and Asian households in 1999. The average risk was almost 13 per cent compared with 15 per cent among Asian households and 17 per cent among black households (Kinshott, 2001) though the raised risk is most likely influenced by other correlates of risk linked with social disadvantage. Apart from these demographic correlates of risk, the place where a vehicle is left also contributes to the likelihood of theft. Controlling for 'parking exposure' related to periods of time spent parked in different locations, Clarke and Mayhew (1996) showed that cars left in public car parks were four times more at risk than those parked in a street outside home or work, a finding which has helped to focus prevention efforts on car parks.

Targeted vehicles

The Car Theft Index, first produced in 1992 and now issued annually (e.g. Home Office 2000a), shows which models and makes of car are most at risk of theft in England, Scotland and Wales, based on information from the Police National Computer and Driver and Vehicle Licensing Agency (DVLA) records. The 1997 index indicated that 81 per cent of vehicle thefts related to cars, 9 per cent to motorcycles and 9 per cent to light commercial vehicles (Brown and Saliba 1998). Heavy goods vehicles accounted for a further small proportion of 1 per cent (Brown 1995).

Vulnerability to theft is also linked with the purpose of the theft, and Clarke and Harris (1992) developed model-specific indices for three forms of US car theft: theft for temporary use (TWOC), stripping of internal and external parts (theft from) and permanent retention (theft of). They found that high-performance, sporty American vehicles were at highest risk among joyriders; foreign-registered, mainly German models were at greatest risk of stripping of parts and contents; and a mix of luxury, expensive cars and cheaper, European cars were most likely to be stolen for permanent deprivation. In the USA, permanent retention theft risk has been shown to vary in terms of relative ease of export, and Clarke and Harris (1992) reported that each of the ten highest theft-risk states in 1987 was shown either to have a seaport or to border the Great Lakes. This may help to explain the high vulnerability of vehicles in Britain.

Older vehicles are consistently found to be attractive to thieves, mainly for the purposes of stripping of parts and contents and temporary use (e.g. Kinshott 2001). This may be due to the non-availability or expense of replacing spare parts from older cars, the familiarity of older models and their incongruence in less affluent areas (Light *et al.* 1993; Sallybanks and Brown 1999), and their relative lack of security features and greater likelihood of being parked in a public area or street (Clarke and Harris 1992). While there may be little consistency in targets across countries owing largely to differences in their availability, estate cars in the UK, Australia and the USA are at low risk of theft (Clarke 1999: 9) probably because of their uncool image to joyriders who comprise the bulk of thieves in these countries.

Vehicle theft for contents and parts

Where vehicles are stripped of their contents, interior fittings or external parts, it may be a matter of convenience whether the vehicle is moved beforehand. If removal occurs then the incident is recorded as a 'theft of' offence, but if it is not moved it is classified as a 'theft from' offence. In other words, taking a vehicle may be for the sole purpose of stealing parts or contents yet it is recorded as an unauthorised taking (TWOC/TDA) or theft of vehicle offence. Thus the most serious offence takes precedence for classification purposes, and only one theft offence is recorded per incident.

Nevertheless, even without the 'theft from' offences that are actually recorded as 'theft of', the former category accounted for around 67 per cent of all recorded vehicle thefts in 2001–2, representing 11.9 per cent of all recorded crime. As noted in Table 4.2 above, only around 31 per cent of such thefts experienced in that year were recorded by police, most victims failing to report the incident because the police 'couldn't do anything' (Simmons 2002: Table 3.07). Yet should victims change their habits towards reporting more of these thefts (or the police recording more of them) there would be serious consequences for recorded crime statistics, and partly for this reason recent research has examined more closely the patterns of theft involved.

What gets stolen?

While received wisdom held that the most frequent target of car thieves was stereo equipment, including radios, CDs, cassette tapes and speakers, an analysis of three British Crime Surveys showed that between 1993 and 1997, external parts took over the top spot. Sallybanks and Thomas (2000: 18) analysed the 1998 BCS to show that stereo systems continued to be stolen at roughly the same rate (just over a quarter of all thefts from a vehicle), but external vehicle part thefts had doubled over the 1993–7 period and in 1997 comprised 36 per cent of all items stolen in thefts from vehicles. By 2001–2, vehicle parts comprised a similar proportion (37 per cent) of items stolen (Simmons 2002: Table 5.05).

Sallybanks and Thomas (2000) showed that though almost three quarters of stereo equipment thefts were reported to police; for external vehicle parts the rate was much lower and in 1997 only 20 per cent were reported. This included bumpers, wheels, hub caps, number plates, exhausts and makers' badges (ibid.: 19). Several possible explanations were suggested. Because older vehicles are most at risk of theft (e.g. Home Office 2000a), it could be that the non-availability of car parts for older models or the expense of replacing them – which might be greater than the value of the whole car – accounts for the high rate of external parts theft. Yet unless the cost of parts or labour rose disproportionately in the late 1990s or the availability of spare parts decreased substantially this would not necessarily explain the rapid increased rate of such thefts in the same period. The removal of vehicle registration plates for the purpose of changing a stolen vehicle's identity ('ringing') might also account for a proportion of external parts thefts but whether ringing offences increased markedly around the turn of the century is unclear. The youth fashion for wearing or collecting badges from various marques, such as Volkswagens or Mercedes, could also explain a small proportion of parts thefts and was especially prevalent in the late 1990s.

Valuables such as bags and money comprised 18 per cent of all items stolen from vehicles in the BCS 2001–2 and telephones 4 per cent (Simmons 2002: Table 5.05), and it is these items that tend to be highlighted in media advertising campaigns warning owners to lock their cars (e.g. summer 2002) rather than the external parts which appear at far greater risk. Inside vehicles, drivers' airbags became the new luxury 'must-have' for thieves (e.g. *The Times* 20.1.01).

Little other research has focused exclusively on theft of vehicle contents and parts, probably because stealing items from vehicles often occurs contemporaneously with stealing the vehicles, which as the more serious offence is the one recorded. Other studies that have embraced theft of contents and parts *inter alia* include Clarke (1999), Spencer (1992) and Parker (1974). Sutton (1998) considered theft from vehicles and provided a wide-ranging description of the ways in which stolen goods were bought and sold, in order to inform his proposed market reduction approach to reduce both demand and supply. Integral to the study were in-depth interviews exploring motivation with different types of offender, including those who stole car contents, especially stereos.

Noting that stereo radio-cassette systems have been present in almost all cars for years, which would seemingly reduce the need for their theft, Sutton asked the obvious question of what then happens to stolen car stereos (ibid.: 73)? In answer he found that among his group of car thieves there was high status attached to expensive, new and sophisticated models of stereo which tended then to be installed in offenders' own cars, but little status attached to older ones which were often removed and sold on to a network of friends for small profit. Stolen stereos were frequently being 'traded up' and on their way to somewhere else.

In sum, it may be thought curious that an offence that contributed a massive 11.9 per cent in 2001–2 to the annual recorded offences in England and Wales (Simmons 2002: Table 3.01) has warranted little exclusive research attention. This is particularly so when less than half of theft from vehicles is reported by victims, illustrating the fragility of the figure which could rise substantially should aggrieved owners change their reporting patterns. Yet, because theft of parts and contents often occurs in conjunction with moving a vehicle for joyriding or stripping purposes, it is included in research into theft of vehicles and this becomes our focus now.

Vehicle theft for temporary use: joyriding

Though the gap between theft for temporary use and that for permanent deprivation may be shrinking, as noted above, the former have more frequently captured the public imagination, media attention and criminological research interest. As noted earlier, these TDA or TWOC offences are commonly referred to as 'joyriding', a term which reputedly was coined to express the joy and pleasure of stealing and driving someone else's car.

Yet there is not always joy associated with the activity and crashes are often associated with stolen vehicles. Weglian (1978) reported that joyriders were between 47 and 200 times more likely than other drivers to become crash-involved, and a Florida study found that one third of hot pursuits by police ended with a crash and 1 per cent in death (Alpert 1987, cited by Clarke and Harris 1992).

One condition for an 'aggravated vehicle taking' charge is a crash in a stolen vehicle that causes damage or injury, and the number of these offences has risen steadily since 1992, when the offence was first introduced in England and Wales. In 2001–2, 'aggravated vehicle taking' comprised 3.7 per cent theft and unauthorised taking of a vehicle offences. Although dangerous driving whilst stolen is the other main condition necessary to meet an aggravated vehicle-taking charge, this means that up to 1 in 27 recorded TWOC offences could involve a crash of some kind.

Who does it?

A true picture of who gets involved in vehicle theft generally and joyriding specifically is elusive since Criminal Statistics include only those who are convicted, and the British Crime Survey excludes respondents under 16. Also, self-report and offender-interview studies often suffer from sampling biases, as they draw participants mainly from sources linked with the criminal justice system. Those who get caught are over-represented and those who do not under-represented.

A more accurate picture of the demographics of young people's involvement in car crime can be found in the results of a nationwide interview survey of a representative sample of 1,721 young people aged 14–25 in England and Wales and of a representative similar-aged booster sample of 808 ethnic minority young people (Graham and Bowling 1995). *Inter alia*, respondents were asked if they had ever carried out any of a list of 23 offences; if so, whether this had been within the last year, when they first began and when they had stopped. Theft from a car and theft of a car were included. Although the results refer to 1992, when a peak in vehicle thefts occurred, Table 4.4 shows that males were roughly six times more likely ever to have stolen a car than females and more than four times as likely to have stolen from a car than females. The picture for involvement in car crime during the 12 months up to the survey shows a similar pattern, with the expected lower proportion of 'active' offenders.

These findings are interesting for several reasons. First, although self-reported offending in general is predominantly male dominated (2.7:1 males to females admitting ever having offended), the ratio was more pronounced with respect to car theft (5.9:1 for 'theft of' and 4.4:1 for 'theft from'). A similar pattern was evident for offending within the previous 12 months (active offenders). It could be that female car thieves are less likely than males to be the instigators, being present as one of a group, since car theft is usually a group activity (e.g. Spencer 1992: 8), or

Table 4.4: Prevalence of involvement of young people in car theft in England and Wales in 1992*

	'Ever offenders'				'Active offenders'			
	All (%)	M (%)	F (%)	Sex ratio	All (%)	M (%)	F (%)	Sex ratio
23 listed offences**	43.0	55.0	31.0	2.7:1	20.0	28.0	12.0	2.3:1
Theft of car	2.0	3.4	0.6	5.9:1	0.9	1.5	0.2	6.5:1
Theft from car	2.8	4.6	1.1	4.4:1	0.5	0.8	0.3	3.0:1
Unweighted *n****	1,648	738	910		1,538	676	862	

*   Derived from Graham and Bowling (1995: Tables 2.1, C1 and C2).

**   Drug offences are excluded.

*** This table uses data only from their core sample.

that females are less interested generally in car theft than in other crimes. Secondly, in accord with the large absolute drop in vehicle theft since 1991 (see Table 4.3), the proportion of young people who admitted to 'theft of and from' in 1998, compared with 1992, also declined. As Table 4.4 shows, 0.9 per cent admitted to theft of a car and 0.5 per cent theft from a vehicle in 1992, but this proportion fell to 0.3 per cent for both offences in 1998 when a similar survey was conducted (Flood-Page *et al.* 2000: Table A.3).[7]

Joyriding is apt to be viewed as a white man's crime since, as Groombridge (1994) points out, if there were grounds to implicate black men as culprits to foment a panic the tabloid newspapers would have done so. He postulates that either racist policing deters young black men from driving cars unless they own them, or else black masculinity makes different use of the car such that its significance cannot be encapsulated in short-term reckless use but rather in possessing a car on a longer-term basis and proving ownership when asked (by police). On the other hand, blacks and Asian groups are not precluded from other professional vehicle theft. Graham and Bowling (1995) did not find an over or under-involvement of young black men (or black women) in car theft (ibid.: 113), although small numbers were interviewed even with the booster sample. Similarly, Asian groups (considering only Indians, Pakistanis and Bangladeshis) were not significantly over or under-represented in having 'ever' participated in car theft (ibid.). The common perception that vehicle theft is predominantly the work of white, working-class youth may result from the much lower population rates of the ethnic minorities.

Many offenders begin their criminal careers with vehicle theft when relatively young. Light *et al.* (1993: 7) found that almost half of their sample began at 14 or 15, and Spencer's (1992) school sample and McCullough *et al.*'s (1990) probation sample threw up examples of children starting at age 10. Light *et al.* concluded from existing research that car-related theft is one of the most specialised offences, and noted in their own study that car-crime specialists (just over half their sample) were strongly interested in cars from an early age. However, not all researchers agree that most car thieves are specialists (see Wilkinson 1997; Rose 2000; Soothill *et al.* 2002).

Whether or not young offenders are specialists in car crime, a career progression is common, with young children quickly progressing from lookouts (co-opted by their older brothers and friends), to passengers, to stealing contents or parts as perks of driving the stolen vehicle. These proceeds can be for their own use or sold on. Indirect involvement can lead to direct theft of a car for joyriding. Entry skills are learnt and showing off one's driving skills can be manifest in performance driving displays, a phenomenon associated with the early 1990s. As a developmental step, a stolen car (or stolen parts) may be resold for profit, or more professional, fraudulent activities such as ringing, chopping or insurance scams may ensue. Stealing a car to use for other criminal purposes such as burglary can also mark a progression. Thus a large proportion of those who commit different kinds of car theft will share similar demographics as they simply progress through the range, though a profile of the smaller proportion engaged in car theft for professional and financial purposes is less clear particularly where organised crime gangs are concerned.

The backdrop to car theft for most known offenders seems to be a socially deprived home life, poverty, unemployment, underachievement and low aspirations located within a lower socioeconomic environment (Spencer 1992; Webb and Laycock 1992; Light *et al.* 1993). Family involvement in car crime seems common, with one third of Light *et al.*'s (1993) offender sample saying that other family members, usually a brother or cousin, also took cars (ibid.: 15) and Sutton (1998: 108) noting the willingness of family members to receive stolen goods. Such a picture is fairly typical for young offenders of all kinds and reflects a bleak future with restricted opportunities. Stealing cars provides a meaningful diversion. Indeed, the employment aspirations of over a third in Light *et al.*'s sample focused on legitimate work involving cars or driving, revealing a passion for cars that often accompanied the excitement of stealing fast models.

Explanations for joyriding

Some of the more common conceptualisations of joyriding will be considered now.

Rational choice

This perspective, as noted in Chapter 1, arose from government interest in preventing crime through situational measures and is founded on the view that offenders are by and large rational, free-thinking beings. Evidence to support a rational choice perspective in decisions to commit car theft comes from government-funded research, including Light *et al.*'s (1993) study of young offenders, in which different motivations are revealed to explain the career stages of initial involvement, continuing in and desisting from theft activities. So key benefits of getting involved – e.g. relief from boredom and the financial perks of stealing a car radio or stereo (ibid.: 23–5) – could outweigh the perceived costs like getting caught, which many young 'apprentices' underestimated (ibid.: 61–2) or discounted (ibid.: 89). As offenders progressed, the motivation to continue partly switched from expressive reasons to functional ones so the financial incentive provided by stealing parts or contents or reselling the vehicle (ibid.: 29) might vie with the thrill of a police chase (ibid.: 60) or the status accorded to those who progress to performance driving (ibid.: 29–30); and reasons for desisting might centre on a changed perception of costs transcending the perceived benefits which might lessen with changing needs such as settling down or finding a legitimate job (ibid.: 42–4).

Career progression has been identified in other government-sponsored studies of car thieves which suggest that offenders often reassess the benefits, costs, needs and opportunities as they develop from apprentices to skilled operators (e.g. Smyth 1990; Spencer 1992). A general conclusion from studies of rational choice is that event decisions are most amenable to prevention by situational measures and that opportunity reduction is likely to be more fruitful than reducing motivations for many kinds of crime.

The rational choice perspective has been closely associated with routine activity theory because of a shared emphasis on similar key qualities determining the suitability of criminal opportunities. Clarke (1999) has an updated model of the features of target suitability that can be applied to consider why cars and their contents are 'hot products' so attractive to thieves.

Car theft as compulsion

However rational the activities linked with car theft, the themes of compulsiveness and addiction frequently surface in studies documenting what offenders say. Though this is central to the notion of the criminal compelled to offend in early biological positivist models of offending (e.g. Lombroso 1876) and fell out of favour as ideological traditions moved on in criminological theorising, remnants of the idea have lingered.

Light *et al.* (1993: 38) noted that offenders' accounts frequently mentioned falling victim to the 'heightened emotional buzz of thieving and driving at speed' resulting from perceived 'unlimited opportunity and personal gratification', which tended to make car theft more compulsive than other kinds of theft. Certainly, offender-based studies have confirmed the high frequency of offending by some. For instance, Light *et al.* (ibid.: 11) showed that around half their participants reported more than one hundred thefts each. More worryingly, McCullough *et al.*'s (1990) study of joyriding in West Belfast showed that almost two thirds said nothing else felt as good as stealing cars, and a further 17 per cent said that only the effect of drugs compared. This may help explain why the extent of car theft in Belfast was uninfluenced even by the risk of kneecapping and shootings of car thieves carried out by the Irish Republican Army in community-ordered control initiatives (ibid.: 4).

However, several studies (Gulliver 1991; Light *et al.* 1993; Chapman 1994) liken car theft more to adolescent infatuation than addiction and are quick to caution against discussing compulsion in the clinical sense (e.g. Light *et al.* 1993), though others have done so. Kilpatrick's (1997) depth interviews with a small sample of persistent joyriders indicated that the bulk were diagnosed as psychologically dependent on joyriding according to six commonly agreed characteristics of addiction to chemical substances (e.g. increasing tolerance, withdrawal distress, craving to reengage, and relapse of a decision to stop). While a consensus regarding compulsion is unlikely, the huge tally of thefts built up by some persistent young offenders clearly underlines the scale of the problem.

Juvenile drift into car theft, neutralisation and normalisation

The notion of adolescents drifting into and out of delinquent activities, as originally proposed by Sykes and Matza (1957), is supported by Spencer's (1992) self-report study of car-theft offenders. Among her general school sample of 86 boys from a car theft-prone Sunderland estate, all car thieves reported that they had got sucked in by their brothers or friends and would not have got involved on their own (ibid.: 13).

Sykes and Matza's (1957) techniques of neutralisation can be applied to car theft. Light *et al.* (1993: 69) showed that few of their sample felt that stealing cars was serious and that status and respect rather than stigma were attached to the activity, suggesting that wrongfulness was neutralised by justifications to assuage any guilt. Moreover, for largely white working-class youth living in deprived or marginalised conditions in poorer areas, the everyday nature of stealing cars was normalised as part of the ordinary, routine way of life. Most youths knew someone who was entangled in car crime (Spencer 1992: 8), family and friends might also be connected (e.g. Sutton 1998: 105), and personal involvement was thought unexceptional. The drift to delinquency in this way rather decries positivist projections of some being compelled to offend. Yet while the concepts of drift and addiction seem polarised opposites, they could describe sequential stages in some car thieves' careers where initial casual interest later transforms into an all-consuming passion.

Gender-based theories

Consideration of gender in relation to car theft was for a long time a non-issue in mainstream theorising. This has most likely resulted from the androcentric focus that still dominates mainstream criminology which tends to assume a masculine arena for researchers and their subjects, coupled with a general lack of female interest in stealing cars, contents and their parts. That said, interest in issues and theories around masculinity has enjoyed a revival in response to feminist inquiry about gender concerns, and several of those embracing a gender focus will be considered now.

An early grasp of the problem of joyriding borrowed from a psychoanalytic approach that was intersected by class. Groombridge (1994: 30) summarised what he saw as the middle-class 'mummy's boy' hypothesis put forward by the subcultural theorist, Albert Cohen (1955: 164), as one where 'joyriders are "mothers'" boys trying to prove themselves men'. Adolescent boys are under strong pressure to establish their masculinity, and since conduct norms and 'good behaviour' tend to have been inspired by the care of mother these acquire feminine significance. In order therefore to establish a masculine gender identity, good behaviour must be rejected (to deny femininity) and replaced with 'bad behaviour' or delinquency (associated with masculinity). Class was involved in the early formulations of delinquency and Gibbens (1958) found it was middle-class youth that tended to take up joyriding around puberty as deprived, lower-class boys seemingly began stealing money and other things at an earlier age. In keeping with a psychoanalytic approach, Gibbens considered stealing cars as a compulsive behaviour with its roots in a neurotic family relationship particularly with the mother; hence the strong tendency to repetition despite court sanctions. Though the involvement of middle-class boys in joyriding may have been true in the 1950s, joyriding became very much linked with white, lower-class youth, as noted above. With this in mind, the notion of the tearing of adolescent boys away from the mother's grasp has been updated by Jackson (1992) and Campbell (1993), and though class is salient, a middle-class focus is not.

The difficulties of growing up male in a deprived neighbourhood and establishing an appropriate masculine identity are covered by Chapman (1994) in describing the problem and attempted solution of the Probation Service to joyriding in an area of West Belfast in Northern Ireland. He outlines a struggle where maternal control, usually accompanied by erratic or little paternal responsibility, gives way to young men breaking free to lead a marginalised existence in a street culture which is suffused with distorted and immature images of adult masculinity and male role models, and is typified by the characteristics of toughness, competitiveness, egocentricity and dominance. This scenario is entwined with feelings of being 'waste material' as few jobs are on offer, and resorting to crime, especially joyriding, is the most effective means of satisfying the needs and wants of these young men. Chapman likens their situation to an extended childhood, separated from responsible adulthood, where the toys they choose to play with have been designed for adult purposes. In one neat package, joyriding provides challenge, risk, competition, violence, escape, release from boredom, achievement, attention, audience applause, money and sex. The best solution to joyriding is often found in a 'good woman', but Chapman questions whether forming a relationship in this context just leads to the domesticisation or privatisation of criminality, whereby the young women partners are victimised by the attitudes and behaviour the community is now spared.

Themes addressing the individual and social delights of engaging in the strongly masculine joyriding culture surface repeatedly in offender-interview studies, and enjoyment of a shared culture is well illustrated by the thrill of the chase, experienced not only by the pursued but also the pursuers.

Light *et al.* (1993) found that, while 31 per cent thought that being chased by the police was the worst thing about their experiences of stealing cars, being chased and getting away was the best experience for

14 per cent, and feelings of shared fear and excitement in adrenalin-bolstered situations added to the thrill. Mirroring the accounts of some car thieves, those who chase them may also experience a sense of a shared masculine culture. The Policy Studies Institute (PSI) study of the Metropolitan Police spotlighted the jesting, self-congratulation and camaraderie enjoyed by officers after a shared hot pursuit of a stolen vehicle; the thrill of a chase enlivened more routine activities and imbued them with satisfaction and purpose (Smith and Gray 1985: 340). Interviews with male police traffic officers for Corbett *et al.*'s study of the deterrence of speeding (1998) revealed similar sentiments, reinforcing the notion that showing off high-speed skills to the 'enemy' in high-powered cars not only could bolster officers' self-esteem but also the feeling of being a good team player in multi-handed pursuits.

These two sides may of course reflect the same story: that shared masculine experience in this context is just part of the broader car culture in which most men (and now most women) have a role. Groombridge (1994, 1998) concluded from his research that the joyrider's use of cars is too close to the everyday and advertised use – i.e. to experience freedom and control on the road, to solve personal transport problems and realise male dreams which may include cars acting as a prop to their masculinity. He adds that these things link joyriders with other drivers and what separates them is that joyriders are just too young, drive too badly and are unsponsored. Indeed, in questioning whether joyriding is a male driving disorder he concludes that it is but one of them. The joyrider's disorder is to do it at the wrong time and the wrong place, yet many 'legitimate' drivers act disorderly – e.g. drink driving, speeding or using the car unnecessarily. Thus in critiquing car culture, Groombridge's view is that joyriders need more ways to be a man and more choice in means of transport.

A final point can be made about the search for masculine identity in connection with a study undertaken by Campbell (1993) of Blackbird Leys in Oxford, which experienced high levels of performance driving, torching of vehicles and youth disturbances in the early 1990s. She observes that where self-esteem is already in crisis and young offenders' identity as men is at stake, the pleasures of joyriding and its cult status may lead to a fearlessness which can reach the point of being suicidal (ibid.: 268–9). Hence the risks taken by some joyriders in West Belfast. In the face of these factors, she considers that the criminal justice system can do little or nothing to counter the invitation offered by joyriding, and perhaps these factors more than anything else underscore the problem posed by the most prolific joyriders.

Campbell's observations also underline a basic fact: that men are more attracted to risk than women, who are more attracted to safety than men, and these deeply entrenched cultural stereotypes of men as risk-seeking and women as safety-seeking are prescriptions of expected behaviour that mould and constrain our gender and social identities (e.g. Messerschmidt 1993; Barjonet 1988). Not only are men more likely to consider risk a pleasure and be more prepared to take risks when driving (Barjonet 1988: 135), male attraction to risk may also help to explain their strong dominance in vehicle-related theft, especially in activities such as ramraiding and performance driving, and indeed in other kinds of risk-involved mainstream crime such as robbery. (Risky driving behaviours are discussed further in Chapters 5 and 7 in relation to the general theory of crime.)

Theoretical abstractions of joyriding have ranged from the psycho-analytic model through the addiction model, to the rational choice approach associated with the attraction of hot products, while recent discourse has focused on broader considerations concerning the search for masculine identity among vulnerable youths in a shared male culture. Though each of these explanations has shown some applic-ability and relevance in understanding joyriding, the linking – and sometimes unstated or unquestioned – theme is society's immersion in car culture. Until cars become less central to our lives, and become less functional and symbolic, the desire and need to use cars lawfully or otherwise will continue unabated. If reducing this motivation is therefore unlikely, then increasing the difficulty of theft may be the key means to reduce its incidence, however unsatisfying this may be. This will be discussed further in the final section of the chapter.

Vehicle theft for permanent deprivation: professional theft

Stripping, ringing, dumping and reselling vehicles and their parts is big business, the proceeds of which would make it one of the most lucrative international industries were it legitimate (*The Times* 17.2.97). Yet though the costs involved are substantial, best estimates for the USA and England and Wales suggest professional car crime accounts for a minority of all vehicle theft (e.g. Clarke and Harris 1992; Webb and Laycock 1992). Together with knock-on effects felt by all motorists, through raised insurance premiums, and a growing concern by governments to stop the violence accompanying such thefts, preventive efforts are being targeted on these crimes. In Britain, the government hopes to meet one third of its car theft reduction target by 2004 through legislative measures geared towards cutting professional theft and fraud.

The Home Office (2000d) estimated that around 44 per cent of stolen vehicles in England and Wales in 1999 remained unrecovered, and it is believed that a quarter of these vehicles are 'rung' every year. Ringing is where scrapped, accident-damaged or low-value legitimate vehicles, together with their registration documents, are bought by thieves so their identities can be swapped with those of stolen vehicles. This is done by transferring the chassis number to the stolen car, and having the vehicle registered as if it were the repaired version of the damaged, legitimate one. The stolen vehicles are then resold at much higher prices to unsuspecting purchasers.

Insurance fraud by owners who have their vehicles scrapped accounted for an estimated 8 per cent of total theft of vehicles in 1990 (Webb and Laycock 1992: 9) but may have risen since. The remainder of unrecovered vehicles are either exported to order or stripped of engines, gearboxes, axle and suspension units and body panels for export or onward sale to suppliers or scrapyards.

Research on those who permanently deprive owners of their vehicles is limited. The culprits seem roughly to divide into several main groups: those who move from joyriding to ringing and associated activities; those who gravitate to permanent vehicle theft to fund a drug habit; owners who are unable to pay for repairs or who decide for other reasons to scrap their vehicles and then fraudulently make an insurance claim; and organised professional gangs who take advantage of lax vehicle documentary and registration procedures.

Hinchliffe (1994), a serving police officer, gathered information from 58 other officers who were experienced in investigating this kind of vehicle theft. Their experiences suggested that most 'ringers' worked in teams, the large majority were ex-joyriders progressing up the criminal ladder and most had connections with the legitimate motor trade. A smaller group comprised people engaged in a lawful car business, some of whom were of previous good character, who had moved up to ringing when times got hard or another financial motive arose. Their point of sale had all the appearances of a legitimate business, with a high proportion of genuine second-hand parts for sale, unlawful and lawful business operating side by side.

Popular scams uncovered by police are highly diverse, as detailed by Hinchliffe (1994) and the media. They include the following:

Chassis numbers of unsold luxury cars are used by corrupt staff or dealers to apply for registration documents for them. Once a registration document is obtained the vehicle is stolen to order for export and hidden in underground tunnels or lock-up garages with steel roofs which block out signals to satellite tracking devices that are fitted as standard to luxury vehicles. Onward exportation in steel shipping containers to distant destinations outside the reach of satellite systems complete the thefts. Estimates suggest up to 25,000 luxury cars are shipped abroad annually at a cost of £700m, most of which is shouldered by insurance companies who pass on the cost to policy holders (*The Sunday Times* 15.11.98).

Illicitly obtained credit card information may be used over the telephone to buy a new car through paying a deposit and then arranging instalments. Hire car companies have also fallen victim when hirers pay with stolen credit cards, show false documentation and fail to return the vehicle. By the time such scams are detected, the stolen vehicle has a new identity and has been sold on (*Daily Telegraph* 11.11.00).

Foreign-made cars are seen as desirable status symbols in former Eastern bloc countries. In Moscow organised crime syndicates sell luxury cars below market value to customers who are aware from the price that they are buying a stolen car. After a few days the cars are stolen back from the buyers, who fail to report the theft. This scenario can be repeated many times with each vehicle (*The Times* 17.2.97).

And the scam can be played out on the international stage wherever there are willing customers. Britain's potential for theft is enhanced by its island status and numerous seaports. Stolen European vehicles arrive in Britain by ferry and are transported to distant markets with shipping connections (*The Times* 26.5.95). Two other factors compound the situation. First, shipping companies are not required to verify that the cars carried are legitimate (*The Sunday Times* 15.11.98); and, secondly, it is relatively easy for professional thieves to obtain false documents from the Driver and Vehicle Licensing Agency (England and Wales). The DVLA admitted to issuing 25 million bogus licences and registering several more million vehicles than are on Britain's roads (ibid.). It is clear that regulatory and documentary procedures must be tightened if target reductions are to be met.

Unfortunately for those whose luxury cars are stolen, improved in-vehicle security features have led to criminals using more violence and threats of violence. This may help account for the switch in police focus to target organised vehicle theft gangs (e.g. Clarke and Harris 1992: 15).

It is ironic that the advances achieved in vehicle security appear to have deterred some joyriders while making the professional thief more determined permanently to deprive by resorting to violence, since this places well-off luxury car owners at greater risk of 'carjacking' than those with less valuable and protected cars (e.g. *The Times* 17.4.01). This tends to fit Beck's thesis of 'risk society' (1992) whereby as a consequence of our increasing mastery of the environment, middle-class citizens are no better able to protect themselves from humankind-manufactured problems than other citizens.

Crime control efforts

In the late 1990s, the Labour government began a multipronged attack on car theft, recognising the political danger posed by car theft figures, A Vehicle Crime Reduction Action Team was set up at the Home Office to co-ordinate the skills and experiences of police, car manufacturers, insurance industry experts, other government departments and agencies (Sallybanks and Brown 1999: 1). In addition, a £1.6 billion sum was allocated to the task of realising the initial target of a 30 per cent reduction in vehicle theft by 2004 (e.g. *Guardian* 19.7.00).

Efforts to reduce car theft should be supported, but the large sum allocated appears to prioritise it over other types of 'car crime', indicating that safety of property seems more important to government than the safety of pedestrians and other road users. Indeed, it underlines the point that the state's focus appears less on crimes by drivers and more on crimes against cars!

Raising awareness: publicity campaigns

The new initiative also included a major two-phase multimedia publicity campaign, backed by a large budget, which was aimed at the responsibilisation and empowerment of car owners to take practical measures against becoming theft victims, and at demystifying car thieves in the public perception (*The Times* 23.6.00). This 'Don't give them an easy ride' campaign was seemingly a consequence of a regular BCS finding that many thefts occur after owners fail to lock doors and windows. The 2000 survey showed that 10 per cent of thefts from vehicles arose through unlocked doors (Kershaw *et al.* 2000: 29). At a deeper level, this message fits in well with what O'Malley (1992: 252) calls privatised 'prudentialism' whereby the burden of responsibility for minimising crime risk has gradually shifted from the state to citizenry. This is part of the deeper transition in society towards the management of risks associated with neoliberal ideology (e.g. Stenson and Sullivan,

2001). Victims, like offenders, are seen as rational, responsible and free individuals; prevention becomes their responsibility, and victimisation their own fault.

Whatever the intended message of this campaign, it contrasts sharply to that promulgated in the 1992 high-profile multimedia campaign, which showed hyenas swarming over the shell of a victimised car. That enterprise was criticised for bestialising offenders, treating them as vermin and unhelpfully denying them connection with their community (Campbell 1993: 266), and of raising public fears that the culprits were savage villains rather than the mainly youthful opportunists who actually comprise the bulk of car thieves. The campaign also drew fire from feminists who likened it to subliminally gendering the car as woman because of its image as a rape victim (ibid.).

Theoretical interpretations apart, owner carelessness may seem an obvious focus for prevention campaigns, but previous 'lock-your-car' publicity had little success (Clarke and Harris 1992: 32–3). It could be that a natural threshold is reached whereby owner forgetfulness can be reduced no further, and even if some individuals act to reduce their own risk an abundance of other unlocked vehicles is unlikely to dent overall theft figures (ibid.). Nevertheless such campaigns help to raise driver awareness of the problems and show that government is seemingly 'doing something' about car theft, although not all are impressed (e.g. Chapman 1995: 130).

Enforcement tactics

In the Home Office initiative, Britain's 43 police services were all given individual targets for reducing different high-priority crimes, defined as car crime, burglary and robbery (*Guardian* 15.2.00). In response to fears expressed by police of insufficient resources to deliver the new target figures, extra monitoring powers were given to Her Majesty's Inspectorate of Constabulary to encourage co-operation (ibid.), and much of the £1.6 billion extra cash promised later that year was earmarked for police (e.g. *Guardian* 19.7.00).

In addition, the police have used innovative grass-roots methods to enforce car theft laws with limited resources. South Wales Police used scare tactics to mount an elaborate, horrific and realistic 'road crash' stunt for joyriders on a youth project day-out. The 'crash' was hailed an unqualified success, despite the shock and tears of the youngsters (e.g. *The Independent* 10.3.00). Another controversial strategy is the use of decoy or trap vehicles left in crime 'hotspots'. Unsuspecting thieves can be trapped inside the vehicle, or caught by tracking devices or surveil-

lance. Accusations of agent provocateur tactics or unlawful imprisonment might be levied at such deployment, although seemingly these
criticisms would not find much support in court (Sallybanks 2001), and
70 per cent of police forces interviewed for an evaluation of the strategy
reported use of decoy vehicles. Perhaps unsurprisingly only a short-
term reduction in vehicle theft was found (ibid.).

Tracking technology

A bigger thrust, however, is towards deploying new technology.
Recognising the high recidivism rate among car thieves, police forces are
increasingly taking DNA samples from all suspects charged with
vehicle-related offences and collecting DNA evidence in routine
examination of stolen vehicles. Although this has reportedly brought
considerable successes (e.g. Forensic Science Service 2000), these
strategies raise fears of possible abuse. Some criminologists are
concerned that measures like these represent another step towards a
surveillance society (e.g. Ericson and Haggerty 1997; Norris *et al.* 1999)
and a culture of control (e.g. Garland 2001).

The increasing number of CCTV cameras installed in theft hotspots,
such as car parks (e.g. Kershaw *et al.* 2000: Table A5.6), has also yielded
success (e.g. Clarke and Mayhew 1996) and has probably reduced
drivers' fear of theft. Moreover, since most drivers use public car parks at
least occasionally, CCTV protection is widespread rather than only for
those who can afford it. These are salient points since the same discourse
of the creeping tentacles of state surveillance machinery infiltrating even
the everyday activities of citizens can be applied here.

Situational measures and the implications of displacement

The mounting of CCTV cameras in hotspots is one of many strategies
based on the original tenets of situational prevention. This was
championed by the Home Office from the mid-1970s to counter the
limited success of offender treatment programmes (e.g. Brody 1976).
Situational prevention relies simply on reducing opportunities for crime
at a broad societal level rather than on improving institutions or society
Opportunity reduction is based on a range of strategies designed to
make crime more difficult, more risky or less rewarding. Situational
prevention was later refined by the work on routine activity theory and
rational choice, and in accord with the latter Clarke and Harris (1992: 44)
concluded that reducing motivation for vehicle theft was less likely to
reap rewards than focusing efforts on increasing the difficulty involved.

Two classic examples of how situational measures can work were provided by West Germany in the early 1980s. First, the requirement to install steering column locks into all new and used cars produced substantial short- and long-term reductions (e.g. Mayhew *et al.* 1989). Secondly, the mandate for motorcyclists to wear helmets reduced motorcycle theft considerably, probably because helmet-less opportunist thieves would be conspicuous, and this did not displace interest to cars or cycles which suggested that the combination of opportunities and needs was not equally met by these alternatives (ibid.).

Yet the fortunes of other preventive measures have been mixed, with some displacement occasionally reported although, as Felson and Clarke (1998) state, no studies have found displacement to be complete. When steering column locks were fitted in new British cars in 1971, the theft of new cars decreased but thieves' attention was displaced to older cars (e.g. Mayhew 1990: 41). If preventive strategies merely shifted patterns of crime around, rewarding those better able to protect their property and victimising the less able, such measures should not become the focus of public policy and instead should be left to the private sector (Clarke and Harris 1992: 25). In this regard, the mandatory practice of installing electronic immobilisers into all new vehicles in England and Wales since 1998 (in accord with EU law) raises uncomfortable issues for government. For instance, because of the reported success of these anti-theft devices (e.g. NHTSA 1998; *The Independent* 23.9.99), owners unable to afford immobilisers are put at a disadvantage – though it might be argued that security improvement has to start somewhere. Tracking devices are another technological development fitted into many newer and luxury vehicles that send signals traced by satellite technology when there is unauthorised movement of the vehicle. Similar arguments apply since those unable to afford them are less likely to have their stolen vehicles returned, as police may be more inclined to devote resources to easily traced vehicles than to those requiring greater investigation.

Sentencing deterrent strategies

A more traditional effort to control car theft concerns sentencing policy. Although an attempt to strengthen the negative consequences of apprehension for aggravated taking and stealing was made in 1992, sanctions for car theft have not been regarded as particularly onerous, and in 1998 the Home Secretary announced that tougher and swifter measures would be introduced against vehicle theft (e.g. *The Times* 30.4.98). In 2000, the Home Office issued a consultation paper on revised penalties for a wide range of road traffic offences, including aggravated vehicle taking (Home Office 2000b). The proposal was for the maximum term of imprisonment to be increased to five years from two years and for disqualification from driving to be for a minimum of three years. Both proposals were supported in the government's response to the consultation (Home Office 2002a).

However, in view of past unimpressive sentencing deterrent efforts with car thieves (Clarke and Harris, 1992: 27) and bearing in mind the West Belfast experience where even the risk of kneecapping was seemingly accepted by some prolific joyriders (McCullough *et al.* 1990), more stringent sentencing policies are unlikely to reduce the motivation for vehicle theft, although longer incapacitation of the worst car thieves might cut actual thefts. Another kind of deterrent strategy, championed by the Home Office from the late 1980s, involves sending offenders to motor projects.

Motor projects: growing up and into car culture

Young car thieves sent to motor projects usually go there as part of a probation order and sometimes as a last-ditch attempt to avoid custody. Many such projects now operate and their key aim is to challenge offenders' attitudes and behaviour through the use of cognitive-behavioural techniques. Offenders are encouraged to consider the consequences of their actions for themselves and their victims, to 'own' responsibility rather than to shift blame and to develop values and strengths that empower rather than hinder maturity and growing-up (e.g. Chapman 1995). In the earlier 1990s, roughly half such schemes included a car maintenance workshop whereby attendees could increase their knowledge of car repairs and restoration which was intended to encourage more responsible driving. Other schemes offered a racing element whereby off-road opportunities, such as 'banger' racing, were provided for legal fast driving (Sugg 1998). First appraisals of the projects were not encouraging with 80 per cent of the 1,087 offenders engaged on 42 schemes being reconvicted of an offence within two years of being sentenced, the majority of these for motoring offences (ibid.).

Some projects obviously fared better than others. In the early 1990s, the TURAS project in West Belfast combined several elements: an outreach component to engage the most prolific young joyriders in organised activities late at night (when they were most likely to offend); a personal development plan to lead youths away from joyriding towards social action, co-operation and empowerment; and help and support to direct the effort to change (Chapman 1995). An evaluation of the scheme showed that 30 of 70 high-risk offenders who had participated apparently stopped stealing cars (Marks and Cross 1992), which is encouraging though could reflect natural maturation by some of them.

A reconviction study of the much vaunted Ilderton motor project in east London showed that compared with a matched comparison group of 40 probationers who did not attend the project, after two years significantly fewer (65 per cent) of the 35 Ilderton probationers had reoffended compared with 91 per cent of the other group, and they had reoffended less often than the others (Wilkinson 1997). Findings like these led Smith (1999) to opine that motor projects showed potential if carefully targeted, managed and run professionally according to exact criteria, since earlier failures had been partly attributed to staff who were insufficiently well trained in the underpinning theory and cognitive-behavioural techniques (Hedderman and Sugg 1997).

Nevertheless, it is noteworthy that motor projects make no attempt to divert young joyriders away from car culture. The implicit assumption is that cars are here to stay and it is better to inculcate young people into car culture legally than leave them to do it illegally. Not all accept this assumption. Jackson (1992) commented that sending young joyriders to motor projects is like sending alcoholics to a brewery. Ultimately, however, joyriding fulfils so many needs for young people growing up in deprived environments that no measure is likely to solve the problem on its own. Changing the social, cultural and economic conditions that underpin their lives may be less readily achievable but should still be striven for.

Legislating against fraudulent deals

Long-overdue legislation designed to reduce vehicle theft for permanent deprivation in England and Wales was introduced by way of the Vehicle (Crimes) Act 2001. The main provisions of this Act were expected to deliver 10 per cent of the government's target of reducing vehicle theft substantially by 2004 through cutting ringing offences by up to 33,000 annually (Home Office 2000d: para. 2).

More specifically, powers were introduced that would require motor salvage businesses to (1) register with local authorities and (2) to keep records, which would make it more difficult to dispose of stolen vehicles and would facilitate police investigations when offences occurred. Hitherto, anyone could operate a motor salvage outlet, and partly because no documentation was required these outlets in Britain were believed to pass up to 78,000 stolen cars and up to 12,000 insurance fraud cars every year (Home Office 2000e: para. 1). Secondly, there were no controls on the supply of registration 'number plates', and to rectify this a secure number plate system was provided for under the Act that would require suppliers to register with the Driver and Vehicle Licensing Agency (DVLA). That system would check the identity and entitlement of applicants to ensure supply only to those with genuine reasons and for the correct vehicle. Once operational, it was hoped that these measures would reduce the number of 'rung' vehicles (where the identity of a written-off vehicle is swapped with that of a stolen vehicle that is resold with new number plates) and the practice of using false plates to disguise vehicles used to commit other crimes. However, if plates were harder to come by then one wonders whether the number of vehicles stolen in which to commit other crimes would rise. Thirdly, it was planned to strengthen regulations concerning vehicles written off by an insurer to prevent new registration documents being issued for a repaired vehicle before an identity check was made. This was intended to prevent offenders passing off stolen or ringed vehicles – for which in future they would generally not have the registration document – to unsuspecting purchasers. According to police estimates, these activities involved up to 40,000 or 10 per cent of vehicles stolen annually (Home Office 2000f: para. 23).

Given the high volume of fraudulent vehicle activities that have dogged the crime statistics in England and Wales, it is curious that insurers and the salvage industry have coexisted on voluntary codes, and many legal loopholes have enabled fraudulent activities like ringing and insurance scams to endure on a large scale. In these circumstances, strengthening the regulations around the sale and purchase of motor vehicles could hardly fail to cut thefts involving unrecovered vehicles.

Concluding comments

It is clear that vehicle theft in its many disparate guises will remain a big problem internationally. This is because the underpinning linking feature is car culture, in which most citizens participate and in which society is heavily embedded, so the problem is mainly constructed as one of discouraging illegal car use rather than encouraging less car use. Consequently markets for stolen vehicle parts and stolen vehicles continue to flourish, and the problem of car culture is merely more acute for those who do not have legal access to a vehicle. For disenfranchised youth growing up with little hope of a full stake in society, the attraction and equalising power of driving fast cars may seem particularly strong, though joyriders usually want the same things that legal drivers want.

In other words, vehicle theft is simply a byproduct of car culture and as the world citizenry increasingly lives by the car, the motivation for car theft could grow rather than recede. Ironically, while manufacturers are encouraged to improve vehicle security to thwart intending thieves, an unplanned and worrying consequence of it could be an escalation in violence and threats of violence to secure the handing over of ignition keys, thus raising the stakes and seriousness of vehicle theft. A greater irony could be that as many such incidents are classed as robberies in England and Wales (and in other countries, for instance, the USA) officially they disappear from vehicle crime figures although they could represent the most serious problem associated with it.

In view of the world's continuing demand for cars (lawfully and unlawfully obtained), opportunity reduction is probably the best overall preventive strategy rather than a hope for motivational change. In this regard, current legislative efforts to increase the difficulty of fraudulent, professional theft are welcome if overdue. In addition, vehicle security improvements signal a promising way forward although displacement implications go hand in hand, and here it is useful briefly to revisit the notion of 'car crime'.

Car crime, as noted, has traditionally been socially and politically constructed as crimes against cars rather than crimes by drivers. This largely means 'car theft'. A critical view might posit that the emphasis in England and Wales on reducing this substantially by 2004 might not be unconnected with political expedience. On balance it could be safer politically to earmark funds for more property protection than more people protection, because following a utilitarian argument, more vehicle owners become victims of theft than people are injured or killed by vehicles. Indeed, promoting technological advances in vehicle security protection might be wiser than chastising the majority of drivers who occasionally fall short of required driving standards. Hence there could be a sense that the car-owning masses should be courted not alienated, and that it would be more expedient to demonise the thieves who cause the distress than the bulk of the electorate who drive cars.

Yet in obliging police to divert limited resources to safeguard vehicles, less protection might be available for the car-less, including women, children and the poor who are vulnerable to personal crimes and vulnerable as pedestrians. In addition, poorer car owners are more vulnerable to victimisation because older models are at greater risk of theft than newer ones, and thus disadvantage could accumulate.

In all, the extent, nature and solutions to vehicle theft raise uncomfortable and difficult issues for governments worldwide, and in view of the sheer scale of these crimes, there can be no turning away.

Summary of main points

- 'Theft of and from vehicle' offences tend to represent stereotypical representations of 'car crime'.
- 'Theft of a vehicle' is one of the most numerous recorded crimes worldwide, and has a strong emotional and practical impact on victims and economic impact on states.
- Classification of vehicle theft incidents is a grey area that needs tightening up.
- Comparison of British Crime Survey and Criminal Statistics figures illustrates high attrition rates in recorded theft offences and a general decline in both distributions over the last decade.
- Risk of victimisation varies widely, and car-owners in England and Wales in 2001 were at highest risk of victimisation compared with 17 other countries.
- 'Thefts from a vehicle' comprise around 1 in 8 of all recorded crimes in England and Wales yet only around 3 in 10 are recorded. A change in reporting or recording habits could have serious consequences for target reduction figures.
- External parts and vehicle components represent the most frequent class of items stolen in 'theft from' offences, replacing stereo equipment as favourite.
- Joyriders tend to comprise young, white males from deprived backgrounds. They frequently progress to other kinds of vehicle theft so that the bulk of those involved in fraudulent activities such as 'ringing' are similar.
- Theories abound as to the causes, motivations for and solutions to, temporary vehicle theft, but they do not necessarily address society's immersion in car culture. This must limit the effectiveness of long-term solutions.
- Vehicle theft is a byproduct of car culture.
- Multi-pronged efforts are in progress to reduce vehicle theft, the most promising focusing on opportunity reduction by vehicle design and technological advance and new legislation to cut vehicle fraud.
- Financial input by the British government to reduce 'car crime' underlines how safety of property appears to be seen as more important than safety of road users – i.e. the state's focus seems more on crimes against cars rather than by drivers.

Notes

1 Derived from Tables 1 and 1.5 in Barclay *et al.* (2001).
2 Derived from ibid.: Tables 1.3, 1.4 and 1.5.
3 However, while those whose vehicles were stolen were more angry they were much less fearful and tearful than those who experienced a domestic violence incident.
4 For more on penalties and legal provisions for vehicle theft offences, *see* Gordon *et al.* (1998).
5 This figure includes aggravated vehicle-taking offences.
6 There is anecdotal evidence to support this contention.
7 Further breakdown of the 0.3 per cent figures was not provided, though a corresponding fall in young people admitting any of the 23 listed offences in 1998 was noted, with 26 per cent males and 11 per cent females admitting 1+ offences within the previous 12 months.

Chapter 5

Impaired driving: alcohol, drugs and fatigue

A one-armed driver using his good arm to hold a mobile phone to his ear was stopped for driving through a red light and found to be almost two times over the legal blood-alcohol limit

(The Independent 24.11.01).

Introduction

Attempts to control the incidence of drink-driving have often been hailed a success in recent years as the number of drivers killed in crashes has reduced by two thirds over the last three decades (DETR 2000a: 33). In parallel, sympathy and commiseration for those caught driving over the prescribed limit diminished substantially over that period as anti-drink-drive campaigns helped change public attitudes and raise aware-ness of the risks. Yet despite the considerable educative and enforcement efforts made, around 1 in 7 road deaths in 2000 involved drivers or motorcyclists who were over the legal alcohol limit (DTLR 2001a: 34), 6 per cent of drivers still admit occasionally to driving over the limit, which translates to two million likely drink-drivers in the UK (Waddon and Baker 1998) and, among those convicted are judges, magistrates, police officers and Members of Parliament (e.g. Light 1988; *Guardian* 28.7.99). Drinking alcohol before driving – sometimes to excess – thus seems a widespread, culturally entrenched behaviour spanning the social spectrum, although as we shall see it is predominantly a male activity. Worryingly, in the last few years the falling trends in overall crash and casualty numbers injured through drink-drive impairment have reversed with these figures rising, and further longer-term reduction in the incidence of drink-driving may require redoubled efforts.

Recently, another driving impairment problem has surfaced. Reportedly, illegal drug-driving is more common than alcohol-impaired driving among young drivers (RAC 2000) which resonates with the growing usage generally in society of legal and illegal drugs (Sherwood 1998). Key issues raised are (1) the difficulty of testing whether, which and when illegal drugs have been taken before driving, and (2) the difficulty of establishing driving impairment as a consequence of illegal drug-taking. In law it is an offence to take illegal drugs irrespective of the activities undertaken under their influence (e.g. driving), and it is an offence to drive while unfit through illegal or legal drugs. Yet it is another matter to prove the double digression that illegal drug ingestion has caused driver impairment, since the links between them are not yet well established. Indeed, one review concluded there was insufficient evidence to support an association of raised crash risk with cannabis ingestion (Ward and Dye 1999).

Legally prescribed drugs are primarily taken to alleviate medical conditions and symptoms, and where these conditions are left untreated the ability to drive safely can be affected (e.g. AA Public Policy Group 1998: iv). The hope is that medication will improve the condition and return driving performance to normal safety levels. Yet the situation is more complex and, while, for example, tolerance to a drug is building, side-effects may render a person unfit to drive through impaired functioning. Although the onus is on a driver not to drive while unfit, impairment may not be realised until too late. Medication labels warning of the dangers of operating machinery while taking the drug may be unheeded or forgotten, or the medication eschewed to avoid the possible side-effects, ultimately to the detriment of the driver and others.

There are other forms of driver impairment that do not concern the use of alcohol or drugs. One might contend that British motorists' widespread ignorance of the *Highway code*, where many road signs are misinterpreted, amounts to impairment that could place themselves and others in great danger (RAC Foundation 2001). Restrictions to driver mobility as a result of illness, injury or surgery are other impairments that can reduce driver safety, and simply the consequences of ageing may bring reduced cognitive functioning like slower information processing and hazard perception (Rabbit 2001). Sensory impairment through deafness or defective vision can also impede safe driving and raise crash risk. For instance, crash-involved drivers were significantly more likely to suffer from reduced visual ability than a matched control group in a German study.[1]

Drivers are obliged by law to report changes in their well-being that may affect their ability to drive, and most likely will have to surrender their licence if diagnosed with particular conditions like epilepsy, dementia and some neurological disorders. Other medical conditions are subject to regular review where licences may be issued for one, two or three years, although issues remain about illness developing between medical examinations, and about disclosure where a person's job or mobility is at risk (Carter 2001). Although complex regulatory controls have been in place since the 1930s, medical standards are generally based on expert judgements unsupported by published research data. In recognition of the need for more evidence-based criteria and standards, a government programme of research on medical aspects of fitness to drive began in 2000 to help determine the criteria to inform licensing decisions and possible challenges to them (Carter 2002).

Over the age of 70 drivers must relicense every three years but do not require a medical examination unless their ability to drive could be compromised. Responsibility for sending a completed medical report signed by a doctor to the Driver and Vehicle Licensing Agency (DVLA) rests with the driver. However, where memory or mental state is affected the report might be forgotten and driving could continue, even though failure to notify the DVLA can result in prosecution and a monetary penalty. Driving while impaired by a medical condition is not traditionally regarded as 'crime', though its consequences might occasionally be prosecuted as a 'bad driving' offence.[2]

Except for the effects of advancing age on driving ability, the impairments mentioned above have received little research attention. By contrast, another type of impairment generating much governmental concern is driving while fatigued.

Fatigued driving is implicated as the principal factor in 10 per cent of crashes (DETR 2000a: 37), and is a main cause of motorway crashes (e.g. Horne and Reyner 1995). Indeed, some estimates suggest fatigued driving may cause more crashes than alcohol or drug impairment (e.g. *The Sunday Times* 13.8.00). Interestingly, the act of driving while tired is not a criminal offence unless the consequences amount to a careless or dangerous driving charge, such as happened in Selby in 2001 when a driver fell asleep causing his vehicle and trailer to career down an embankment on to a main railway line, where it impacted with a high-speed passenger train resulting in ten deaths (e.g. *Guardian* 14.12.01). Although regulations restrict the hours worked by heavy goods vehicle drivers in Europe, they do not cover those who drive as part of their job and who are shown to be most often affected (DETR 2000a).

Because some of these impairments are likely to affect the ability and safety of most drivers from time to time, uncomfortable issues are dodged – i.e. just how fit society requires its drivers to be, and whether specific safety-threatening impairments should attract criminal status. Part of the problem could be that so much variability exists *between* people in their standards of driving that changes *within* individuals, either permanently or temporarily, may be less. Alternatively, it might be posited that since there is no widespread public clamour for change, why rush to introduce probably unpopular restrictions on the driving electorate's latitude to drive on impairment grounds? In the mean time, such awkward questions are rather left on one side until further research, media or public pressure require the government to act.

This chapter will begin with an outline of the historical and legal context to impaired driving. It will then consider drink-driving, drug-driving (divided into illegal and legal drug-taking) and fatigued driving in turn, detailing the extent and trends (as far as these are known), which drivers are most frequently implicated and possible theoretical explanations. Efforts to control the different types of impairment are also considered. As drink-driving has attracted the most legal and research attention, the bulk of discussion will centre on this offence.

Historical and legal context of impaired driving offences

Before reliable, objective measures were introduced in England and Wales, in 1967, assessing driver impairment caused by alcohol or drug consumption had been an imprecise art. Part of the problem was in determining an agreed standard of drunkenness that made a driver dangerous in charge of a vehicle – and determining what 'in charge of a vehicle' meant. The milestone Road Traffic Act 1930 grappled with this and produced a definition of an impaired driver as one who 'when driving, attempting to drive or being in charge of a vehicle on a road or other public place was under the influence of drink or drugs to such an extent as to be incapable of having proper control of the vehicle'. This definition based on unfitness was the standard until 1967, although the definition proved vulnerable to frequent legal challenge for its subjectivity and for penalising drivers for their condition or appearance rather than their driving (Willett 1964: 92–6).

All that changed in 1967 when suspicions were exchanged for evidence under the Road Safety Act, which made it an offence to drive or be in charge of a vehicle with more than 80 milligrams of alcohol in 100 millilitres of blood or in 107 millilitres of urine. Three new offences were enshrined under the Act:

- Driving or being in charge of a vehicle having consumed a quantity of alcohol over the prescribed limit.
- Refusing to take a (roadside) breath test.
- Refusing to provide a urine or blood specimen for a laboratory test.

This Act also introduced the 'breathalyser', a roadside device used by police to indicate the likelihood of a driver being over the prescribed threshold. Although objections were raised in Parliament by some MPs pondering the difficulty of remaining below the legal maximum at official functions (Black 1993: 2), an initial 11 per cent reduction in road casualties ensued from the 1967 legislation (Sabey 1989). Despite the promising start, a subsequent waning effect of the new measures, combined with a tendency to legal challenge, led to a rethink under the Blennerhasset Committee of Enquiry in 1976. The resulting Transport Act 1981 increased penalties for impaired driving and introduced less time-consuming evidential breath testing (using approved breath-analysis devices) in place of urine or blood specimens. Thus failure to provide a breath specimen (for a laboratory test) became an offence, as did driving or being in charge of a vehicle with a breath-alcohol concentration (BrAC) in excess of $35\mu g/100$ ml of breath. Unsurprisingly there followed a raft of case law that tried to expose legal loopholes and challenged the reliability of the new breathalyser and the procedures themselves (Black 1993).

Since 1981, several Acts have consolidated and strengthened the statutory provisions for drink-driving *inter alia*, the Road Traffic Act 1988 (ss. 4–11) which remains the main Act to prosecute impaired drivers and the Road Traffic Offenders Act 1988. In 1988 also, a committee chaired by Sir Peter North delivered the 'North report' comprising a detailed review of road traffic law. Many of its recommendations regarding new and reformulated offences and penalties were subsequently enshrined in the Road Traffic Act 1991, and enhanced powers to deal with convicted impaired drivers were introduced – e.g. the rarely used forfeiture of vehicle. In particular, this Act created a new offence of causing death by careless driving while above the legal limit or while unfit through drink or drugs, which carried a maximum prison sentence of five years (raised to ten years under the Criminal Justice Act 1993). Careless driving is considered in Chapter 7.

No further statutory reform was deemed necessary in the 1990s although in 1998 a consultation paper (DETR 1998) mooted a sliding scale of penalties for errant drivers and a downward realignment of blood-alcohol limits to those of many European countries. Subsequent newspaper editorials on behalf of their readers weighed in with general opposition (e.g. *The Times* 2.2.98), and medical advice suggested more casualty savings would come by prioritising the worst offenders (e.g. *The Times* 27.4.98). Although the bulk of consultees later favoured lowering limits (DETR 2000d), the government announced it would deal with the proposed reductions 'in the European context' as part of an EC review (DETR 2000a: 35), hence reducing the heat temporarily. Simultaneously, the Home Office set up a review of road traffic penalties inviting consultation to examine the range of penalties for drink-drive and other offenders (Home Office 2000b).

With respect to driving or being in charge of a vehicle while intoxicated through drugs, no device has yet been approved to measure accurately the extent of impairment, there being no breathalyser equivalent. Reliance continues on the subjective 'unfitness' criterion, so much challenged last century, whereby under the Road Traffic Act 1988 s. 4(1) it is an offence to drive or attempt to drive while unfit through drink or drugs. Tests of hand–eye co-ordination or motor skill co-ordination assess impairment rather than breathalyser evidence. Interestingly, once convicted the law makes no distinction between impairment caused by licit or illicit drugs, and in theory drivers may receive similar sentences whether the ingested drugs are legal or otherwise.

Although the role of fatigue in crashes is becoming clearer, tiredness cannot be measured directly, so a quantum of allowable fatigue cannot yet be debated and legislated. Faced with this problem, international efforts have focused mainly on educating the driving public about the dangers of fatigued driving, with British regulation restricted to setting minimum requirements for breaks and rest periods for HGV, bus and coach drivers. Additional regulations exist to monitor distances driven while on duty and ensure tachographs are fitted to vehicles, and further realignments with European directives are likely. Ultimately, driving or being in charge of a vehicle when fatigued is not a criminal offence, even when people drive knowing they are liable to fall asleep through tiredness, although the behavioural consequences of fatigued driving such as dangerous or careless driving can be prosecuted.

Since 1967, conviction for driving or attempting to drive under the influence of drink or drugs in Britain carries a mandatory minimum period of 12 months' licence disqualification; being 'in charge of a vehicle' in this condition attracts discretionary disqualification. In addition, a first-time offence can result in six months' custody and a fine up to £5,000. Repeat offences carry heavier penalties. Yet there are other consequences to drink or drug-related driving convictions, including the considerable lifestyle effects of disqualification (e.g. loss of mobility, independence or a job), and much higher insurance premiums following licence renewal, occasional difficulties finding an insurer and problems hiring a car for up to 10 years through remaining penalty points. For these reasons, some convicted impaired drivers do not inform family, friends and employers of their disqualification (Silcock *et al.* 1999a). Unlicensed driving is considered further in Chapter 8.

Alcohol-impaired driving

Extent and trends

As no perfect measure exists to determine the extent of and trends in illegal drink-driving, a variety of objective and subjective indices are typically used. The best objective data sources are those linked with annual road accident statistics and police prosecutions, although these obviously omit undetected instances of drink-driving.

STATS 19 breath test figures provide the main data on injury accidents in Great Britain where the driver or motorcycle rider survived and was breath-tested at the roadside. Refusals and instances where drivers were too seriously injured to provide a specimen are included and treated as test failures, but drivers whose crashes were unattended by police or who left the crash scene – usually 'fail-to-stops' – are missing from STATS 19 data. When traced by police, between a quarter and a third of such drivers have been found 'over the limit', and Broughton (1993) estimated that an additional 23 per cent of serious accidents and 35 per cent of slight accidents should be added to STATS 19 1991 drink-drive totals.

Other data come from coroners' figures and procurators' fiscal figures in Scotland of fatally injured casualties who died within 12 hours of a crash in which the driver or rider exceeded the legal alcohol threshold.

Table 5.1, based on STATS 19 and coroners' data, shows that the number of casualties involved in drink-drive accidents decreased steadily from 1980 to 1998, strongly suggesting that drink-driving levels also fell over this period. Since 1999 a reversal in this trend is seen with slight and overall casualties rising.

Table 5.2 uses STATS 19 data to show the number of drivers screened (for all reasons), those who fail or refuse the breath test and those who are convicted. Although refusals in these figures include a small unknown proportion who are unfit through drugs rather than alcohol,

Table 5.1:   Estimates of all GB road accident casualties where illegal alcohol levels were found among drivers and riders, adjusted for under-reporting

	Fatal	Serious	Slight	Total
1980	1,450	7,970	20,420	29,830
1985	1,040	6,810	19,380	27,220
1990	760	4,090	15,550	20,400
1995	540	3,000	12,450	16,000
1997	550	2,940	13,310	16,800
1998	460	2,520	12,610	15,590
1999	460	2,470	13,980	16,910
2000	530	2,540	14,990	18,060

From: DfT (2002: Table 2a).

the data indicate that proportionately fewer drivers failed or refused in 2000 than in 1990, although the failure rate of those tested has remained stable at around 13 per cent since 1995.

In addition, Table 5.2 shows that the number of convicted drink-drive offenders (including a small proportion unfit through drugs) fell between 1990 and 2000, excluding a temporary rise in 1997. Yet interpretation of Tables 5.1 and 5.2 together is not clear cut. While an overall decline in drink-driving is suggested over the 1990s, evidenced by reduced casualties, crashes and convictions involving alcohol (or drugs) and the continuing decline in convictions since 1997, the climb in overall drink-drive casualties and crashes since 1999 needs investigation. It is possible that because only around a quarter of drink-drive convictions arise after an injury accident (extrapolated from Tables 2c and 2d, DfT 2002) – the remainder arising from non-injury accidents, traffic offences and suspicion of alcohol incidents – discretionary road stops by police

Table 5.2:   Drivers and riders screened in roadside breath tests: England and Wales (000s)

	1990	1995	1997	1998	1999	2000
Total tests required	597	703	800	815	764	715
Total failed/refused	102	94	104	102	94	95
% test failures	*17*	*13*	*13*	*13*	*12*	*13*
Convictions: alcohol + drugs	113	93	100	93	89	86

From DfT (2000: Table 2d)

have fallen in recent years with attention focused on injury-accidents where breath testing is routine. Such an explanation would fit overall rising casualty and crash figures, falling numbers of roadside breath tests and drink/drug-driving convictions towards the end of the 1990s, and could indicate a corresponding rise in alcohol (and perhaps drug) impaired driving rates.

The data so far represent only those detected while driving with illegal alcohol levels. *Undetected* drivers do not appear in these figures. The best means of estimating the extent of drink-driving among the general driver population is through roadside surveys of all drivers making a representative sample of journeys. A series of these was conducted between 1988 and 1991, and the 1990 survey covered drivers travelling in ten counties (Everest *et al*. 1990). All drivers travelling between 19.00 and 02.00 on Thursdays to Saturdays were stopped at hundreds of selected sites and invited to give a breath sample and interview, and an amnesty was offered to any driver found over the breath-alcohol limit (provided they did not continue to drive). Fewer than 1 per cent refused, mainly through reasons of haste, so no undue bias is likely in the samples, and just over 1 per cent were found to be driving illegally (range 0.5–1.6 per cent in the ten areas). Almost 12 per cent were found to have drunk some alcohol including 2.3 per cent of the total who had breath alcohol levels equivalent to blood alcohol between 40 and 80 mg/100 ml, which although legal is linked with higher crash rates. For instance, in 1999 2 per cent of fatally injured drivers had blood-alcohol levels between 50 mg and 80 mg/100 ml (DTLR 2001a: 42). Unfortunately, similar roadside surveys have yet to be repeated so trends cannot be measured in Great Britain, but the 1 per cent provides a good *objective* indication of the proportion of drivers travelling above the legal alcohol limit in the evening drinking hours in the early 1990s.

The 1 per cent figure, however, does not tell us what proportion of drivers admit to driving while over the blood-alcohol limit and their frequency of so doing. For this information, we must rely on self-reported *subjective* data obtained from surveys of drivers.

The SARTRE project (Social Attitudes to Road Traffic Risk in Europe) mainly comprised surveys of opinions and reported behaviour of car drivers in all ten EU and five other European countries in 1991–2. A follow-up, SARTRE 2 (SWOV 1998), was conducted in 1996–7 and data provided by at least 1,000 active drivers in each country. The sampling for the surveys was geographically representative of all regions and individually representative of sex, age and occupational status. Respondents were interviewed at home.

Table 5.3: *'Over the last month how often did you drink and drive when you may have been over the legal limit for drinking and driving?'*

	BAC limit	Never drink before driving %	Never drive over limit %	Once a week or more %
UK	(.08)	72	24	1.9
Greece	(.05)	51	31	13.1
Ireland	(.08)	74	18	2.7
Sweden	(.02)	90	9	0.1
EU	(.02–.08)	63	29	3.8

From SARTRE 2 (SWOV 1998: Figures 4.7 and 4.8)

Self-reported information given face to face about a socially unacceptable behaviour is almost certainly subject to under-reporting. Even so, Table 5.3 shows that 1.9 per cent of UK drivers admitted to driving over the alcohol limit at least once a week, which compares favourably with the EU average of 3.8 per cent. Sweden boasted the lowest proportion of drivers (0.1 per cent) while Greece admitted the highest proportion (13.1 per cent).[3] The surveys revealed that on average more than 6 in 10 EU drivers (63 per cent) always abstained from drinking alcohol before driving, and almost 3 in 10 (29 per cent) reported never driving over their respective limits. Nevertheless, some estimates could be optimistic, as shown by 6 per cent of EU respondents who believed they could drink five or more units of alcohol and still remain under the limit (no higher than .08 anywhere in the EU). Among certain groups at greater risk of drink-driving, a higher proportion may hold unrealistic estimates. For instance, Corbett *et al.* (1991) found that in a sample of 225 English pub patrons drinking alcohol and intending to drive on departure from the pub, 16 per cent believed they could drink six or more units and remain under the legal limit.

Who does it?

A review by Maycock (1997: 14) concluded that rather more C2s and DEs (skilled, semi-skilled, unskilled manual workers, casual workers and the unemployed) and rather fewer ABs and C1s (senior and junior managerial, professional, administrative, supervisory and clerical workers) were found among drinking drivers than in the driving population as a whole. Samples of offenders drawn from police prosecution files in three forces (Everest 1993)[4] showed a further distinctive bias towards C2 and DE involvement. Considering that police discretion produces the bulk of breathalysed drivers (stopped on suspicion of alcohol or for a traffic offence) rather than the much smaller proportion involved in crashes, Maycock opined (ibid.: 13–14) that selective police targeting is likely to account for the under-representation of ABs and C1s in the numbers prosecuted when compared with the proportions shown to drive illegally. This is supported by a self-report study of young people (Graham and Bowling 1995) that showed an over-representation of the middle-classes in drink-driving involvement.

Demographic data consistently show that men are much more likely to drive with legal and illegal levels of alcohol than women. In the 1990 roadside surveys (Everest *et al.* 1990) twice as many men were found to have drunk some alcohol (13.3 per cent v. 6.8 per cent), and among drivers who admitted in a postal questionnaire to at least occasional alcohol consumption before driving, 65 per cent were male (Lennox and Quimby 1990). Men figure even more prominently where illegal levels occur. Of those over the limit in the roadside surveys, almost 9 in 10 were male; of those prosecuted for drink-driving more than 9 in 10 are male, and of breath-test failures among car drivers involved in injury crashes, almost 8 in 10 are male (DTLR 2001a: 40). Nevertheless, women are gradually catching up as more become drivers, illustrated by the slower decline among women in the overall trend towards falling positive breath-test rates (Maycock 1997: 15).

It is not straightforward to calculate the risk of involvement in drink-driving by age since this varies according to exposure (e.g. average mileages driven, proportion of licensed drivers by age). For instance, middle-age groups have the highest annual mileages; the youngest age group has the fewest licensed drivers and drives fewest miles (ibid.: 15–23). This apart, the 20–24 age group is most likely to drive with illegal alcohol levels, most likely to drive far above the limit, and is at greatest risk of drink-drive crashes among both women and men, with the age groups either side at next greatest risk (DETR 1998: Annex 3). Risk thereafter tails off with age (ibid.: 15–17). Nevertheless, if account is taken of the lower mileages travelled by 17–19-year-olds, this age group becomes most at risk of drink-drive collisions because of their greater involvement in crashes generally, usually attributed to a lack of driving experience (DTLR 2001a: 40–1).

High Risk Offenders (HROs) in England and Wales, first defined under the Transport Act 1981, are those disqualified for a drink-driving offence after being 2.5 times over the permitted limit, or those who have been disqualified twice for a drink-drive offence within a ten-year period, or those who have been disqualified for refusing to give a sample for analysis. The aim of the HRO scheme is to keep habitual drink-drivers off the road until they no longer pose a safety threat, as assessed by a medical examination. Davies *et al.* (1999b) found that about two fifths of convicted drink-drivers in Great Britain were registered under this scheme. Their characteristics were similar in gender and occupational terms to the profile of drink-drivers produced by STATS19 data but they were slightly older.

An attempt to categorise drink-drivers according to their attitudes and lifestyles (Research Services Limited 1994) identified five groups from an apparently representative sample of 293 convicted male offenders in a large metropolitan area of Britain. These groups were as follows:

1 *Persisters* (23 per cent of the sample): aged 25–44, typically beer-drinking in a pub or at home before offending. Often unemployed or lower occupational status, with previous convictions for drink-driving or mainstream crime.
2 *Refuters* (19 per cent of the sample): aged 25–54 and as above. Denied that drink-driving is wrong; felt they were good drivers unaffected by drinking.
3 *Devastated professionals* (19 per cent of the sample): aged 25–44, mostly beer but some wine and spirit drinkers. Predominantly middle classes who were shocked by treatment as criminals. Felt capable of driving after drinking.
4 *Young irresponsibles* (17 per cent of the sample): aged 25–36, typically strong beer-drinking, skilled or semi-skilled manual workers, with carefree attitude to life and easily influenced by peers though knowing their driving was impaired.
5 *One-offs* (7 per cent of the sample): aged 35–54, middle or lower occupational status. Often unusual circumstances (e.g. a celebration led to the offence). Severely affected and claimed to be reformed by conviction.

A weakness in this typology is that none of these groups is aged below 25, but it shows that drink-drivers reflect a range of lifestyles. This resonates with an important study that asked whether those who commit serious kinds of traffic offences such as drink-driving are otherwise law-abiding citizens. Using the Home Office Offenders Index, it was found that drink-drivers had half as many previous convictions for mainstream offences as dangerous drivers or disqualified drivers, but were still twice as likely as members of the general population to have a criminal record (Rose 2000). This indicates not only that drink-drivers are generally more criminal than the average person, but also that serious traffic and mainstream offending overlap.

Explanations for alcohol-impaired driving

As summarised by Strand and Garr (1994), early research explaining drink-driving focused on personality traits like aggression, self-esteem and risk-taking orientation in order to distinguish those who drove while alcohol-impaired from those who did not. This chimed with the positivist tenet that specific acts have specific causes. Later research focused on classically based deterrence and found, for instance, that deterrence is a fragile, dynamic process contingent on changing circumstances like shifting evaluations of perceived enforcement practices (e.g. Homel 1993).

Rational choice perspective

The development of the rational choice perspective provided another angle from which view to drink-driving, and Homel (1993) considered the applicability of this in light of his own research on the deterrent effect of random breath testing (RBT) initiatives in Victoria, Australia (Homel 1988). He concluded that its premises would explain well his own findings from a survey of New South Wales residents. Among these he concluded that media publicity of police enforcement activity was not as important as direct exposure in drink-drive decisions, and that perceptions of arrest certainty had a much bigger influence on drink-driving behaviour than perceptions of penalty severity. The greater influence of detection risk over likely punishment severity is often noted in deterrence research (e.g. Paternoster 1987; Åberg 1997); Corbett et al.'s (1991) pub study showed that most drinking patrons who thought they would be over the limit but intended driving away from the pub feared the penalty of disqualification and a high fine if caught, but perceived the risk of detection as very low.

Interestingly, Homel found that non-legal sanctions on behaviour were at least of equal importance to legal ones. Invoking predictions of prospect theory (Tversky and Kahneman 1981) – that people tend to act in a risk-seeking manner when choices are framed in terms of losses rather than gains – Homel 1993: 71–2) estimated that in most cases potential offenders would select the *possible* loss of detection, arrest, conviction or a crash against the *certain* loss of inconvenience in seeking an alternative means of transport and, among some male groups, the informal punishment of peers for failing to drive after drinking. Only very strong feelings of guilt would be likely to bias the decision towards not drink-driving. Indeed, among those who drank in groups, the sure loss of being seen as incompetent by one's drinking companions outweighed the possible losses involved in breaking the law, to lead to more episodes of drink-driving reported in a follow-up interview held after the introduction of RBT (ibid.: 75).

Masculine constructions of fitness to drive

Being seen in one's own and others' eyes as competent to drive after drinking features in Gusfield *et al.*'s (1981) observational, ethnographic study of drink-driving carried out in four Californian bars. Drinking, driving, and both together, involved risk, but in American society competent people, especially men, were expected to take risks. In fact drink-driving was normal; it was failure to drive after drinking that needed explaining, underlining the culturally embedded, masculine element to risk-taking while driving. Incompetence was implied in a drinking group by refusing a drink, getting drunk, getting caught or causing crashes after drinking. Yet there were several acceptable excuses for not drinking that deflected the threat to masculine self-image as a competent driver able to handle alcohol, such as having to get up early for work. (Being female could also be an excuse!) In Homel's view, one exculpatory defence would be police carrying out RBT. Since few can avoid a police stop – it can happen to anyone – there would be no disgrace in not drinking or not driving.

The notion of competence links in with Corbett *et al.*'s (1991) study of pub patrons, where the main reason expressed for driving home among those believing they might or would be over the legal limit was 'fitness to drive'. Alarmingly, 60 per cent of this group thought they would be fit to drive after more than 10 units of alcohol, suggesting unrealistic optimism, male bravado or the illusion of being in control (see Corbett and Simon 1992b; McKenna 1993, for more on the illusion of control). As most drivers think they are more skilful (e.g. Svenson 1981) and safer than the average driver (e.g. Corbett and Simon 1992b: 546) which cannot of course be logical, it is easy to see how decisions to drink and drive are made. (Illusion of control is discussed further in Chapter 6.)

The general theory of crime

Other theorists have tried to apply Gottfredson and Hirschi's (1990) general theory of crime to explain decisions to drive while alcohol-impaired and to posit that drink-driving does not require a specific explanation. Keane *et al.* (1993) tested aspects of this theory in a secondary analysis of Ontario data taken from a large roadside sample of male and female drivers, who had completed an interview and given a breath sample. Using objective and subjective indicators of self-control, a relationship was found between driving under the influence of alcohol and low self-control for both men and women. To illustrate, they found that drivers who had been discouraged from driving by others had higher BAC (blood-alcohol concentration) readings than those not discouraged, and that the higher the perceived certainty of detection the higher the BAC. Thus driving while impaired was confirmed as impulsive, hedonistic and short-term orientated behaviour where the worst offenders did not seem to care about the consequences of their actions. Strand and Garr (1994) tested the notion that people do not specialise in particular deviant or criminal acts. They looked at high-school seniors aged 17–18, for whom drinking alcohol was illegal, and found that those who drove after drinking alcohol were more likely to smoke marijuana, to get traffic penalty tickets and to have traffic accidents. Thus drink-drivers were more likely to engage in other risky behaviours suggestive of low self-control. Interestingly, this partly supports Rose (2000), who found that people who engage in serious traffic offending, including drink-driving, are more likely to have a criminal record than the rest of the population.

In summary, a main explanation for drink-driving centres on the use of limited rationality – making less than optimal decisions to engage in a behaviour which is seen as a good idea at the time. Yet while the rational choice perspective says that the perceived choice-structuring properties for each crime are unique, so that potential offenders will find different crimes to be differentially attractive, the general theory of crime holds that no special explanation is needed to distinguish the appeal and commission of different crimes because all deviant behaviours are determined by low self-control. Both theories also provide explanations for illegal drug-driving, to which we now turn.

Drug-impaired driving: illegal drugs

Extent and trends

As with drink-driving, there exists no direct measure to determine prevalence and trends in drug-driving, and our state of knowledge relies on crash fatality statistics and survey data to give approximate answers. Meanwhile tests are being developed to facilitate detection of a wider range of drugs.

Road accident fatality figures show a six-fold increase in illicit drug use over a decade – from around 3 per cent in the late-1980s (Everest et al. 1989) to 18 per cent in 1999 (Sexton et al. 2000), the figures including all casualties (drivers, riders, passengers and pedestrians). This suggests a six-fold increase in illegal drug use by drivers during the 1990s (Tunbridge *et al.* 2001). Cannabis appears to be the main culprit, detected in two thirds of the casualties (ibid.). Yet the presence of cannabis does not prove that impairment has occurred or impairment caused the crash for a number of reasons. First, the drug ceases to be active (to produce a 'high') shortly after ingestion although it may remain in the system for over four weeks (Tunbridge 2001); secondly, individual variability in performance impairment is high after cannabis ingestion, making predictions and conclusions difficult (Sexton *et al.* 2000); thirdly, compensatory strategies may be used by cannabis-intoxicated drivers to offset their impairment, making their driving behaviour more cautious in contrast to the more risky behaviour associated with alcohol-impaired driving (Ward and Dye 1999); and, fourthly, there is no evidence that impairment from cannabis use causes crashes (ibid.). Prosecution for unfit driving is therefore problematic in these circumstances, and following the British Home Secretary's proposal in 2002 to reclassify cannabis from a Class B to Class C drug, prosecution for possession of small amounts will be unlikely. Possible implications of this are taken up later in the chapter.

Survey data from populations of drivers and passengers not necessarily involved in crashes broaden the picture. An RAC report (2000) that canvassed a representative sample of 1,563 drivers showed among drivers of all ages that more had been given lifts by a driver who had taken drugs, most commonly cannabis, than by someone over the legal alcohol threshold. Among those aged 17–34, 1 in 10 claimed a lift by a drug-influenced driver and 1 in 25 by a driver over the legal alcohol threshold in the previous 12 months. Amphetamines were the next most commonly reported drug taken before driving, followed by ecstasy, cocaine and heroin. However, these drug and alcohol incidences are not strictly comparable since any non-medicinal drug-taking is illegal but drinking alcohol at least by adults is not, and ingestion of illicit drugs does not necessarily equal driving impairment, as noted, so caution is needed in interpretation.

Among drivers themselves, a survey of Scottish drivers' self-reported incidence of taking drugs before driving found almost 1 in 10 of those aged 17–39 claiming ever to have driven while under the influence of cannabis or harder drugs, with 1 in 20 doing so within the previous year (Ingram *et al.* 2001). A European review of general driving population surveys concluded that the prevalence of illicit drug use was in the range of 1–5 per cent when driving, with cannabis the most frequently used (de

Gier 1998). So the evidence overall suggests that taking drugs before driving is increasing in line with the pervasiveness of legal and illegal drug usage in society generally.

Who does it?

Because it is well known that some drivers consume alcohol below the legal threshold in combination with illicit drugs before driving (de Gier 1998), inevitably there will be some overlap between the profiles of drug-taking drivers and alcohol impaired ones. Evidence from survey and crash data suggests that drug-driving and drink-driving occur more frequently among younger age groups and among men, yet how well drug-driving groups fit the five main groups identified in the Research Services Ltd (1994) study above remains to be seen.

Explanations for illegal drug-impaired driving

Illegal drug-impaired driving is such a recent concern that no tailored theory is available. Any theory should be set within the broader frame of illegal drug-taking in society generally and its links with other kinds of crime, and have regard to associated criminological and sociological theories – be they focused on individual or social forces or connected with structural factors. Those mentioned in Chapter 1 might all find resonance. In particular, a rational choice framework could be used to model and investigate the decision stages of drivers who take illegal drugs before driving. The fact that some use low amounts of alcohol and take illicit substances before driving raises questions about the cognitions of such drivers in regard to the legality of these combined activities, and research to illuminate these matters would be useful.

Drug-impaired driving: legal drugs

Extent and trends

Driving while taking medicinal drugs prescribed by a physician or sold over the counter is not an offence unless it is shown that the person is unfit to drive as a consequence. This is not a straightforward matter. In any event, drivers are legally responsible to ensure that any resulting impairment caused by medication does not render them unfit to drive.

De Gier's (1998) review of European surveys of the general driving population concluded that the prevalence of licit drug use fell in the range 5–15 per cent, depending on which classes of drug were included and drug use patterns. Benzodiazepines were the most frequently taken drugs. This by itself means little, but a panel of experts concluded that fewer drivers were killed with traces of medicinal drugs in their bodies than were taking these medications in the general driver population (AA Public Policy Group 1998: iiv), which indicates that drivers on medication are not over-represented among driver fatalities. Moreover, the numbers of drivers killed who were taking prescribed drugs remained stable at around 5 per cent of all driver fatalities in the decade to 1998, unlike the rise shown of illegal drug traces among driver fatalities (ibid.: iv; Tunbridge *et al.* 2001).

However, the possibility remains that drivers taking some medicines are at raised risk of accident compared with drug-free drivers, although this is not easy to determine because so little is known about the interactive effects of different drugs on different medical conditions and how these interact with existing driving impairments. In addition, results of drug studies are often critiqued on methodological grounds. For example, laboratory and observational studies of medicinal drug effects often use healthy volunteers rather than the target populations for whom the drugs are designed (AA Public Policy Group 1998: iv), so volunteers may feel worse with the medication (causing unfitness to drive) whereas patients might feel better (recovering their fitness to drive); and establishing whether any driving impairment is due to the drug or underlying symptoms of the condition can be problematic. Moreover the trajectory of the effect of medicinal drugs on driving ability can vary over time as drug tolerance increases with dosing and side-effects disappear or driving ability might deteriorate on withdrawal of the drug. Alternatively, the effect of drugs on performance may be so minimal that this is less than the variability in driving skill among the general driving population.

Nevertheless, evidence exists that raised risks are caused to and by drivers on certain medications (e.g. Hindmarch 1986; Alvarez and Del Rio 1994). A report for the European Community suggested that at least 10 per cent of all those killed or injured on the roads were taking psychotropic medicines that were likely to have been a contributory factor (de Gier 1993). The crash risk associated with tranquillisers based on benzodiazepines (valium, mogadon and librium) can be considerably higher than for drivers not taking these sedatives, and it is estimated that annually 110 fewer road deaths would occur in Britain if such sedated people did not drive (Barbone *et al.* 1998). Moreover, tranquillisers react with other medicinal drugs, further impairing performance, and those drinking alcohol while taking these drugs are at greater risk than those drinking a similar amount without the drugs (ibid.).

A review of over-the-counter (OTC) medicines by Horne and Barrett (2001) concluded that the impairment caused by the recommended doses of at least two kinds of classical H^1-receptor antihistamines, often used to treat hayfever, was greater than that caused by the legal blood-alcohol concentration limit for driving in Britain.

Explanations for legal drug-impaired driving

This subject has not been much theorised, but could encompass the unwitting nature of some impairments. Driving performance is likely to be negatively affected by even temporary handicaps like headaches, pain, migraine, hayfever or anxiety, and any side-effects of medication to alleviate these conditions must be balanced against the likely improvement in driving performance. Yet assessing the net effect on driving performance of symptoms and medicines may not be easy, and drivers are not always helped by the labelling on their medication. Horne and Barrett (2001) found that labelling on the packages of standard OTC medicines sometimes omitted warnings of potential side-effects such as drowsiness, blurred vision, nausea or dizziness. This information may have been available on the package insert, but in some cases was misleading. Worryingly, the warning labels recommended by the British National Formulary for use with medicines are just that – recommendations – and manufacturers do not always comply. Consistency and accuracy in labelling are left to the consciences of pharmaceutical companies – an arguable point. As a result, unwitting impairment while driving is possible, especially among the elderly, who can be especially vulnerable to the sedating effects of OTC medications (ibid.).

By contrast, some people may realise their skills are impaired but they continue to drive, thinking or hoping they are still within the bounds of safety and fitness. Others will realise they are unfit but will continue to drive for reasons similar to those who drive while impaired by illicit drugs or alcohol. As such, individual-level theories like the general theory of crime, emphasising risk-taking and low self-control, and the rational choice perspective centred on assessments by potential offenders of the costs, benefits, needs and opportunities of particular crimes could apply. Clearly this matter is ripe for investigation although many ethical and practical issues are involved. Because of the lack of research it is not possible to profile the kinds of driver who may wittingly and unwittingly drive while impaired by legal medication.

Fatigue-impaired driving

Extent and trends

Driving while fatigued is another behaviour which cannot be measured directly, and estimating its prevalence rests as much on drivers' subjective self-reports as on objective crash data. This is so because to determine that falling asleep is a key cause of a crash it is necessary to eliminate others, such as drunk or drug-driving, mechanical defects or suicide attempts, and to establish that up to around 10 seconds prior to the impact the driver could see the point of run-off or the vehicle hit (Horne and Reyner 1997). Determining this is not so easy, although lack of hard braking or skid marks up to point of impact can be a main clue. That aside, the UK's national database of STATS 19 accident reports has no category to record cause of accident, and sleep-related crashes are often attributed to 'driver inattention' (ibid.).

Objective indices have mainly arisen from analyses of crashes to which police have been called. Horne and Reyner (1995) studied all crashes occurring on non-urban roads in Devon and Cornwall over a five-year period and estimated that 16 per cent were attributable to driver sleepiness. Urban roads are usually too stimulating for falling asleep, but in an analysis of crashes occurring on less stimulating motorways 20 per cent were attributed to drivers falling asleep (ibid.). A study of 60,000 single-vehicle crashes confirmed driver fatigue as a key contributory factor in 20 per cent of crashes on French motorways (Philip *et al.* 2001). Overall, Horne and Reyner (1995) estimate that sleepiness may be a factor in 10–25 per cent of crashes. Other data on sleep-related collisions show clear time-of-day effects with peaks between 02.00–06.00 hours and 14.00–16.00 hours reported in various countries (e.g. Summala and Mikkola 1994; Horne and Reyner 1995) whereas road crashes generally peak around 08.00 and again around 17.00 hours.

Self-reports are the other main source of data on driver fatigue, and several surveys confirm its high incidence. A postal survey of a structured sample of male car drivers, yielding 4,600 responses, revealed that 29 per cent reported having felt close to falling asleep at the wheel in the previous 12 months (Maycock 1996). Of the accidents they reported in the last three years, tiredness was implicated in around 9–10 per cent.

An RAC (2001) survey of 678 British motorists found that 60 per cent admitted driving while sleepy in the previous year, and of these 8 per cent revealed having nodded off, which is the equivalent of four million drivers in Britain having fallen asleep at the wheel in one year. Another survey by BRAKE (2001) showed the same proportion admitting driving while tired, and 14 per cent had 'ever nodded off while driving'. Its prevalence may therefore explain the 'there but for the grace of God go I' sentiment expressed by many drivers when high-profile crashes result.

Who does it?

Unsurprisingly, those under pressure from employers to get to a destination on time are more likely than others to have driven when tired (RAC 2001). Another survey found that 22 per cent of 2,100 company-car drivers from six European countries (including the UK) admitted ever having fallen asleep at the wheel (Leaseplan 2001).

The small minority of drivers who suffer from impaired breathing during normal sleep (sleep apnoea) have twice the risk of falling asleep while driving than other drivers (e.g. Maycock 1996) and they have up to three times as many crashes as others (George 2001; see Connor *et al.* 2001, for a review). HGV (heavy goods vehicle) drivers who snore every night or have a larger collar size (!) are also at higher crash risk – perhaps linked with their greater propensity to daytime sleepiness (Maycock 1996). Generally, men under 30, those from skilled manual occupations and those chronically sleep deficient are at greater risk (Horne and Reyner 2001). While it may be thought ridiculous to ban drivers who are more prone to daytime sleepiness, the issue resurfaces about just how fit society requires its drivers to be and just how much impairment can and should be tolerated.

Explanations for fatigue-impaired driving

People who drive while tired either start their journeys knowing they feel sleepy or they do not realise they are sleepy until too late. Horne and Reyner (1997) report that most drivers involved in sleep-related crashes usually deny having fallen asleep (possibly out of fear of prosecution or loss of insurance indemnity) so evidence must be sought elsewhere. However, drivers have to be asleep for 2–4 minutes before at least half will admit to falling asleep (Bonnet and Moore 1982), yet it is virtually impossible to fall asleep while driving without being forewarned by sleepiness (Horne and Reyner 1997).

Because sleepy drivers mostly put much effort into remaining awake, Horne and Reyner (ibid.) hypothesise that sleep onset may be more rapid and more likely than many drivers appreciate when feeling tired, or it could be that a particular quality of sleepiness clouds perception of fitness to drive, perhaps by affecting mood to make a driver more optimistic, less cautious or more reckless. Alternatively, it could be that since drivers generally overestimate their driving skill and safety, which may lead to overconfidence and over-optimism, a special quality of sleepiness is not required to explain fatigued driving.

Although the cited research demonstrates that psychologists are making inroads into explanations for fatigued driving, criminologists have left this activity – which is not specifically criminalised – out of their theorising. Nevertheless, rational choice once again could model the behaviour and the processes and factors feeding into it. In particular, the distorted judgements that may have a role in fatigued driving could exemplify the less than optimal decisions that people are held to make using limited rationality, which is a cornerstone of the perspective. Supporters of the general theory of crime, by contrast, might point to driving while knowingly fatigued being just another risky behaviour with self-interest and low self-control at root that would probably correlate with other risky driving behaviours and deviant activities were this to be tested. Alternatively still, failure to admit fatigue or to continue driving regardless might be understood as just another cultural manifestation of masculine risk-taking behaviour not requiring a more complex theoretical underpinning.

When asked retrospectively, drivers often explain sleepy driving by citing pressures of work (RAC 2001). An American study compared the responses of 467 accident-involved drivers whose crashes were identified by police as having resulted from fatigue or falling asleep with those of control groups of non-fatigued accident-havers and drivers un-involved in recent crashes (Stutts *et al.* in press). Telephone interviews with them shortly after the crash found that routinely sleeping fewer than six hours nightly and building up a sleep debt, being awake for 20 hours or more before the crash, or working night shifts or long hours characterised the tired drivers more than the control groups. In fact it seemed that the former group tended not to plan ahead to make up sleep deficit to avoid drowsiness, and instead tended to neutralise the risks of driving while tired, thinking it a routine rather than serious activity. No specific theory was tested in that study, though seemingly the general theory of crime, rational choice and some aspects of masculinity might all find support here.

Indeed, while people may know that it is not a specific crime to drive when tired, not all may know the consequences of surviving a crash caused by fatigue could be serious driving charges, unless a high-profile case such as the Selby rail crash (e.g. *Guardian* 14.12.01) raises their awareness. Thus while the consequences of fatigued driving can be serious, drivers may feel the act cannot be serious because it is not unlawful.

Crime control efforts

The traditional triumvirate of measures used to control undesired driving behaviours comprises enforcement, education and engineering techniques. These will be considered in turn.

Enforcement and sanctions for drink-driving

Enforcement is linked with the detection of traffic law transgressions and the sanctions and penalties that may apply afterwards, and the theoretical framework applied in enforcement is mostly based on deterrence, noted in Chapter 1.

For the most part enforcement initiatives designed to reduce traffic offending through general and specific deterrence initiatives get mixed results (e.g. Homel 1988: Ch. 3). Deterrence may work in the short term where multi-pronged initiatives using a variety of strategies are set up, but is not usually sustainable in the longer term (Ross 1985; Homel 1988). In particular, it appears that the perceived threat of detection must have some correspondence with the actual threat posed (e.g. Shinar and McKnight 1985), so if few police are deployed on an enforcement initiative involving stopping drivers any deterrent effect achieved is soon likely to wear off. The experiential effect of seeing others caught or being caught can be a very strong deterrent (e.g. Homel 1993), so hearing that a friend has been arrested for drink-driving may have a stronger effect than seeing and hearing publicity announcements during an enforcement campaign.

Random breath testing embodies a general deterrent philosophy by aiming to influence the behaviour of all potential drink-drivers. It has been operational in New South Wales (NSW), Australia, since 1982, and more than one in three drivers have been tested annually for drink-driving at randomly set-up road blocks (Homel 1993). Laws are vigorously enforced and the campaign is accompanied by intensive, ongoing publicity. Although the fall in alcohol-related crashes has been sustained in NSW for many years (ibid.) and RBT is generally regarded as a success there (e.g. Assailly 1999), similar intensive initiatives involving random stops and widespread publicity in other countries, such as Canada and New Zealand, have not met with such fortune (ibid.).

In Britain, the picture is less clear. While breath tests increased substantially from 1995 corresponding with a lower breath test failure rate that has remained stable around 13 per cent since then (see Table 5.2 on p. 79) – suggesting a possible deterrent effect – Table 5.1 shows that overall drink-related casualty numbers rose in 1999, contradicting a deterrent effect, although alcohol + drug-related convictions have fallen (Table 5.2). This latter fall could result from fewer discretionary police stops since roads policing has yet to be identified as a core police function, and is unlikely to be resourced as well as other types of enforcement activity (e.g. PACTS 1999: 63; Corbett 2000b).

Pressure by many to reconsider the adequacy of traffic penalties for a wide range of offences, including alcohol and drug-impaired driving, was eventually rewarded by a Home Office Traffic Penalty Review, set up in 2000, which invited consultation. The measures to be considered by the review indicated tougher sanctions for the worst offenders, including longer disqualification periods, yet the government's official response (Home Office 2002a) left any changes for the consideration of a new sentencing guidelines body planned under the government's *Justice for all* White Paper (2002). In the meantime, PACTS (1999) notes that the average sentences of magistrates' and crown courts for drink-driving offences rarely reach the maximum fines and disqualification lengths allowed, so it is perhaps an academic exercise to raise penalties.

Of course heavier sanctions may better serve retributive and denunciatory functions, but there is little general evidence that more onerous penalties act as better deterrents (e.g. Willett 1973; Pearce *et al.* 2002: 82–3). Certainly there is evidence that some convicted drink-drivers are not averse to driving while disqualified despite the likely penalty if caught – which can include imprisonment (e.g. Davies *et al.* 1999b; Silcock *et al.* 1999a; *The Times* 5.1.02; and see Chapter 8). It is probable that the low perceived risk of detection may outweigh the fear of punishment in some drink-drive decisions (e.g. Corbett *et al.* 1991).

As indicated above, amendment to the legal breath and blood-alcohol limits has been mooted by the British government and been put on hold in face of strong opposition from expected quarters and because such changes were expected to be considered in a European context. Yet the government points out that up to 50 lives and 250 serious injuries would be saved annually if the British threshold was reduced from 80 mg to 50 mg per 100 ml blood (DETR 1998: para. 37), although it is possible that a higher level of non-compliance might simultaneously occur and no more resources would be available for enforcement.

Indeed, given the continuing likelihood of limited police resources and the urgent need to tackle the problem of alcohol-impaired drivers more effectively, targeted enforcement has been proposed by the British government though is likely to be challenged in the European courts should this become law. The proposal is to give powers to police to breath test people driving at specific locations where it is expected that an amount of alcohol has been consumed (DETR 2000a: 35). At present police have powers only to test for alcohol level following a crash, if a road traffic offence has been detected or if the driver is suspected of drinking, although anecdotally police say these powers are normally sufficient. While many would support this proposal for targeting, others might be less quiescent, fearing abuse of police powers could amount to surveillance of certain locations where driving after drinking could be expected.

Another attempt to use resources more efficiently is the proposal for evidential roadside breath testing, designed to streamline the process to gain admissible evidence (ibid.). This would remove the requirement to have a second test at a police station using a driver's blood, urine or breath sample and instead would allow a roadside breath test to provide the admissible evidence. This would allow police to target more drivers for the same level of resources.

Controls on drug-driving

By contrast with the means available to measure alcohol consumption, no roadside meter has yet been authorised to measure the presence of illicit drugs, although these are in development. This means that roadside testing consists of hand–eye co-ordination and motor skill co-ordination exercises administered by police, which leads to laboratory drug-screening tests if drivers fail. The difficulties are that drug effects can wane very quickly, the screening tests sufficient to produce a conviction are expensive, drugs such as cannabis may remain inert in the body for several weeks and drug presence does not necessarily signify that driving impairment has occurred.

The reclassification of cannabis resin to Class C status may also have deleterious knock-on effects for crash figures as police enforce less vigorously for possession of small amounts, and users perceive it to have gained virtual legal status and therefore is not a problem when driving, which may not be true (e.g. Ward and Dye 1999; Tunbridge et al. 2001). Although this change helps circumvent the problem of prosecution when cannabis may have been ingested legally in another country, drivers' revised perceptions of its semi-legal status could obscure issues around fitness to drive with potentially serious consequences.

Drivers taking prescribed medication may not perceive a problem if the dangers of the potential effects of the drug do not come to their attention. Medicines are dispensed with authorised patient information leaflets detailing how medicines act, any possible side-effects and influence on the ability to drive, but drivers may ignore or forget the information, and pharmacists are not legally required to give warnings. As a result some may unwittingly drive impaired by the side-effects of their medication. Alternatively, others may not take the medication to avoid possible side-effects that could impair their driving, to the ultimate detriment of themselves and perhaps other road users.

If controls were introduced as a precautionary measure, to prevent driving while tolerance to a drug was developing, this could be seen by drivers as an unnecessary restriction (if side-effects were absent or minimal), and some drivers might eschew the medication to avoid the restriction. These are difficult issues and, while there are plans to introduce a European-wide symbol on medicines known to affect driving ability (DETR 2000a: 37), some would say this is not enough in view of research findings that drivers on some medications have a higher crash risk (Horne and Barrett 2001). In the meantime, ultimate responsibility for fitness to drive is left with those taking the medicines, and it is unclear whether there have been legal challenges to pharmaceutical manufacturers by drivers who did not realise the extent of their impairment.

Measures to reduce fatigued driving

Efforts to tackle driver fatigue have mainly come through restrictions on the driving hours and working hours of HGV and bus or coach drivers, and regulation of their rest periods. European harmonisation of the regulations is pending (DETR 2000a: 37) and could impose further working and rest time limits on such drivers. Yet rest periods may not always be spent sleeping, and where two coach drivers share the driving, resting or sleeping in the adjacent seat, this system does not produce adequate, quality sleep according to Horne (cited in *Guardian* 8.8.00). Further, company car drivers, a key group at greater risk of sleep-related crashes, will remain unaffected by these rulings, as will shift workers whose body clocks never properly adjust to the shift system (e.g. Stutts *et al.* 2002). Others will be untouched by European regulations but at a greater risk of SRVAs – those with undiagnosed or untreated sleep disorders (e.g. Connor *et al.* 2001), those who are sleepy for a range of domestic reasons and those who regularly have less than six hours sleep. This again raises the question of how fit ordinary drivers must be, and what (if any) controls should be placed by legislators on fatigued driving to prevent 'accidents waiting to happen' and more unnecessary deaths.

A related, important point that turns the spotlight from the driver to the state is that every year when clocks go forward, more car crashes occur over the following few days as drivers proceed to make up the loss of one hour's sleep caused by changing to summer time from standard GMT time (*The Sunday Times* 17.1.99). When clocks change back again in the autumn to give lighter mornings and earlier hours of darkness, between 104 and 138 deaths annually, often of schoolchildren, are attributed to the darker afternoons when visibility is more dependent on car and street lighting and children are less attentive to road conditions after lessons (Broughton and Stone 1998). Although the time change is reportedly kept for political reasons, to appease those in opposition to abolishing it (e.g. Hillman 1993; *Hansard* 25.11.94[5]), the foreseeability of these extra deaths raises questions about the state's failure to halt the bi-annual change.

Whether or not drivers begin their journey realising the extent of their tiredness, typically long distances between motorway junctions and service areas, can only add to the likelihood that crashes will happen, and questions must be asked of road planners. For instance, one stretch of the M40 motorway in Warwickshire saw far more than its expected share of crashes when service stations were few and far between, according to Reyner and colleagues (2002). More frequent opportunities to pull off motorways would help those prepared to take rests when tired.

Raising awareness through publicity

Moving on to education as a control strategy, many opportunities exist to influence the extent of impaired driving. Ignorance of the raised crash risk for different types of impaired driving, how to reduce it by preventive strategies and ignorance of the sanctions for breach of the laws where they exist and for the consequences of the impaired-driving where they do not, is likely to account for a fair proportion of impaired-driving behaviours. Preventive education is therefore crucial and roadside posters and other media campaigns often accompany enforcement initiatives. Indeed, the cumulative, long-term effect of state-sponsored multimedia publicity campaigns that have endured for over 26 years is attributed by government as a key factor in inspiring the widespread cultural attitude shift away from the social acceptability of drink-driving that has occurred over that period (e.g. DfT 2001). A decline from more than 1,600 drink-related fatalities in 1976 to around 520 in 2000 is held as evidence of the positive tangible effect of such publicity (ibid.). Yet despite this encouraging trend, it is probable that those drivers most needing to heed publicity messages are the least likely to take notice of them (e.g. Keane *et al.* 1994: 42), so educators face an uphill struggle with the worst offenders.

For instance, as it is known that there is a general fear of disqualification among drivers (e.g. Corbett *et al.* 1998: Ch. 4), it may be that drink-drive offenders are unaware of the likely penalty if caught. Harland and Lester (1997) found much ignorance among ordinary drivers about the maximum length of disqualification for drink-driving and the requirement for the worst offenders to undergo a medical examination before regaining a licence. Over a quarter of those registered under the High Risk Offender Scheme claimed not to know about the medical examination requirement (Davies *et al.* 1999). Both examples suggest that typical sentences and subsequent requirements could be more of a deterrent if publicised to the target audience. Moreover, publicity could be useful to counter the suggestion from anecdotal evidence that some do not realise that drinking below the breath-alcohol threshold and taking drugs like cannabis may result in unfitness to drive and is therefore illegal.

A rise in positive breath tests among younger motorists[6] also suggests that educational publicity is not reaching its target, and that renewed efforts are needed to engage a new generation of young people who were earlier thought to be among those most convinced of the dangers of drink-driving.

Yet perhaps this is not just an example of young people ignoring safety messages. There has been a growth in the merchandising of 'alcopops' – usually white spirits with exotic mixer drinks in trendy bottles – as fun drinks for young people. Not only might the alcoholic content be masked by the strongly favoured mixers used, confusing drivers in the alcohol amount consumed, but also the drinks' cool status might encourage a dismissive attitude to alcohol rather than something to be taken seriously. Thus some reflection by drinks manufacturers on their marketing strategy in inadvertently encouraging irresponsible attitudes to alcohol among young people and drivers could help stem the worrying breath-test figures and rise in drink-drive crashes. A similar example arose in the USA where a large clothes chain irresponsibly encouraged the consumption of potent cocktails among returning students, and was obliged by public pressure to relaunch its catalogue with suitable cautionary advice (*The Sunday Times* 2.8.98).

With regard to fatigue, permanent signs, posters, leaflets and *Highway code* advice exhorting drivers to take a break, a nap and caffeine drinks have been around for several years in Britain as reminders that tiredness kills. Such messages maintain drivers' awareness of the matter since, as Horne and Reyner (1997) point out, invariably drivers are forewarned about their sleepiness but typically struggle to keep awake. One might suspect that SRVAs are a greater problem in big countries with long interstate highways, and similar educational campaigns against fatigued driving have been prominent in the USA, Australia, France and Germany (DTLR 2001b).

Rehabilitative education

Once convicted, drivers may revise their attitude to the sanctioned behaviour. Whether or not this occurs spontaneously, many drink-drivers are now offered the opportunity of attending an educational rehabilitation scheme, which if completed attracts a discount of up to a quarter of the licence disqualification period. These courses, based on cognitive-behavioural principles, attempt to change attitudes and beliefs about the behaviour and address the motivations for it by developing knowledge and insight. Initial results were encouraging and an assessment of schemes around the country showed that participants were almost three times less likely as non-participants (3.4 per cent v. 9.6 per cent) to be reconvicted of drink-driving in the following three years (Davies et al. 1999). Yet drivers must pay the course fee themselves, attracting comments that this allows the better-off to pay their way out of a longer disqualification, and indeed affluent drivers were over-represented in Davies et al.'s (1999a) evaluation. Once subject selection bias had been factored into the Davies study, to account for the possibility that offenders more predisposed to offend were less likely to be offered and to accept training, courses appeared to have reduced reconviction rates by around 50 per cent (ibid.: 1).

In sum, many opportunities remain to inform drivers and passengers of the perils of impaired driving, and even if the messages fail to reach all members of the different target groups the attempt should never be abandoned. To assist the effort, advances are continuing in the development of technology that may prevent those at risk of drink-driving from so doing.

Technological controls

Breath-alcohol interlock ignition devices (BAIIDs) sample breath to provide a readout of a driver's alcohol level before a vehicle's ignition is switched on and at repeated points during a journey. Only alcohol-free readings would allow a driver to start or continue. Although development and evaluation are still in progress, their installation in the vehicles of repeat drink-drivers for whom other deterrents seem ineffective has been suggested as a half-way stage between end of a disqualification period and regaining a full licence. BAIIDs would need to be tamper-proof and secure against misuse, such as breath samples being given instead by a sober accomplice. While the public recognise the dangers of drink-driving, compulsory installation in all vehicles to prevent anyone driving above the BAC threshold would probably be unacceptable.

Concluding comments

This chapter has focused on the impairments that afflict people's ability to drive and has raised the key issue of just how fit society requires its drivers to be. While a legal BAC threshold is the main measure to determine driver fitness after alcohol consumption, even this threshold varies between countries, highlighting cultural and attitudinal differences to alcohol and drink-drivers. This confirms that constructions of fitness to drive vary by jurisdiction.

In regard to legal and illegal drug-driving in Britain, only the unspecified 'unfitness to drive' criterion exists to determine impairment, and the underlying issue of how much can be tolerated tends to be put to one side. Thus uncomfortable questions remain, particularly concerning the possible side-effects of medications interacting with symptoms of the condition for which the drugs are prescribed, and the impairing effect of either or both on driving ability. In any event, the prevalence of legal and illegal drug use of all kinds is destined to grow (e.g. Sherwood 1998) and more research is urgently needed to help determine the trajectories of drug effects on people with and without a medical condition and on their ability to drive safely.

Finally, if, as the figures suggest, fatigue is at least as deadly as alcohol, should we leave control of it to mild exhortations that tiredness kills and to recommendations to take a break? Sleep disorders like sleep apnoea may only affect small proportions but does this mean we should do nothing? And what about insomnia which is likely to affect the driving ability of large sections of the community on occasion? In fact, it is unlikely that the bulk of the driving population always gets enough sleep. Yet if fatigue could be measured, would we wish the impairment caused to attract criminal status and at what point? Perhaps because of this limitation, society seems to favour the status quo of dealing only with the consequences of fatigued driving rather than trying to determine how much tiredness is unsafe. It appears reluctant to delve deeper in view of the considerable implications for the smooth functioning of the economy which depends greatly on night-time workers and long-distance commercial drivers whose sleep may often be compromised.

Although we have identified a range of problems associated with defining and measuring most kinds of impairment and determining their impact on driving, societal reluctance to confront some of these impairments and to constrain motorists' freedom to drive has nevertheless been detected. The motor car's sociopolitical roots may be instrumental since car ownership in the early 1900s was associated with society's elite and the car was king. A century later much remains unchanged but vehicle ownership now extends to the masses and most British adults hold driving licences, making this constituency one to be courted rather than alienated by government. Yet the growing realisation that extra injuries and deaths can be foreseen from some kinds of impaired driving raises questions about our continuing reliance on drivers' self-assessments and responsibility as to their fitness to drive, and about the low priority hitherto accorded to this. As in other areas of crime control policy, increasing reliance on actuarial techniques to determine tolerable levels of risk posed by different kinds of danger is likely to follow for driving impairments in tandem with new evidence-based research in this area. Yet a fine balancing act will be required to weigh the the needs of individual drivers to remain mobile against the risks acceptable to society to remain reasonably safe.

Summary of main points

- The incidence of alcohol-impaired driving seems again on the increase.
- The incidence of illegal drug-taking before driving is increasing, though it is not straightforward to prove that impaired driving is a direct consequence.
- The effects of legal medication on driving ability are not well known and their interaction with the conditions for which prescribed needs further research.
- Fatigued driving is a main cause of crashes and is a common lawful behaviour, though its consequences may not be.
- Other cognitive and physical impairments can affect driving ability, and the assessment of consequent fitness to drive is often left to self-regulation.

- Because some impairments are common and difficult to measure, the issue of just how fit society requires its drivers to be is sidestepped.

Notes

1 Buser, A. (1996) 'Sehleistung an Verkehrsunfällen beteiligter Personen', as reported in *European Road Safety News*, 7–8, July 1998.
2 See Davis [2002] 1 Cr App R (S) 579, where a diabetic lorry driver was convicted of killing three people as a result of culpable failure to control his medical condition. A contrasting case is seen in *The Times* (4.7.02).
3 Unsurprisingly, proportions admitting ever drink-driving in *anonymously completed* questionnaires are greater. Waddon and Baker (1998) found 6 per cent of 1,013 drivers admitted at least sometimes driving over the limit. Lex (1989) found that 5 per cent of a representative British driver sample admitted drink-driving within the last six months, and Corbett *et al.* (1991) found in a sample over-represented by accident-havers that 22 per cent admitted at least rare drink-driving.
4 Unpublished TRL report: 'A comparison of drink/drive offending between three police force areas.'
5 Parliamentary comment by Mr Waterson (25.11.94). *Hansard*: col. 884.
6 For example, by comparing Tables 36 in DETR (2000e) and DfT (2002).

Chapter 6

Speeding

Introduction

Traffic speed constitutes a major social dilemma facing all developing and developed countries. From one vantage point, speed is valued, attractive and desirable, it arouses passions, it embodies luxury cars, it enhances mobility and we want more of it. From another, it kills and injures, it causes environmental pollution, noise and illness, it reduces the quality of life for the car-less and other road users, it has negative connotations with road building through greenbelt areas, and we want less of it. This paradox causes tensions to run high, and a compromise solution to the problems of speed has remained elusive. Yet speed underpins more than discourses on driving and car culture. Its ethos infuses most other facets of modern life from electronic mail and microwaved meals to a position where 'instant access' to everything has become expected. The desire for speed now seems endemic.

This may help us understand why driving too fast for the circumstances and breaching speed limits still tend to be seen as minor infractions rather than serious crimes like, say, violence or theft (e.g Corbett and Simon 1992a: 37–42), why it is admitted by the bulk of drivers (Lex 1997) and without social stigma, and why tabloid sympathy is shown to 'ordinary drivers' who are often portrayed as unfairly victimised by the system for exceeding limits (e.g. *Daily Mail* 18.11.99; *Daily Express* 5.3.02).

The facts on traffic speed suggest something different. It is well established that speed is a main contributory factor in around a third of fatal road traffic crashes (e.g. Farmer *et al.* 1999; Taylor *et al.* 2000), which means that in 2000 in England and Wales around 1,100 avoidable deaths and more than 100,000 casualties resulted from exceeding limits and inappropriate speed for the conditions; speed is by far the most common single contributor to road casualties (DETR 2000a: 48). Children are disproportionately represented as victims of speed (DETR 2000b: 11), and have a far higher risk of being killed by a vehicle going too fast than by a stranger assailant (extrapolating from Sustrans 1997). The EU rate for speed-related road deaths is around 15,000 annually (extrapolated, for example, from DTLR 2001c: Table 8.7), which is roughly equivalent to a large planeload falling out of the sky weekly; one in nine Europeans will need hospital treatment for injuries received in a speed-related crash during their lifetime (TRL 1998).

Yet a difficulty with speed is that individual instances are only very infrequently negatively reinforced and the rarity of harm may help drivers to justify all other speeding occasions. Moreover, even though a high number of speed-related casualties are predicted and research shows positive correlation between speed and crashes (e.g. Finch *et al.* 1994), the relationship is complex and depends on a range of factors such as speed limits, road type and variability in drivers' speeds (e.g. Taylor *et al.* 2000). Where speed limits are lowered and considered 'unreasonable', some drivers decide for themselves what are safe speeds and these may considerably exceed the new limit (e.g. Bucks County Council 1992). This may raise the dispersion of drivers' speeds which in turn raises the consequent crash risk (Maycock *et al.* 1998; Shinar 1998). However, the notion that 'speed variance kills' and is a direct causal factor in crash risk is disputed (e.g. Davis 2002). The complexity of the relationship between speed and crash risk is further illustrated by the finding that raising or lowering a speed limit does not necessarily change the crash rate associated with it and depends on the road type (e.g. Stuster *et al.* 1998: 17).

Some opponents of speed cameras and reduced speed limits use the complexity of the relationship between speed and crash risk, and the occasionally conflicting evidence, to argue for fewer curbs on speed choice and the raising of some speed limits (e.g. Association of British Drivers 2002a). However, the facts remain that faster vehicle speeds are not matched by faster driver reaction times, that higher speeds require longer stopping distances and the risk of death or serious injury increases at higher impact speeds (Ashton and Mackay 1979; Hobbs and Mills 1984). A general rule confirmed by Taylor *et al.* (2000: 2) is that reducing average speeds by 1 mph cuts average crash frequency by around 5 per cent – more on slower, urban roads and fewer on faster, arterial roads.

Cars and speed are part of the broader fabric of society, and their social and political contexts are important. For instance, if 'deviants' were targeted for speed control purposes this could in fact mean those who refrain from speeding. According to media reports of prosecutions, no one is exempt from exceeding limits; thus government ministers, senior officials, royalty and celebrities have been detected (e.g. *The Times* 5.8.00), along with the regulating authorities (see below). Further, the motor industry remains the nation's largest retail sector, employing 600,000 and raising billions of pounds in tax revenue (Retail Motor Industry Federation 2002), and car production figures contribute significantly to national and global economic health. Thus the high speed capabilities of many vehicles in production may be ignored in efforts to attract and keep foreign trade and investors on 'home' soil. In efforts to curb this kind of car crime – neutralised though it may be – one wonders ultimately how much political will exists.

The word 'speeding' is problematic too, since it is commonly used both in the general sense of 'travelling inappropriately fast for the prevailing conditions' and in the restricted sense of 'exceeding the posted speed limit' (often termed 'excess speed'). In this chapter both these areas of meaning will be covered by the term 'speeding' – subject to an important caveat. Most drivers occasionally exceed speed limits but most are not convicted of dangerous driving offences that may include a speeding element. While not implying any condonation of inappropriate or excess speed, this chapter will focus on the more typical and generalised acts of speeding rather than those which may be labelled aggressive and/or dangerous, such as tailgating, inappropriate overtaking or racing other drivers. Such behaviours will be discussed in Chapter 7 under the general heading of dangerous driving.

This chapter will first examine the historical links and legislative controls on speeding, then consider what we know about those who speed most and how speeding is connected with other behaviours. Following that, key factors and frameworks for understanding fast driving will be discussed. This section will be arranged in terms of individual, societal and structural factors. A detour will be made to consider the respective contributions to speeding and other traffic offending by women and men. Thereafter the range of control measures introduced to restrict speeding will be addressed, particularly the use of speed 'safety' cameras, before concluding comments and a summary of key points.

Historical and legal context of speeding

In Chapter 2, speed control was considered in its social context alongside the regulation of other unwanted driving behaviours. Here, some key points from the social history of speeding are highlighted to remind readers that speed has been a valued commodity since the start of production, that car ownership was initially the province of the elite, that penalties for speeding were hardly a financial burden for the recipients and that there was much early opposition to the car and increasingly higher speed limits. Among the statutes passed was the Road Traffic Act 1930 that abolished speed limits altogether after the roads lobby was able to convince Parliament that limits were a likely factor in raising crash risk, and that drivers would behave more responsibly when deciding safe speeds for themselves (Emsley 1993: 25). Unsurprisingly, speed limits were reintroduced under the Road Transport Act 1934 and have been amended several times since to reflect prevailing vehicle and road conditions, though the 70 mph maximum on motorways has remained in force since the Road Safety Act 1967.

Despite an arguably mild stance being taken with speeding motorists in the first decades of the twentieth century, the Automobile Association was set up partly to support and protect wealthy motorists from over-enthusiastic police officers, who often brought motorists into contact with the criminal justice system for the first time. The notion that drivers who exceed speed limits are hardly real criminals has endured for a century, and regularly surfaces in newspaper stories which promulgate their continuing image as ordinary, otherwise law-abiding, much-maligned victims of the system.

Such a construction emerges when additional curbs on speed choice or sanctions on drivers are proposed. Under the Criminal Justice Act 1991, fines adjusted to net income and to the seriousness of the offence were introduced for many summary offences in Britain, including speeding; yet within eight months, following a public outcry about the resulting 'unfair fines', the then Home Secretary ordered a rapid abandonment of the unit fine system to prevent further erosion of support for the then Conservative government (*Daily Telegraph* 14.5.93). Another U-turn in tackling speed emerged in 1999 when plans for a zero-tolerance policy regarding the 30 mph speed limit were quickly quashed on account of impracticality (*Guardian* 5.2.00). Further, instead of widely rumoured speed limit cuts (*The Sunday Times* 19.9.99), the government's Speed Policy Review promised to develop a national policy on speed limits (but not necessarily to deliver it) and encouraged local authorities to take greater responsibility for deciding local speed limits (DETR 2000b: 31–5). The government's uncertainty about how to tackle speed without alienating the driving and voting public was apparent.

More recently, media indignation turned to the hypothecation debate, whereby part of the fine revenue generated from speeding prosecutions set in motion by camera detection can be used to bid for more camera equipment for the police force concerned rather than the money returned to the Treasury. This was seen as a further means to victimise motorists (e.g. *Daily Express* 5.3.02). The image of the oppressed driver was restored, while the speeding crimes committed tended to be ignored.

In view of the social history of speeding, it is understandable that some fail to appreciate that exceeding speed limits is a crime. Yet road traffic law is an integral, though separate, part of criminal law, and is handled by the courts in the same way as for mainstream offences. Most speed limit offences are punishable under various sections of the Road Traffic Regulation Act 1984 and Schedule 2 to the Road Traffic Offenders Act 1988, where there are also provisions for prosecuting drivers for contravening *minimum* speed limits.

It is one of the few offences in law where corroboration must be given by more than one witness except when a limit is exceeded on a motorway. This can be provided by another officer, but more usually these days comes from a hand-held electronic device which uses laser technology or an in-vehicle VASCAR system using computer technology. However, the evidence from an automated speed camera does not require corroboration under the Road Traffic Act 1991, and this has become the most common means of detecting speeding motorists in recent years as police time is released for other duties and speed cameras can work 24 hours daily.

Registered vehicle keepers must be provided with a warning of intended prosecution within 14 days of the offence occurring. If the driver is someone else, it is the keeper's responsibility to contact that person, and non-disclosure may result in prosecution (s. 21, Road Traffic Act 1991). Thereafter a warning letter may follow or a summons to appear at a magistrates' court if the speed is such that disqualification from driving may be considered. More usually a conditional offer of a fixed penalty is made. If the penalty is accepted, and the driver has not reached 12 penalty points under the 'totting' rules (s. 35, Road Traffic Offenders Act 1988), in which event the case must go to court and the driver is liable for disqualification, the payment should be sent to the court along with the licence, which is endorsed with three to five penalty points. Interestingly, licence disqualification is discretionary for speeding offences, unlike the mandatory requirement to disqualify for drink-driving.

Extent and trends in speeding

Observed incidence

In contrast to most other road traffic offences, there is good-quality *objective data* available on drivers who exceed posted speed limits in the UK. Two main sources will be considered here: (1) official speed monitoring data; and (2) numbers of speeding prosecutions. Both sources can be used to consider patterns over time, though the former is more reliable.

Table 6.1 shows data on vehicle speeds collected during 2000 from a wide number of sites on urban and non-urban roads, comprising observations from hundreds or thousands of vehicles (depending on the volume of traffic) passing each site daily. Even so, it cannot be assumed that observations at the survey sites are necessarily representative of drivers' speed choice generally, but this is about as good as monitoring data get. The survey sites were typically ones where free-flowing traffic was likely, better to reflect the proportions of drivers who intended to exceed the posted speed limit. Since free choice of speed would not

Table 6.1: Proportions of cars travelling in excess of speed limits in 2000 (%)

	Urban roads: 30 mph	Urban roads: 40 mph	Non-urban dual carriageways: 70 mph	Motorways: 70 mph
Average speed	32 mph	37 mph	70 mph	70 mph
Percent exceeding:				
30 mph	66	[88]	–	–
35 mph	32	[61]	–	–
40 mph	11	25	[100]	[100]
45 mph	2	7		
50 mph	0	2	[98]	[97]
60 mph	–	0	[83]	[86]
70 mph	–	–	52	55
80 mph			13	17
90 mph			0	1

From DTLR (2001c: Tables 1 and 5).

always have been possible, the proportions wishing to exceed these limits, had road conditions permitted, are likely to be greater than those who actually did. Nevertheless, the table indicates that more than half the car drivers on motorways and dual carriageways, two thirds on 30 mph urban roads and a quarter on 40 mph urban roads exceeded the respective speed limits on the observed occasions. The proportions exceeding by more than 10 mph were 11 per cent on 30 mph urban roads, 2 per cent on 40 mph urban roads 13 per cent on non-urban dual carriageways and 17 per cent on motorways.

Not shown in the table is that other types of vehicle are implicated in this pattern of excess speed. On non-urban dual carriageway roads, 90 per cent of articulated heavy goods vehicles exceeded their 50 mph limit, and on non-urban single carriageways, three quarters (76 per cent) of them exceeded their 40 mph limit. Over a third of buses/coaches (38 per cent) exceeded 30 mph urban road limits, and almost half (49 per cent) exceeded their dual carriageway 60 mph limit. More than half of motorcycles exceeded the limit on 30 mph roads and motorways. Thus widespread flouting of speed limits is not restricted to cars.

Table 6.2 presents the trends for cars in exceeding limits over a recent five-year period on different types of roads, and the similarity of the proportions speeding on the different road types – except 30 mph urban roads – over this period is striking. Although it is seen that there is a welcome downward trend for speeding on 30 mph urban roads, the propensity of British drivers to exceed limits on other types of roads appears largely undimmed.

Another source of objective trend data is provided by the number of speeding offences prosecuted in England and Wales, although this may say more about police resources available and the level of enforcement applied to speeding offences than to their incidence. It was noted earlier that speed limit breaches were the only kind of motor traffic offence for

Table 6.2:   Proportions of cars exceeding posted limits on different road types, 1996–2000 (%)

	1996	1997	1998	1999	2000
Urban roads: 30 mph	72	70	69	67	66
Motorways	57	54	55	56	55
Non-urban dual carriageways	49	53	54	53	52
Non-urban single carriageways	10	9	10	10	9
Urban roads: 40 mph	25	27	26	26	25

From DTLR (2001c: Tables 4 and 8).

Table 6.3: Numbers of speed limit offences prosecuted in 1997 and 2000

	1997		2000	
	n	*%*	*n*	*%*
Number camera-detected speeding offences	336,700	*38*	733,500	*61*
Number police-detected speeding offences	554,500	*62*	468,800	*39*
Total speeding offences prosecuted	891,200	*100*	1,202,300	*100*

From Table D, note 31 and Table 2 in each of Wilkins and Addicott (1999) and Ayres and Hayward (2001a).

which prosecutions had risen in the five years to 2000 (Ayres and Hayward 2001a: Table 2). Table 6.3 illustrates that the increase in speeding prosecutions since 1997 is largely accounted for by greater speed camera activity, because the number of speed limit offences detected by police has fallen. Speed limit enforcement will be considered below.

Reported incidence

To complement the high incidence of observed breaches of speed limits, *subjective data* obtained from self-report surveys show correspondingly high levels of speeding admitted, indicating that there appears little stigma attached to the activity. Actual figures depend on how the questions are posed and which drivers are asked. In Britain, a Lex survey (1997) found that most of its representative sample of drivers admitted exceeding speed limits at least on some occasions; Silcock *et al.* (1999b) discovered 85 per cent of their sample admitting the same; and Corbett and Simon (1992a: 74) found that only 1 per cent denied ever breaching a speed limit in their sample of 457 drivers in which the crash-involved were over-represented.

High levels of speeding are also revealed in other countries. The European-wide SARTRE 2 driver survey (SWOV 1998), discussed in Chapter 5, included a range of questions about speed-choice behaviour, and some of its findings are given in Table 6.4 which shows reported levels of speeding recorded for selected EU countries in the 1997 survey, along with the percentage change in reported incidence since 1992 when the earlier SARTRE 1 survey was conducted.

This table reveals wide variations between countries in proportions admitting speeding either 'often', 'very often' or 'always' (and excludes those admitting rare or occasional speeding). However, a general pattern emerged whereby more drivers in each country revealed speeding on

Table 6.4: Proportions of European drivers who reported speeding at least 'often' on different kinds of roads, and percentage change between 1992 and 1997: selected countries

Country	Motorways	diff.	Percent admitting Main roads	diff.	Built-up roads	diff.
France	22	–5	18	–2	8	3
Germany	18	–2	16	1	7	4
Ireland	18	–7	14	–3	4	2
Italy	23	–7	23	4	11	4
Portugal	48	20	31	18	15	11
UK	29	0	19	–1	6	1
EU	24		19		8	

From SARTRE 2 (SWOV 1998: Table 5.1).

motorways and main roads than in built-up areas. Portugal emerged with the highest proportion of self-confessed speeders in the EU on all road types, few in Ireland admitted speeding in built-up areas (only Sweden and Switzerland had fewer), and several countries, including France, Germany, Italy and the UK, had profiles that matched the EU average fairly closely. An EU-wide percentage change in proportions speeding was not available, yet for countries where this was measurable, two thirds overall reported fewer drivers speeding in 1997 than in 1992 on motorways, and all reported more speeding on built-up roads. No clear pattern emerged for speeding on main roads. The largest increase in speeding drivers was found in Portugal for all road types. To correspond with these high levels of reported speeding breaches, 9 per cent of all EU drivers agreed that they 'enjoyed driving fast' 'very much' (ibid.: 71).

The accuracy of self-reported speeds

The above figures show that 1 in 4 Europeans admit to exceeding motorways limits at least often, and 1 in 12 to speeding in built-up areas often. They are worrying, but their accuracy may be affected by their self-reported origins. Despite apparently little stigma attaching to confessions of speeding, it is likely that reports will reflect to some extent what is thought socially acceptable. So to check the accuracy of self-reported information, researchers have compared the extent of the association between observed instances of speed choice, which can be measured accurately, and drivers' subsequent reports of their speed on the observed occasion or in general on the surveyed road.

Such studies have revealed that respectable and statistically significant correlations can be obtained between observed instances of speed-choice behaviour and self-reports of the same (e.g. de Waard and Rooijers 1994; Åberg et al. 1997), which indicates that drivers do report their speeds reasonably accurately. Nevertheless, other research shows that drivers' speed choice reports are coloured by a range of influences. For example, Corbett (2001) showed that drivers observed to travel below the 30 mph limit in a series of large surveys tended to report their speeds as higher than those observed, while those seen to travel above the 30 mph limit were apt to report their speeds as lower than those observed. This systematic bias towards under- or overestimates of speed could not be easily explained. However, psychophysical limitations connected with reporting accurately (e.g. Recarte and Nunes 1996) and the automaticity of some well learnt driving manoeuvres, whereby little or no attentional processing is needed to steer at speed (e.g. Brown et al. 1969), could lead to 'best guesses' of prior speed (e.g. Haglund and Åberg 2000) that may explain some of the bias.

In any event, physical limitations are likely to be mediated by social and cognitive processes, such as the perception that exceeding limits may be complying with normative behaviour and may therefore be safer than adhering to the posted limit (Corbett 2001: 148). Moreover, negative stereotyping associated with both overly slow and fast drivers might not be welcomed by those so characterised. Thus while drivers seem able to report fairly accurately their own speeds, there appears latitude for some massaging of speed estimates – unconscious or not – to enhance one's self-image as a good citizen and driver.

Who does it?

Speeding is a pervasive behaviour which few drivers deny. Indeed, the majority of 'gatekeepers', including magistrates, junior and senior traffic police officers and (a small group of) authorised driving instructors, whose role includes helping to regulate and discourage the incidence of speeding, admitted to the behaviour when interviewed (Corbett et al. 1998: 37, 40, 45). Most may exceed limits occasionally, but some have a greater propensity.

Studies show that those who exceed limits most often and by higher margins tend to be young males (e.g. Corbett and Simon 1992a: 19; Lex 1997; Stradling 1999), higher mileage drivers and those with higher opinions of their own driving skill (Corbett and Simon 1992a: 42; Stradling 1999). Research also finds that those who drive for a living, such as company sales representatives, are high speeders (Gallup 1990;

Lex 1997), and Stradling (2001) found that company-car drivers were more likely than others to have been prosecuted for speeding (see also Quimby *et al.* 1999; Webster and Wells 2000).

Speeding is the most commonly reported moving road traffic offence (e.g. Corbett and Simon 1992: 74; Lex 1997; Stradling 1999), and unsurprisingly it is linked with other kinds of traffic breaches. Corbett and Simon (1992a: 18) found that high speeders were more likely than either medium or low speeders to commit a wide range of traffic offences, a finding reinforced by Corbett and Simon's (1999) study of speed cameras.

In the latter research, high speeders, as measured by self-reports in each of seven large surveys, were significantly more likely than medium or low speeders to:

* overtake crossing into hatched white lines;
* pull out from side roads without giving way to traffic;
* overtake on the left-hand side;
* fail to indicate when they should;
* park on single yellow lines;
* drive through amber and red traffic lights;
* drive when over the blood-alcohol limit;
* knowingly drive with defective brakes; and
* knowingly drive without a valid MOT certificate.

In Corbett and Simon's (1992a: 27) study, over a third of drink-drivers (36 per cent) were also high speeders. Combined with the finding that high speeders rated 12 kinds of traffic offence as less serious than low speeders (ibid.: 23), it seems that speed choice may be a critical behavioural determinant of the perceived seriousness of other types of traffic offences and perhaps of the decision to engage in them.

There are also likely to be other links with speed. As will be discussed in Chapter 7, those who have more traffic collisions have worse mainstream criminal records, more traffic convictions, worse health and more off-road accidents than those who have fewer traffic collisions (e.g. Junger *et al.* 2001). Because higher speeds are associated with more crashes (e.g. Finch *et al.* 1994) and speed is a key contributory factor in around a third of road crashes, it follows that those who prefer higher speeds will be more frequently crash-involved and will have more criminal and traffic convictions.

Explanations for speeding

Unlike some traffic offences, speeding has received a fair amount of research attention (though not much by criminologists), probably because of its pivotal role in road crashes and because of its transparency. As a consequence it provides a neat example of how explanations can divide into those mainly at an individual level or social/structural level, which broad framework will be used here. That said, since several social and structural factors associated with speeding have already been developed in the early chapters they will be summarised here and the emphasis placed on those affecting individuals, which are considered first. However, the others are no less important.

Personality traits and perceptual distortions

Although an anathema to all but psychologically orientated criminologists, the search for personality attributes as causal factors in offending has been a leading field of study for many decades. In the context of speeding, traits associated with thrill-seeking, sensation-seeking, risk-seeking and Type-A behaviour pattern (characterised by a sense of time urgency, competitiveness, ambition and alertness), are found to be prominent among those preferring higher speeds (e.g. West *et al.* 1992; McKenna *et al.* 1998).

In this regard, Gottfredson and Hirschi's general theory of crime, outlined in Chapter 1, can provide an individual-level explanation for inappropriately fast driving and excess speed. If extrapolated to speeding, their theory would predict that those preferring higher (riskier) speeds are characterised by low self-control, since this attribute characterises those who engage in deviant and anti-social behaviours of all kinds. (The applicability of this theory to dangerous driving will be considered in Chapter 7.)

Cognitive processes underlying decisions to speed have been another main strand of investigation. It seems that drivers do not see the occasions on which they exceed limits as dangerous or risky otherwise they would not do it (Corbett and Simon 1992a: 38–40), and they are prepared only to drive as fast as the speeds at which they feel comfortable – whether or not that is above or below a speed limit (Corbett *et al.* 1998: 11–17). If they feel in control of the driving situation they may go faster. However, various cognitive distortions have been discovered which indicate that drivers' perceptions of being in control can be illusory. For instance, most drivers tend to see their own driving ability as superior to that of others – which in the aggregate is illogical (e.g. Svenson 1981; Corbett and Simon 1992a: 41). They believe the roads would be safer if more people drove like themselves (including the frequent traffic offenders) (Corbett and Simon 1992a); they think they are more likely to have a crash as a passenger than as a driver, which is also illogical (Horswill and McKenna 1999), and that others have more crashes than themselves (Finn and Bragg 1986).

Drivers are also more likely to accept the proposition that there is a positive link between speed and accidents in general than they are to accept that there is a link between their own speeds and crash risk, which again must be illogical (Corbett *et al.* 1998: 15). It is also well known that around 95 per cent of traffic crashes occur through human error (e.g. Sabey 1999: 11–12), so however much drivers feel in control when they are driving fast, there must occasionally be gaps between perceived and actual control where their risk assessments are inaccurate, otherwise crashes would not happen. Feelings of self-confidence and being in control thus appear prominent in drivers' decisions to exceed speed limits, and drivers do not see speeding as morally wrong or dangerous in situations where they do it (e.g. Simon and Corbett 1991; Corbett *et al.* 1998).

Other main reasons given to explain speeding behaviour include the following:

- *Intrinsic enjoyment of fast driving.* More often endorsed by men, especially young men (e.g. Rolls and Ingham 1992; Rothengatter 1988).
- *The need to drive fast.* Often cited by those in a hurry or who drive for a living (e.g. Corbett and Simon 1992a: 29–32; Stradling 2001). This is a very common factor although, when required of company employees in order to meet tight schedules for company profit, it may be considered an occupational crime since driving fast can endanger others.
- *Risk compensation.* Several theories have been espoused (Wilde 1986; Adams 1988) that propose a hydraulic model of drivers' need to seek out risk. Thus if manufacturers reduce the level of perceived or actual risk through vehicle modification such as installing seat belts, air bags, side impact bars or anti-lock braking systems, drivers will compensate for the safer design features by increasing their risk in other ways – usually by driving faster or closer – to a level that seems right to them when driving, hence the hydraulic (and deterministic) image. Research evidence is inconclusive (and see Davis 1992: 44–7 for a critique) though some psychologists subscribe to this view.
- *Inadvertence.* Frequently used to explain speeding (e.g. Corbett 2001: 144–5) and for getting caught by cameras, particularly by infrequent speeders and slower drivers (Corbett and Simon 1999: 37–8).
- *Social pressure* to keep up or go faster, often when being close followed (e.g. Corbett and Simon 1991a: Table A4.1; Stradling 2001: 81).

Interestingly, perceived social pressure to keep up and perception of greater safety by keeping up with the flow were least likely to be reported by the slowest drivers in Corbett and Simon (1991a: 140).

Drivers are motivated by internal and external pressures to exceed limits which can be instrumental or affective, and these are shaped by the purpose of the journey, the opportunities to exceed the limits, drivers' confidence in exceeding limits and remaining in control, and their evaluations of the internal and external restraints on speeding such as the likely negative consequences (e.g. social disapproval, penalty and crash risks).

The perception and treatment of speeding as not real crime

Several studies of the perceived seriousness of traffic offences have shown that speeding is judged as minor (e.g. O'Connell and Whelan 1996). Corbett and Simon (1991b) showed that traffic police and the driving public ranked the offence of driving between 31 and 40 in a 30 mph limit as almost the least serious of 26 traffic breaches offered, and at least half of a sample of traffic police, magistrates and approved driving instructors did not consider speeding to be a crime in the same sense as theft or violence (Corbett *et al.* 1998: 37, 40, 45).[1]

Perceptions of the minor nature of speeding may be reinforced by the consensual nature of the activity (i.e. most drivers engage in it, including those regulating and controlling its occurrence). In addition, drivers may perceive a lukewarm or mixed response to speeding by the authorities. The lack of a strong lead by government, mentioned in the historical section above, is compounded by the failure to boost the profile of roads policing to core function status.

As noted earlier, licence disqualification is still discretionary for all levels of speeding violations, and up to four convictions are possible before sufficient penalty points accumulate for disqualification under 'totting-up' rules. In addition, commentators point to other factors that underline the low importance placed on speeding:

- *Insurance policies against disqualification for speeding.* These are legal despite lobbying by some road safety organisations (e.g. PACTS 1999: 70), and may provide a chauffeur or travel expenses in this event. Apparently they have been popular among business drivers keen to protect their jobs and among companies keen to keep their staff mobile (*The Sunday Times* 21.1.96).
- *Short periods of disqualification.* Of those given for speeding in 2000,

91.5 per cent were for less than six months (Ayres and Hayward 2001b: Tables 13 and 14), and typical fines may be seen as manageable running costs (like petrol and oil) to regular high speeders (Corbett and Simon 1992a: 57).

• *The discourse of 'accidents'*. The structural mechanism whereby the enduring 'thrills and spills' image of crashes has enabled accidents to be viewed as unlucky, chance events was established by the architects of the original speed limit regulations and speed laws. Drawn from the first car owners, these lawmakers were predominantly male. If they, like many men, shared the male proclivity to seek risks and thrills through fast driving (e.g. Matthews *et al.* 1997), then that may have minimised the danger of speed in the construction of the laws and their sanctions. This connects also with the 'car as master' elitism which emphasises the superiority of drivers over pedestrians and the hegemony of the car (see Chapters 3 and 10).

Female and male drivers compared

Men and women tend to have different relationships with cars. For women, cars reduce fear of male crime (London Research Centre 1998) and raise feelings of independence (McKenna *et al.* 1998: 48) both of which probably help explain rising car sales among women (Lex 1999: 54). In contrast, men are more likely to use cars to demonstrate driving skills, prowess and success in life, to feel excitement and to project an ideal self-image (Marsh and Collett 1986). It appears that men are more interested in the intrinsic pleasure of driving for its own sake. Since they are more apt to see driving as fun and exciting, men are more inclined to see speeding and other traffic violations as less serious than women (Corbett and Simon 1991b).

Official data from STATS 19 accident report forms show that male drivers have more crashes than women (McKenna *et al.* 1998: 49). Men have more on bends, while overtaking and during hours of darkness, while women have more crashes at junctions. McKenna also used several observation, simulation and self-report studies to investigate driving differences between the sexes. They found that men drove faster, committed more driving violations such as aggressive overtaking, were more inclined to drink and drive, and to take illegal drugs before driving, and were prepared to drive for longer periods, all of which explain men's higher fatal crash risk.

In seven large surveys conducted by Corbett and Simon (1999) to examine the effects of speed cameras, male drivers reported significantly higher levels of speeding on urban roads and motorways than women, overtaking on hatched white lines, overtaking on the left-hand side and pulling out from side roads without giving way. In six of the surveys, men were significantly less likely to use indicators properly and more likely to park on single yellow lines. In two surveys, men were more likely to drive through red lights and to drive when over the blood-alcohol limit. Even when controlling for age, with drivers split into four age groups, men admitted significantly more speeding in all seven surveys, and many other significant differences remained by gender when controlling for age in regard to the other offences mentioned here.[2]

In addition, Table 6.5 shows that women reported significantly fewer penalty points on their driving licence than men, when controlling for age in the same study (ibid.), and McKenna *et al.* (1998: 27) found that women reported fewer police stops while driving than men. On the other hand, women's driving behaviour is not homogeneous, and evidence suggests that some women, especially career women may exceed limits and engage in other traffic offences as much as men (Simon and Corbett 1996). Reason *et al.* (1990: 1316) reported that around 10 per cent of female drivers aged 36 or more were high violators, who engaged in 'deliberate deviations ... of a potentially hazardous system'.

As noted in other chapters, evidence suggests that men are more likely to steal cars and car parts, to drive unlicensed, to drive under the influence of alcohol, drugs and while tired, and to engage in aggressive and 'bad' driving behaviours, thus confirming that most car crime is male car crime.

The overall picture indicates that male drivers are prepared to take more risks and enjoy more risky behaviour, and this links with their propensity for risk-taking off the roads, especially in regard to mainstream offending. This is true across different age groups. The cultural prescription for appropriate expressions of normative masculinity includes the need to compete, to show competence and coolness, to express assertiveness and individuality and the readiness to take risks

Table 6.5: Penalty points on driving licence by sex and age (%)

	17–25		26–35		36–45		46+	
	M	*W*	*M*	*W*	*M*	*W*	*M*	*W*
Some penalty points	20	10	20	7	19	6	9	4

(*n* = men: 2615; women: 1545; chi-square: M > W *p* at least <.003). From Corbett and Simon (1999).

(e.g. Messerschmidt 1993), which expressions are also likely to manifest in the broad context of car culture and while driving. For instance, McKenna *et al.* (1998: 48) found that the experience of thrill and feelings of competitiveness while driving were greater for men than women. Such displays of masculinity will be interwoven around any biological propensity.

Crime control efforts

Tackling the problems associated with excess and inappropriate road speed runs counter to the general trend in society, where speed is desired and valued, and these problems are unlikely to be easily resolved. Typical countermeasures comprise elements of engineering, enforcement and education. These are summarised below.

Engineering and technological measures

Engineering countermeasures concern the in-vehicle environment and situational measures such as modifications to road design and road furniture. Considerable advances have been made, the most noticeable being the proliferation of traffic-calming installations in residential areas, such as road humps, chicanes and bollards designed to slow vehicles down and reduce vehicle noise. These have achieved average speed reductions of 10 mph and importantly child pedestrian casualties have fallen (Mackie 1998). Indeed, these installations have become popular near schools, a development of the community partnerships required under the Crime and Disorder Act by local authorities, whose crime audits have frequently highlighted community concerns about excessive speed and road safety (Brookes 1999).

Yet there are problems. While modifications to some kinds of road hump have quietened concerns about the passage of emergency vehicles, back and neck problems may be aggravated among users of public transport especially, and the additional braking and accelerating required may cause longer-term pollution from greenhouse gas emissions. Further, not all vehicles are slowed down, and the popularity of four-wheel-drive vehicles in cities may partly arise from the ease with which they straddle many humps and their suspension smooths out the worst effects (*The Sunday Times* 10.3.02). Protest groups have complained that building foundations are damaged by vehicle vibrations from hitting the humps (ibid.). In view of the foregoing, this kind of preventive measure is considered unsuitable for main roads and motorways, although trials are under way to evaluate new road surfaces.

In-vehicle technological developments have led to a new generation of smart speed limiters. These are responsive to changes in speed limits, are deployed in conjunction with satellite technology and are available for voluntary or mandatory mass production. Simulator trials undertaken by Carsten and Comte (2001) showed that more close following and smaller gap acceptance at intersections resulted from increased frustration experienced by drivers whose speeds were restricted, although results from road trials were inconclusive in this regard. Feelings of vulnerability through difficulties of accelerating away from danger and while overtaking were reported by drivers, although enhanced awareness of potential road hazards and increased time to react were cited as safety benefits.

A voluntary system where drivers can choose to engage the speed controls may be appreciated by those prone to inadvertent speeding, and most European drivers surveyed said they would welcome some kind of in-vehicle limiter (SWOV 1998: 78). However, compulsory fitment and use of speed limiters in vehicles could be far ahead of majority public opinion since drivers would no longer be free to choose how fast to travel, and such an explosive issue would need extremely careful handling by any administration. Moreover, crashes caused by inappropriately fast speeds for the conditions but still below the maximum speed limit would not necessarily reduce as a consequence of this situational measure, even though a dynamic system responsive to prevailing road conditions might be developed.

Police enforcement and sanctions

Enforcement can be used to deter speeding infractions through the threat of punishment as general deterrence or through actual punishment as individual deterrence. Yet because speeding is so pervasive, police enforcement patrols can do little more than serve a symbolic function to underline that it is against the law. Ironically, too, since patrols have tended to target the 'top enders' (Corbett 1993), this may suggest that lower margins of excess are condoned. As remarked earlier, the failure to elevate roads policing to core objective status is disappointing and, coupled with the fall in numbers of traffic police, may account for the reduction in prosecutions of speeding drivers from police stops (see Table 6.3).

However, speeding prosecutions are increasing overall, courtesy of cameras, and the government's Traffic Penalty Review, set up in 2001

(Home Office 2000b), proposed changes for speed limit infractions. Under the proposals a new system for speeding offences was planned with two levels of fixed penalty. More penalty points and a higher fixed penalty were designed for those exceeding limits by wider margins – raising the risk of a 'totting-up disqualification', while standard penalties would accompany standard offences. Plans to adjust progressively the penalties, points and speeding levels to encourage and reflect drivers' adjustment to the new system were included. In other words, the aim was for greater efforts to target and restrain the worst speeders, which follows research that greatest casualty reduction would accrue from curbing the speeds of the fastest drivers (Taylor *et al.* 2000).

These proposals for speeding offences proved the most controversial of the review (Home Office 2002a: 9) with safety lobby groups and motor organisations opposed on the issue of higher penalties and risk of disqualification for basic speed limit offences. Motor organisations had difficulty accepting the proposals in light of widespread prevalence of 'inappropriate' speed limits (ibid.), and more extreme responses saw the proposals as an attack on the 'ordinary' motorist (ibid.). Unsurprisingly, in view of the strong and mixed responses given, the government decided to keep the issue under review with a likelihood of further consultation.

Speed cameras and related issues

The introduction of automatic speed cameras under s. 23 of the Road Traffic Act 1991 was supposed to free up police time for other duties, provide a 24-hour enforcement capability, reduce crashes at 'accident hotspots' and give the message that exceeding posted speed limits would not be tolerated. Published evidence suggests that crashes and speeding have reduced on targeted roads in Britain (Hooke *et al.* 1996; LAAU 1997) and elsewhere, such as Canada (Chen *et al.* 2002), Norway (Elvik 1997) and Victoria, Australia (Institute for Transportation Engineers 1999), underlining the usefulness of speed cameras.

Corbett (1995) showed that drivers' initial reactions to cameras had largely been one of four types, as follows:

1 *Conformers:* Normally complied with limits on survey road, so no change for cameras.
2 *Deterred:* Had reduced their speed on survey road to avoid detection.
3 *Manipulators:* Slowed down on approach to cameras and accelerated away downstream.
4 *Defiers:* Continued driving well above the speed limit and ignored cameras.

As the ideal aim of speed cameras is to enlarge the proportion of deterred drivers, to maintain the number of those who have 'always complied' and to reduce the ranks of the defiers and manipulators, a further research study (Corbett and Simon 1999) aimed to find out more about manipulators and defiers in the context of evaluating best methods of camera deployment.

Manipulators were shown as the most calculating and sophisticated in their reactions to cameras. They approved of them less than other driver types, especially if they had been caught speeding by one, but they reckoned they knew where they were, how they operated and how to avoid detection. They tended to be the youngest and had the second highest traffic-offending and speeding scores and the highest crash rate.

Defiers, like manipulators, were most likely to drive company or high- powered cars and were most likely to deny a general link between speed and crash risk. They had the highest speeding and offending scores, and reported the highest speeds after cameras or signs were installed. This could have arisen from defiers being the type most likely to discount the risk of detection, least likely to think police action would follow, and if so, that it would be lenient.

By contrast, conformers presented as generally law-abiding, cautious drivers who approved of cameras. They were the oldest and most experienced with the lowest speeding and offending scores and crash rates. The deterred were much like conformers on many variables, implying that it was the cameras that had made them so.

The study concluded that addressing the problems posed by manipulators and defiers was crucial, since these types seemed least responsive, respectful and fearful of cameras while simultaneously being at the greatest risk of speed-related crashes. Yet other issues were raised. Elasticity in the notion of complying with speed limits was one, and some of those interviewed, especially 'conformers', said that they kept within a margin of up to 10 mph above the limit because they did not like breaking the law. So this elasticity allowed them to maintain a self-image of being a good, law-abiding driver even when they were not. Yet exceeding limits on many roads is hardly deviant (see Table 6.1 above), and keeping up with normative speeds may be perceived as sensible safer behaviour since speed dispersion is reduced (e.g. Maycock *et al.* 1998). This is indeed what the majority of magistrates, driving instructors and traffic police officers implied in Corbett *et al.*'s (1998) study. Presented with a hypothetical situation of driving along a 40 mph dual carriageway in fine conditions where everybody else was doing 50 mph, the majority said they would do 50 mph, too, for reasons of greater safety. This is an anomalous situation where lawful behaviour can be interpreted as riskier and perceived safer behaviour is against the law.

If drivers look to the police for direction on this not unreasonable interpretation, police speed control policy and practice may do little to alter it. Police forces generally have not reduced the tolerance threshold of cameras as much as originally intended (DETR 2000b: 34), though with wider coverage by cameras expected via hypothecation, this may happen as the higher risk of detection becomes more potent, enabling tolerance margins to be cut. The latitude that has been allowed to drivers passing speed camera sites may suggest to them either that police are colluding in ignoring speed limit infractions or that a margin of, say 10 mph above the speed limit is complying with the law (e.g. Corbett 2001: 147–8).

In sum, cameras can be an important means for raising drivers' awareness of the dangers of speed and of inadvertent speeding, and digital cameras that allow detection of excess speed between fixed sites, rather than just when passing them, may be more effective in modifying drivers' behaviour. However, whether attitudes to, and beliefs about, speed and speeding will become less favourable as a result remains to be seen, though it is likely that additional deterrents will be required (e.g. de Waard and Rooijers 1994). While most drivers held positive views of speed cameras in the mid-1990s (Corbett and Simon 1999) and in the early millennium (Mori Financial Services 2001) not all were happy. The public backlash following the proliferation of speed cameras, after more British police forces joined the National Safety Camera initiative allowing hypothecation, included the vandalism of cameras, the setting up of protest groups, a growing unease over camera siting and dispute over the truthfulness of apparent casualty reductions (e.g. Association of British Drivers 2002b), underlining disillusionment with government speed control policy (e.g. *The Sunday Times* 21.4.02).

Controlling the attraction and desirability of speed

Education is the third of the traditional 'three E' countermeasures, and is likely to be the longer-term solution to the problems of inappropriate and excessive speed, although sustained efforts will be needed.

Unlike the social context in which drink-driving has become less frequent, that for speeding is different because drivers generally do not see exceeding limits as dangerous when they do it. Most reasonable people can appreciate that consuming alcohol above a certain level will impair driving performance, but most reasonable people do not appreciate that, for instance, reaction times of pedestrians and drivers are not faster at higher speeds, and that the likelihood of getting killed rises substantially if hit at 35 mph rather than 30 mph (Hobbs and Mills 1984). Unfortunately, because most drivers only exceed limits when it appears safe to do so and they think they are better than others (e.g. Svenson 1981), they may ignore such unappetising crash facts because of their seeming irrelevance.

Thus education is needed not only to encourage individual drivers to acknowledge their vulnerability at higher speeds and that the majority cannot have superior driving skills, but also globally to turn round the value placed on speed and to substitute the greater worth, for example, of smoothness or safety while driving. In this regard, companies and corporations that operate vehicle fleets could take more responsibility for the well-being, safety and health of their driving staff. As yet, drivers may be unaware of their raised crash risk in driving a company-owned vehicle (e.g. Lynn and Lockwood 1998), and companies may do little to discourage their drivers from exceeding limits to meet tight schedules (e.g. Lex 1997). These matters are now being addressed by the British government (e.g. DTLR 2000c; see also Chapter 9).

Steps, however, are being made in the right direction with the adaptation for persistent speeders of cognitive behavioural driver improvement programmes presently offered to drink-drivers and 'careless' drivers (see Chapters 5 and 7, crime control sections).

Concluding comments

Problems connected with speeding are usually cast as problems of individual 'deviant' drivers. While this policy is unlikely to be accidental, it is nevertheless short-sighted by ignoring the fact that speed is highly valued, attractive and desirable in the wider society. The social dimensions of driving and exceeding limits, and the political landscape in which these are located, are also extremely salient factors in the occurrence of speeding. It is now seen that in most European countries and elsewhere, for instance the USA, speeding is a majority activity where the consensus tends to legitimate the transgression, and deviants may be those who deny speeding. Even the elite and regulating authorities admit to speeding and get detected. Certainly, governments must be wary of antagonising the electorate, the majority of whom are likely to be drivers, so controls on excess speed need to be effective and socially acceptable, which is not a simple combination. The upshot has been that European governments and their enforcement agencies have tended to give lukewarm or mixed responses to tackling the problems of speed (see, for example, European Transport Safety Council 1999: 13, 42–3).

Moreover, worldwide car sales are expected to rise, intensifying fierce competition by governments to keep existing motor manufacturing plants on home ground and to attract foreign trade. Indeed, as motor manufacturing figures traditionally provide a key barometer of a nation's health, a low profile on sanctioning speed may continue, particularly in regard to the production of luxury vehicles with high speed capabilities. Despite exhortations to leave our cars at home, governments are actually keen for us to buy new (fast) cars and limply to hope that we shall drive slowly in them or not use them much.

Until some concerted political will can be mustered nationally and internationally, speed-related casualties will escalate as different sections of society and interest groups continue to pull in different directions. Any move towards treating speeding as an administrative infraction rather than as a crime, as has occurred for minor speed limit breaches in Holland, may only exacerbate levels of speeding, and the hope that social education initiatives will succeed in turning inappropriately fast driving and excess speed into perceived anti-social and dangerous behaviours seems far off.

Summary of main points

- Usually regarded as a minor offence but causes major social harm.
- It is the most pervasive moving traffic offence, with authority figures and gatekeepers admitting it and few drivers denying it.
- Drivers do not perceive exceeding limits as dangerous when they do it, and inappropriately fast speeds for the conditions are seen as appropriate.
- The proclivity to speed is connected with exaggerated feelings of being in control, perceiving one's driving skills as better than average, and other cognitive distortions.
- Social and structural factors like the consensual nature of speeding, the influence of the media in promoting the 'victimised driver' (often 'speeder'), the enduring discourse of 'accidents' and ideology of the 'car as master' help to promote the trivial nature of speeding.
- Men speed more than women, which may be linked with their attraction towards riskier behaviour, cultural expressions of appropriate masculinity and their higher levels of offending in general.
- Situational prevention measures such as speed humps and cameras can help in controlling excess speed and resulting casualties, but their uses are limited.

- Long-term education to turn attitudes away from the attraction and desirability of speed towards valuing other qualities like smoothness or safety of a journey will be needed, along with more determined political commitment.

Notes

1 See Corbett (2000b) for more on how speeding is constructed as not real crime.
2 These differences by gender have not been reported elsewhere.

Chapter 7

Bad driving: dangerous and careless offences

Introduction

'Bad driving' is a generic term describing a wide range of actions which when prosecuted are generally classed as either dangerous or careless driving offences. Behaviours constituting bad driving range from minor to very serious, though criminal charges usually only follow crashes (Pearce *et al.* 2002: 43). This chapter will mainly concern three types of bad driving offence: (1) causing death by dangerous driving; (2) dangerous driving; and (3) careless driving.

Although there is an offence of causing death by careless driving while under the influence of alcohol or drugs, a fatality which results from careless driving in other circumstances is treated as an aggravating factor in a 'careless driving' charge. Careless driving comprises two kinds of offence: 'driving without due care and attention' and 'driving without reasonable consideration for other road users'. The key difference is that the latter requires evidence that some other road user was actually inconvenienced. In practice, these two offences are both referred to as 'careless driving'.

Bad driving includes inappropriate speed, unsafe overtaking, driving too close, failure to pay sufficient attention and errors of judgement. Specific examples include falling asleep at the wheel, driving the wrong way on a one-way road, disregarding a red traffic light, failing to observe a stop or give way sign, pulling out unsafely, overtaking on the inside lane, cutting in sharply, using a mobile phone while driving, tuning a radio, and eating or drinking while in charge of a vehicle. However, deciding whether a dangerous or careless charge is the more appropriate in the alleged circumstances seems an inexact science with inconsistencies being noted. Major research by Pearce and colleagues (2002), which is valuable throughout this chapter, has confirmed that key elements of road fatality cases, such as inappropriate speed, unsafe overtaking and lapses of attention, can form part of both dangerous driving and careless driving charges. Very similar circumstances may lead to different charges. Minor cases can be prosecuted under dangerous driving legislation while more serious ones can be prosecuted under careless driving provisions (Pearce *et al.* 2002: 46, 47, 51).

The baseline for determining a bad driving offence is to compare the quality of driving in the particular circumstances with what a 'careful and competent driver' would do and consider dangerous. Despite the different definitions for dangerous and careless offences (see below) and the legal cornerstone that each case turns on its own facts, this leaves considerable prosecutorial discretion in preferring charges, given the subjective element inherent in deciding what a careful and competent driver would do. Nearly all drivers think they are careful and competent, but Pearce *et al.* showed that there was wide variation among legal professionals in the proportion of *other* drivers they perceived to be careful and competent (ibid.: 56). This variability focuses attention on the standard that may be applied in distinguishing dangerous from careless driving actions, and may help explain inconsistent charging practices.

Virtually all drivers consider themselves as careful and competent; most exceed speed limits when they consider it safe to do so and most 'break other traffic rules sometimes' (Corbett and Simon 1992a). To have a reasonable prospect of a dangerous driving conviction, the prosecution would need to show that the driving in question was far below the jury's own standard (Pearce, *et al.* 2002: 55). This may help explain why far fewer charges of dangerous driving are brought and why the acquittal rate is higher for dangerous than for careless driving (see Tables 7.1 and 7.2 below; Pearce *et al.* 2002: 43).

Inappropriate speed and excess speed feature prominently as elements of careless and dangerous driving cases (ibid.: 99), yet there are no guidelines advising whether *speed* in itself is sufficient to justify a dangerous driving charge. Without such guidelines prosecutors and juries must decide for themselves, using their own standards of carefulness and competence, and this introduces much latitude for interpretation.

There are other contentious issues in discourses around dangerous and careless driving, most notably attempts to unpick the obscured relationships between (1) degrees of culpability in all the circumstances of a case; (2) extent of the consequences; and (3) levels of sanctions that are subsequently applied. The debates generate much heat and pain but less resolution.

Where a driver deliberately flouts the law, driving recklessly or aggressively without concern for the consequences to self or others, there is little dispute that the sanction should be severe where serious injury or death results. However, all drivers are fallible as humans, and where serious harm occurs and blameworthiness is judged to be low as, when an error of judgement or minor lapse of concentration happens, there is a sharp clash between the impact on victims and bereaved and typical sanctions applied. Indeed, the award of a small fine and several penalty points or a disqualification may understandably feel insulting to the memory of a relative. Yet sanctions for road traffic offences have largely though not exclusively been linked with culpability not consequences in Britain.

This situation was modified in *Simmonds* [*1999*], where an appeal court held that a fatality can and should be noted in court and taken into account when deciding sentence in careless driving cases in English courts. This means that Scottish courts need not take it into consideration although they are bound by the same Road Traffic Act (RTA) 1991. However, as noted by Pearce *et al.* (2002: 57), not all English courts follow this case law ruling, and some groups are unhappy that *Simmonds* was not incorporated into statute. Even where aggravating factors are many and culpability is high in fatal crashes, courts rarely use their full powers to mark society's disapproval (ibid.: 62), attracting comments that the system is offender-orientated and biased against victims and their families. Explanations for this sentencing stance are unclear.

Lastly, it was noted in Chapter 6 that there were semantic difficulties around the word 'accident'. Unsurprisingly, the same is true regarding the term 'careless', which in everyday usage connotes a trivial omission or error with minor consequences and fails to denote an action that may culminate in death. Those who lobby for change think that 'carelessness' is an inappropriate term to describe substantial negligence in driving, where significant failure in the duty of care to other drivers is distinguishable, say, from a minor lapse in attention. Thus calls have been made for an intermediate offence between 'careless' and 'dangerous' to account for those driving actions that constitute sub-stantial negligence but fall short of the criteria for dangerous driving (ibid.: 98).

The term 'dangerous' is problematic because it has negative and positive associations. On the positive side, danger is linked with the risk-taking, daring and skill that are frequently aspired to in modern culture, especially among young men eager to demonstrate their masculinity. On the negative side, dangerous manoeuvres in theory are unacceptable on the road, yet distinguishing what is skilful from foolish can represent a fine line for some given the favourable associations with danger, especially for the driving majority who prefer to decide for themselves what are safe speeds. Dangerous, inappropriate speeds for some could be viewed as skilful and appropriate for others.

This chapter will deviate from the standard format to incorporate three sections on topical concerns – mobile phone usage while driving, 'road rage' behaviour and police vehicle accidents – and another on the perspectives of victims and the bereaved. Their plight is seemingly dismissed as the inevitable and unfortunate price to be paid for car culture and the abuses, transgressions and 'accidents' that happen within it.

Historical and legal context of bad driving

Attempts to constrain dangerous and careless driving have been recognised in law for longer than cars have been around. Since 1861, drivers can be charged under s. 35 of the Offences against the Person Act for furious and wanton driving, which these days is used for such driving elsewhere than in public places or on roads, or in vehicles other than mechanically propelled ones. Where a vehicle is used in an attack on a pedestrian or other target, the driver can be charged with manslaughter contrary to common law (see *R* v. *Adomako [1994]*), and drivers can be charged with murder where *prima facie* evidence of intent exists.

Specific bad driving offences were first introduced under the Motor Car Act 1903, which created reckless driving, and the Road Traffic Act 1930, which introduced careless driving. Subsequently, the Road Traffic Act 1956 created an offence of causing death by reckless or dangerous driving, which was amended in 1972 under a new Road Traffic Act. The offences of causing death by dangerous driving and dangerous driving were repealed under the Criminal Law Act 1977. This left careless driving offences and those of reckless driving and causing death by reckless driving, all of which failed to allay concern and led to the establishment of the Road Traffic Law Review in 1985 to consider the structure and penalties for these and other offences (see Chapter 2). As a result of the committee's report (Department of Transport and Home Office 1988), reckless offences were repealed under the Road Traffic Act 1991 and new offences of dangerous driving created.

Up to 1991 a main difficulty had been for courts and juries to determine the state of mind of the offending driver as the various legal definitions of recklessness or dangerousness had all involved subjective considerations. The 1991 Act intended to replace the subjective elements with objective ones and to focus on the quality of the driving rather than the driver's state of mind. Thus the new formula for dangerous driving, under s. 2A of the Road Traffic Act 1988 amended by the RTA 1991, rests on two bases: (1) the standard of driving fell far below that expected of a competent and careful driver; and (2) it would be obvious to a competent and careful driver that driving in that way would be dangerous. Section 2A also provides for 'dangerous driving' if it is obvious to a competent and careful driver that driving the vehicle in its current state would be dangerous.

Thus the court now needs to make an objective assessment of the standard that would be applied by a careful and competent driver. If the court decides that the behaviour fell *far below* what would be expected it must decide whether it would be obvious to a careful and competent driver that driving thus would be dangerous. The court does not have to show what was obvious to the defendant but what *should* have been obvious, thereby introducing some objectivity. If either (1) or (2) are not fulfilled the court can decide if a conviction for careless driving is proved instead (Gordon *et al.* 1998: 33), which is a departure from normal criminal procedure.

To prove an offence of driving without due care and attention, the standard of driving must fall *below* (rather than *far below*) the standard expected of a reasonable, prudent and competent driver in all the circumstances of the case (e.g. Sampson 1999: 199). As noted by the Crown Prosecution Service in its charging standards (CPS 2000: para. 4.1), there is no statutory guidance about what constitutes a manner of driving 'below' and 'far below' the required standard. This leaves subjective interpretation to the court.

Where a major element of a case is a lapse of attention, charging officers are advised that 'something more than momentary inattention (which may have minimal or serious results)' generally warrants careless driving, while 'substantial/gross/total inattention (which may have minimal or serious results), even though it may take place over a period of a few seconds' generally warrants dangerous driving (ibid.: para. 4.3). Subjective assessment will clearly be involved here. Pearce (*et al.* 2002: 46–7, 95) found inconsistency in charging, with major lapses sometimes framed as careless driving. They concluded that major lapses should be considered as a separate offence, and guidelines for the court would help reduce inconsistency of approach.

In sum, while the RTA 1991 has succeeded in turning the court's attention away from the mental state of the driver and on to the standard of bad driving, charging officers and the court are left making assessments based partly on subjective interpretations of the quality of evidence.

With regard to penalties, careless driving is a summary-only offence, attracting a fine of up to £2,500, discretionary disqualification and re-testing, and obligatory penalty points. Dangerous driving is an either-way offence – up to two years 'imprisonment or an unlimited fine, obligatory disqualification, penalty points and an extended retest. Causing death by dangerous driving, or by careless driving while under the influence of drugs or alcohol, are indictable offences that carry a maximum of ten years' imprisonment which is rarely used (Pearce *et al.* 2002: 62), and obligatory disqualification and extended retesting (ibid.: Table 1; Schedules 2 and 3, Road Traffic Offenders Act 1988).

Extent and trends in bad driving offences

Trends and offence outcomes

Determining the extent of bad driving is an under-researched topic. The best *objective* source are data from the official motoring statistics that give trends over time and a breakdown of the consequences of cases reported for prosecution. These will be considered first.

Table 7.1 shows the trends over time of bad driving cases in which some official police action was taken. Some care is needed in interpreting the table as offence definitions have altered and the basis on which statistics are compiled vary from year to year. The table nevertheless shows that for roughly every *one* offence of causing death or bodily harm by dangerous driving (CDDD), 18 of dangerous driving (DD) and around 190 of careless driving (CD) were actioned in 2000. Further, it shows that the number of CDDD offences has remained fairly stable

Table 7.1:   Trends in bad driving offences since 1961: England and Wales (thousands of offences)

	1961	1971	1981	1991	1996	1998	2000
Causing death or bodily harm	0.5	0.8	0.4	0.6	0.5	0.5	0.5
Dangerous driving	10.9	10.7	6.8	12.2	10.4	10.1	9.2
Careless driving		84.6	139.4	180.5	128.8	99.0	99.8	94.8

From Ayres and Hayward (2001a: Table 2).

over the last forty years, while they have fallen for DD and CD over the last decade (as have most other road traffic offences). Most notably, CD has almost halved in the last 20 years from 180,500 to 94,800 offences actioned while licensed vehicles on the road have increased considerably by 45 per cent between 1980 and 2000 (DTLR 2001c: Table 9.8). Total road casualties have reduced by 3 per cent during that period from 329,000 to 320,000 annually (ibid.: Table 9.10) for a range of reasons, although the decrease in traffic policing resources, noted in Chapter 6, could account for some reduction in processed CD cases as well as the practice of diverting 'careless' offenders to Driver Improvement Schemes in place of prosecution (see 'Control' section below).

In contrast to Table 7.1, which shows trends in offences, Table 7.2 shows the proportion of cases that end in acquittal, which is far higher for CDDD cases than for the other two offences: in 2000, 33 per cent CDDD v. 11 per cent DD and 2 per cent CD cases ended this way. Thus it appears more difficult to avoid a conviction once charged with careless driving than other bad driving offences: less than 12 per cent of initial CD charges were later discontinued, withdrawn or acquitted compared with 42 per cent of CDDD and 44 per cent of DD cases dealt with by police action. A part explanation could be that guilty pleas to the lower

Table 7.2: *Outcomes of bad driving offences dealt with by official action in 2000: England and Wales (%)*

	Causing death by dangerous driving	Dangerous driving	Careless driving
Written warning	—	<1	12
Fixed penalty notice	—	—	34
Discontinued/withdrawn	9	33	9
Acquitted in MC[1]	—	4	2
Finding of guilt in MC[1]	—	40	43
Acquitted in CC[2]	33	7	0.01
Finding of guilt in CC[2]	59	15	<1
Total (%)	100	100	100
Total *n*	359	9,317*	95,031*

*These totals have been adjusted to include some extra cases carried over from the previous year and changes to guilty pleas at Crown Court for the lesser offences of dangerous or careless driving.
1 = Magistrates' courts; 2 = Crown Court.
Extrapolated from Ayres and Hayward (2001b: Tables 1, 2 and 7).

charge of CD are often accepted instead of commencing trial for DD or CDDD (see Pearce *et al.* 2002: 96; pers. comm. Ayres, 2002). Also noteworthy is that 33 per cent of DD cases were discontinued or withdrawn following the initial decision to prosecute. It is not clear why this is much higher than for the other two offences.

Fatal crash outcomes

The study by Pearce and colleagues (2002) included an analysis of 5,870 fatal accidents files from between 1989 and 1995 in several police force areas in England and Wales (where only 1 per cent had been excluded because of insufficient information). Using their data (ibid.: 25–6), initial and final case outcomes are combined in Table 7.3.

Table 7.3 shows that more than two in five drivers at fault were killed (44 per cent) and one in five pedestrians at fault was killed (20 per cent). In only 10 per cent of the total cases was someone reported for CDDD or CDRD; in 20 per cent someone was reported for CD, and in 1 per cent for DD. Combined with 4 per cent cases in which no prosecution resulted, this left only 32 per cent of the total cases available for further action, and of these between 10 per cent and 26 per cent were later discontinued (Pearce *et al.* 2002: 25–6).

Table 7.3:   Initial and final outcomes of a sample of fatal accident cases occurring between 1989 and 1995 in England and Wales (%)

Initial outcome		Final outcome % convicted of offence prosecuted	
		Before RTA 1991	*After RTA 1991*
Driver at fault killed	44	—	—
Pedestrian at fault killed	20	—	—
No prosecution	4	—	—
Reported for CDDD/CDRD**	10	CDRD: 89	—
		CDDD: —	79
Reported for CD	20	CD 87	92
Reported for DD	1	nk*	nk*
Reported for unrelated offences	2	nk*	nk*
	100%		
Total *n* = 5,870			

*Not known.
**Causing death by reckless driving, superseded by CDDD in the RTA 1991.
   Extrapolated from Pearce *et al.* (2002: 25–6).

Of prosecutions, different conviction rates resulted before and after the RTA 1991 for both causing death and careless driving offences. After the Act, a lower conviction rate resulted for CDDD cases than for CDRD before the Act, while the reverse was true for CD cases involving a fatality. Unsurprisingly, disappointment was expressed by lobby groups (e.g. RoadPeace 1997) who were hoping that the objective criteria used by juries in CDDD decisions would result in proportionately more convictions after the Act rather than fewer.

Extrapolation from the Pearce findings indicates that following the RTA 1991 less than 1 in 14 fatal crash cases led to convictions for CDDD and around 1 in 7 led to convictions for CD. So roughly twice as many cases ended in CD as CDDD convictions. Since few CD cases were discontinued or ended in acquittal, criticism arises that prosecutors are apt to reduce dangerous charges to careless driving in order to secure an easier and less demanding conviction (e.g. Pearce *et al.* 2002: 96).

Who does it?

In view of the inconsistency noted in charging cases for bad driving offences, knowledge about characteristics of convicted drivers must be treated with some caution.

Careless driving

Little is officially known about who commits the many different acts comprising careless driving save what is known about the gender and age breakdown of those convicted of the offence from official statistics. In 2000, 84 per cent were male – slightly fewer than for mainstream offending – and 16 per cent were aged under 21, which suggests younger drivers are over-represented (Ayres and Hayward 2001a: Table 12).

Also, 'more than momentary inattention' and 'minor errors of judgement' comprise core features of careless driving charges (CPS 1996), and there is some evidence that minor lapses of attention are more frequently experienced by female drivers and that errors of judgment are experienced fairly equally by all types of driver (Stradling 1997). However, this adds little to knowledge about convicted careless drivers, and further research is needed. Considerably more attention has been paid to convicted dangerous driving offenders.

Dangerous driving

Table 7.4 shows that a higher proportion of men and those under 21 are convicted of dangerous than of careless driving offences (Ayres and

Table 7.4: Profile of offenders convicted of bad driving offences 2000: England and Wales

	% male	% under 21
Causing death or bodily harm	95	25
Dangerous driving	97	34
Careless driving	84	16

From Ayres and Hayward (2001a: Table 12).

Hayward, 2001a). Since 1996, dangerous driving has been a standard list offence, which means that conviction records are included in the Home Office Offenders' Index (OI). The OI now provides conviction information on mainstream, serious traffic and some serious summary offences so that more comprehensive criminal history research can be conducted. One such study (Rose 2000) examined the criminal records of a large cohort of offenders convicted in 1996. Three groups of serious traffic offenders were distinguishable, including 396 dangerous drivers whose records could be compared with those of mainstream offenders.

The study confirmed that dangerous drivers were predominantly male and up to three quarters were aged between 18 and 32. Almost half had a previous conviction for a mainstream offence, almost a third had one for vehicle theft, more than four in ten were first convicted before age 16 and over a quarter were reconvicted within a year (ibid.: 32–3). Dangerous drivers were also linked with other serious driving offences; where this was the principal offence, in 18 per cent of cases a drink-drive conviction and in 15 per cent a disqualified driving conviction also resulted. Yet two main kinds of dangerous driver emerged – the bulk appeared similar to most drink-drivers, having few previous criminal convictions and none for car theft; the other third had many convictions, including car theft, and were otherwise similar to recidivist mainstream offenders and disqualified drivers (Rose 2000: x).

Pearce *et al.* (2002) analysed 5,744 drivers convicted of dangerous driving in 1999 whose details were held on the database of the Driver and Vehicle Licensing Agency (DVLA). This confirmed the predominance of young male perpetrators, who were twice as likely to live in areas of lowest social classification and half as likely to live in areas of highest social classification as the proportion of the general population living in those areas (ACORN categories F and A, respectively; ibid.: 76).

While the OI excludes most summary offences of all types, the DVLA database excludes all mainstream offences. Yet the picture suggested from the latter tended to confirm the profiles suggested by the Rose analysis in that two main types surfaced: those without any previous convictions comprising a third of the sample, and the majority who had some. Forty per cent of the total had been convicted for a previous insurance offence, 22 per cent for a licence offence, 20 per cent for a drink/drugs offence and slightly fewer for driving whilst disqualified (Pearce *et al.* 2002: 79–80).

The combined findings suggest that dangerous drivers are nearly all male, mostly young and may either have no or few previous criminal convictions mainly for other traffic offences, or to have a comprehensive criminal career spanning mainstream and traffic offending that often includes car theft. For those with more than one conviction, little hint of specialisation is apparent, dangerous drivers largely presenting as generalists on and off the road.

Explanations for bad driving

The limited attention given to traffic offending by criminologists means that no specific theory has been proferred to account for bad driving, although control theories have been used to explain recent findings that link risky road behaviours with road and other accidents and with mainstream and traffic crime.

Social control theory and the general theory of crime (low self-control)

Social control theory was briefly considered in Chapter 1 and argues that people are prevented from crime to the extent that they are attached to the social bond. Yet Suchman (1970, cited in Junger *et al.* 1995) argued independently of Hirschi that social controls protected people not only from crime but also from other harms such as accidents and injury, since the more that social controls were violated the greater would be the additional risk of harm to the individual. Thus should there be a relationship between crime and accidents a common aetiology could be shared.

To explore the link, Junger *et al.* (1995) undertook a nationally representative survey of 2,918 Dutch adolescents using interviews and written questionnaires, asking about delinquent behaviour, accident involvement of all kinds, injuries suffered and the extent of social controls in their lives. They found that the higher the delinquency score the higher their accident risk of all kinds, whether as a pedestrian, cyclist, motorcyclist or driver. This relationship held when controlling for age and gender and applied for different kinds of criminal involvement comprising property, violence, vandalism, alcohol and drug crime. They found that social control measures based on Hirschi (1969) predicted accident and criminal involvement, and concluded that social controls protected individuals from involvement in both. They also concluded that the general theory of crime was supported since the predicted inter-relationships between broad categories of accident and criminal behaviour were found (Junger *et al.* 1995: 50–1). In sum, the study indicated that involvement in different kinds of mainstream crime predicted traffic crash and other accident involvement and that low self-control and/or low social controls could provide a common causal mechanism.

Junger *et al.* (2001) built on these findings to test the hypothesis that accident-involved drivers who were judged to display risky behaviour immediately preceding the crash would have a more extensive criminal record than accident-involved 'passive' drivers. The analyses were based on a random sample of 903 crashes involving 1,531 traceable drivers. The names of drivers obtained from the Dutch accident registration system were then cross-referenced with the National Database of Offenders, and the extent of risks taken was assessed by researchers using police reports. These risks included speeding, right-of-way violations, ignoring traffic signals, driving under the influence of alcohol or drugs, illegal overtaking, close-following, cutting in and driving the wrong way down a one-way street, which are behaviours that often appear in careless and dangerous driving charges.

They found that drivers judged at fault by risky actions directly preceding the crash had a higher likelihood of a criminal record than the general population. Specifically, risky drivers had an odds ratio of 2.6 for violent crime in their conviction record, 1.5 for property crime and 5.3 for involvement in traffic crime (which comprised different crimes from the traffic violations noted in the crashes). This was a methodologically sound study, and the results supported the notion that a common factor underlies risky traffic behaviour and criminal behaviour. The researchers suggested that this dimension might be labelled as risk-taking, impulsiveness or low self-control, which if confirmed would help to support Gottfredson and Hirshi's (1990) theory of the generality of deviance and crime causation, discussed in Chapter 1.

Theoretical explanations for careless driving are scarce. This may be partly because careless driving is difficult to define in practice. The guidelines are not sufficiently clear to all legal professionals and inconsistent charging can result (Pearce *et al.* 2002: 34, 38). To the extent that careless driving comprises risky and deliberate or intentional actions, the general theory of crime might apply, though to the extent that errors of judgement and minor lapses of attention embody careless driving, no specific criminological explanation exists. However, the nature of driving errors and lapses, and who commits them, has been the subject of much research used to develop the well-validated theory of planned behaviour (e.g. Reason *et al.* 1990).

Low self-control superficially seems to provide a reasonable explanation for many risky driving behaviours and other crimes, though as noted in Chapter 1, many criminologists have reservations about the applicability and some tenets of the general theory of crime. Yet it may be unwise and premature to dismiss the theory since if a common aetiology is accepted between wide-ranging (but not all) deviant behaviours and accidents of many kinds, then as Junger *et al.* point out (1995: 52) there are policy implications for the authorities involved. This is because health, accident prevention and crime prevention agencies will be dealing with the same people and focusing on the same background variables. In this case, the introduction of multi-agency co-operation under the Crime and Disorder Act 1998 will have been especially timely.

Expressions of youthful masculinity
Interestingly, Junger *et al.* (2001: 452) found an age effect whereby younger drivers who displayed risk-taking preceding the crash were *more* likely to have a criminal record than the general population of young people, but they were *less* likely to have one than older risky accident-involved drivers. This suggests that the link between risk-taking on the road and other criminal propensity among younger people may be less well established than among older risky accident-involved drivers, for whom risk-taking on the road might be part of a wider lifestyle of injudicious behaviours. In other words, to some extent dangerous driving among some young men could be a manifestation of their inexperience, bravado, overconfidence and attempts to impress others by displaying perceived normative masculine attributes. Even so, a tendency to risky behaviour generally would seem to be a key predisposing factor.

The Pearce *et al.* analysis of key elements in fatal crashes revealed that driver aggressiveness was a prominent feature in 15 per cent of the 84 cases tracked and this was more frequently associated with dangerous rather than careless driving charges (2002: 45). Aggression on the road is more commonly known as 'road rage', and to this we now turn.

Road rage

Definitions and prevalence

Driver aggression on the road is hardly a new phenomenon, but the term 'road rage', coined to describe driver aggression, is believed to have been first attributed to events in Los Angeles during the 1980s (Brennan 1995). There is no single agreed definition though it appears to range from minor aggressive acts such as rude hand signals and verbal abuse, to more serious pursuits of cars for intimidation, acts of 'dangerous driving', physical abuse including common assault, actual bodily harm (ABH), grievous bodily harm (GBH), causing serious injury or death by dangerous driving, and using the vehicle as a weapon which may comprise manslaughter or murder.

Recorded statistics are not a reliable index of its incidence since only the more serious incidents will be reported and they could be recorded under various offence categories, but self-report surveys of both victims and aggressors may provide a better measure, depending on who is sampled. The nationally representative 1998 British Crime Survey (BCS) found that over half (54 per cent) of those who had driven a van or car during the previous 12 months reported some form of road rage incident, most experiencing verbal abuse or gestures and almost one in ten (9 per cent) being forced to pull over or off the road completely. Three per cent had been threatened by violence from another driver who had got out of their car (Marshall and Thomas 2000). These figures are lower than others reported elsewhere (e.g. Joint 1995), where almost 90 per cent of motorists experienced road rage incidents and 60 per cent admitted losing their temper behind the wheel in the previous year. However, the BCS figures should allow trends over time to be assessed.

Importantly, the fear of road rage has led many drivers to carry weapons in their cars. An Arriva survey in Britain (BBC News Online 6.4.99) found that nearly a third kept crowbars, repellent sprays or knives there, and 42 per cent women drivers carried personal alarms. The latter finding is ironic since many women use cars to escape the fear of crime experienced when walking and using public transport (London Research Centre 1998).

Yet fear of road rage, albeit fuelled by media treatment that tends to focus on the more serious incidents (Marshall and Thomas 2000), and growing fears of 'carjacking' in Britain, where drivers have been forced out of their cars, attacked and even murdered for their car keys to enable the theft of their (mainly) luxury cars (e.g. BBC News Online 17.3.02), are now serious issues that chime with discourses of concern around street crime.

A survey of 2,100 company-car drivers in six European countries (Leaseplan 2001) found that not only was road rage the most disliked behaviour committed by others, but that over half (53 per cent) admitted 'ever' behaving aggressively towards other drivers themselves, men slightly more than women (53 per cent v. 46 per cent) and younger drivers slightly more than older ones (61 per cent of <35-year-olds v. 44 per cent of 46+ drivers). Interestingly, this survey found that road rage was engaged in mainly to respond to the poor driving of others and to other drivers' aggression, though unsurprisingly few saw themselves to blame (ibid.).

A general point, however, is that driver aggression is a cross-cultural problem occurring in many countries (e.g. Traffic Safety Village 2000; Parker *et al.* 2002), and is especially prevalent and lethal in the USA, where high levels of gun ownership suggest that restraint in face of driver provocation is particularly sensible. A study by Mizell (1997) showed that at least 1,500 US citizens annually in the early 1990s were injured or killed through aggressive driving, and in that country racism/religious hatred and domestic violence were identified as key motivations in 2.5 per cent and 3 per cent respectively, of violent crime reports where traffic altercations and vehicles used as weapons were involved (ibid.: 8).

A unique phenomenon or a reflection of our times?

As noted, men appear to be aggressors more than women and the young more than the old, and as for mainstream crime this situation is mirrored in victims, with all men (and younger men) significantly more likely than all women (and younger women) to be at risk of a road rage experience (Marshall and Thomas 2000). Yet outside the general trends, all kinds of formerly peaceful drivers can show aggression, with road rage being no respecter of religion, ethnicity, social class or celebrity status (e.g. Mizell 1997).

Because of the involvement of atypical 'criminals' in road rage incidents, this has led some to suggest that road rage is not normal social violence and comprises a unique phenomenon requiring a specialised explanation. Certainly, traffic congestion does not seem to provide such a direct explanation of driver aggression as superficially might seem obvious (Lajunen *et al.* 1999), although traffic density may play a part (Parker *et al.* 2002). Further, related research suggests that aggressive driver behaviour is a complex phenomenon with a range of psychological causes (Lajunen and Parker 2001).

The false attribution of others' apparent aggressive or careless behaviour to internal rather than to external situational causes (Jones and Nisbitt 1972) could be another explanation for road rage, leading to the recommendation that re-education along the lines of trying to see the other driver's viewpoint could help (Levelt 1998).

While research continues to seek for causes of road rage within the individual, an acknowledgement of society's dependence on the car and what it represents and symbolises in our lives could broaden understanding of the phenomenon. In other words, the car provides a safe, private space in the public domain, and defence of one's perceived territory when threatened by others' actions may provoke an angry response. The car is often a key to freedom, independence and control, it may facilitate one's livelihood, it can be an expression of status and self, and owning one may be at great financial cost. So the burden of responsibility to prevent crashes caused by the mistakes of others may add to a driver's susceptibility to aggression (Connell and Joint 1996).

Lastly, at a structural level it was found some time ago (Porterfield 1960; Whitlock 1971) that traffic fatalities are strongly positively correlated with homicide and suicide rates, and multiple regression analyses by Sivak (1983) confirmed that the homicide rate predicted the US traffic fatality rate (along with the proportion of young drivers). This led him to conclude that society's level of violence and aggression affects the extent of aggressive driving and consequently the frequency of fatal traffic crashes. In the present context, this means that road rage could be a situation-specific reflection of society's general level of aggression and this would be interesting to measure and test.

Current advice to prevent victimisation includes the suggestion to avoid eye contact with the other party where possible, not to behave confrontationally, to lock one's doors while driving in town and to avoid the temptation to carry a weapon (e.g. Joint 1995). This may be sensible advice, but unfortunately it is unlikely to tackle the fear of crime and feelings of unsafety among drivers generated by aggressors on the road, which is linked with the wider difficulties of controlling levels of violence in society.

Mobile phones and other in-vehicle distractions

Is there a problem?

Most adults in Britain own mobile phones and most are drivers. Since experienced drivers find that conversations can be fairly comfortably held with passengers in normal driving conditions, it is hardly surprising that many feel it acceptable to make and answer mobile phone calls when driving, estimates varying from around a third in the general driving population (Direct Line Insurance 2002) to three-quarters of higher mileage drivers (BRAKE 2001). Yet another reason why motorists may not be overly concerned about mobile phone use when driving is that no specific offence has so far been legislated in Britain prohibiting their use despite considerable media attention, a private member's bill in Parliament and some damning fatal crash reports (e.g. *The Times*, 4.2.99; *The Times* 15.2.01). Although new drivers should know that the *Highway code* strongly *advises* against their use when driving – as did government publicity campaigns in 2002 – drivers may still believe that their danger could be overstated, which would support the experience of most drivers that harm has not happened to them (yet) while on the phone.

Nevertheless, rare harm does occur although British police accident reports do not record whether mobile phone usage is involved, so the extent to which they may be a contributory factor in road crashes cannot yet be accurately established. In Canada, crash risk has been estimated to increase 400 per cent when talking on a hands-free phone with raised risk extending for several minutes afterwards (Redelmeier and Tibshirani 1997).

Difficulties associated with mobile phone use when driving

Problems associated with mobile phone use when driving include the following:

- Lowered attention through manual dialling, composing and reading text messages.
- Losing control when changing gear in manual transmission vehicle with hand-held phone.
- Lowered concentration through calls tending to be 'intense, complex, business-related and urgent' (ROSPA 1999).
- Social pressure to maintain normal fluent conversation with caller in contrast to passenger conversations where pauses are mutual and accommodated.
- Slower reaction time to hazards (Direct Line Insurance 2002).
- Tendency to 'tailgate' and miss road warning signs through distraction (ibid.).
- Increased stress levels as shown by raised heart rate (Haigney and Taylor 1998).

In sum, distraction is a major problem associated with making and receiving mobile phone calls, which may raise collision risk especially when attentional demands of the traffic environment are high. In particular, one study has confirmed that both hands-free and hand-held phone usage raise crash risk since reaction times of motorists using phones increased during sophisticated simulator tests (Direct Line Insurance 2002). Those using hand-held phones reacted 30 per cent more slowly than those over the blood-alcohol limit and nearly 50 per cent more slowly than normal drivers, and even those using hands-free kits needed longer braking distances than drunk-drivers. Further, drivers using hands-free or hand-held kits were equally distracted by changing signal quality, which reduced attention to road hazards (ibid.).

Even motorists acknowledge that their use can be dangerous. Surveys show that 91 per cent supported a ban for using hand-held phones, and 47 per cent for all mobile phones, when driving (BRAKE 2001), and that this should be the government's priority for crash reduction (RAC, 2002). However, few in the RAC survey (5 per cent) thought this was the best way for themselves to reduce their own crash risk. This echoes a theme raised in Chapter 6 that drivers do not see risky or unlawful actions as unsafe when undertaken by themselves since they are careful drivers able to select safe situations for risky manoeuvres. Most drivers probably think they are being careful rather than careless when using a mobile phone behind the wheel.

Other technological distractions

The mobile phone is not the only in-vehicle gadget causing concern. Electronic traffic information and navigation systems (screen-based and audio-based), complex air-conditioning systems and entertainment technology providing music and satellite-beamed television channels have also been identified as serious distractors, along with fax machines, other office technology and sophisticated dashboard displays. As bad may be hand-held congestion warning systems that allow viewers to flick through a selection of electronic maps detailing congested areas while driving. All these devices can lead to sensory overload as well as failures of attention to the road environment.

Using a national US database, Stutts *et al.* (2001) found that where vehicles were towed from the crash scene 13 per cent of drivers were distracted at the time of the crash and, of these, distraction caused by adjusting a radio, tape or CD player were determined as contributory causes in over 11 per cent of crashes, and adjusting vehicle controls accounted for 3 per cent of distractions. Mobile phones accounted for just 1.5 per cent distractions. In 34 per cent of the crashes where distraction had been a factor, the source was unknown. Given that the driver's attention status could not be determined in a further 36 per cent of the total, these figures for distractions of all types are almost certainly underestimates.

Although navigational products are largely marketed as driver aids and that sensible use 'should be no more distracting than listening to the car radio' (*The Times* 27.2.99), this may depend on the amount and type of cognitive processing needed for both kinds of information, with traffic information possibly demanding more processing and requiring visual attention to be diverted from road to screen. As things stand, nearly all crashes are caused by human error (e.g. Sabey 1999), many of which arise from failures of attention, and tempting drivers to be distracted with ever more sophisticated gadgetry of various kinds could come close to facilitating driver inattention or even negligence, which some, including bereaved relatives, would consider criminal.

Why not a new offence?

Drivers may be prosecuted for any of the bad driving offences or for failure to have control of their vehicle, which in practice usually means where a crash has occurred. Thus it tends to be the consequence rather than the act that is prosecuted. Officially the situation is under constant review and, while plans for specific legislation were resisted earlier by government, a consultation was set up in 2002 to canvass views on introducing an offence of using any hand-held phone while driving.

Government resistance appeared to rest on the premises that the police had sufficient powers to prosecute where necessary, and that even if a law were introduced it would be unenforceable (e.g. *The Times*, 8.5.02). The second point deserves expansion.

Although in theory some drivers might be caught red-handed talking on a hand-held phone by a passing police patrol, say in a traffic queue, proving an ongoing conversation on a hand-held or hands-free phone would be virtually impossible since electronic logging methods can show a phone was connected at a specific moment but not that the driver was talking. Listening in routinely to calls to catch drivers would raise serious objections around privacy and 'creeping state surveillance'. Moreover, since police have insufficient patrolling resources adequately to tackle widespread mobile phone usage when driving, very limited and patchy enforcement could bring the law into disrepute, alienate those apprehended and might make little difference to usage or to overall casualties.

Conversely, failing to legislate despite publicity campaigns warning against the activity could be interpreted as condoning and legitimating the behaviour. Now it is known that mobile phone usage adds to reaction times, braking distances and crash risk and can be more dangerous than drink-driving, lack of firm action might be seen as negligent, especially by crash victims and their relatives, and especially given that the majority of drivers appear to support a ban. A counterclaim is that other types of distraction which cannot be legislated against seem to cause far more collisions, therefore why worry about the proportion caused by mobile phone use. This may be a spurious argument, yet more research on the relative contributions to collisions of mobile phones, other in-vehicle technology devices and other types of distractions, would provide a more solid basis on which to proceed.

Police vehicle accidents (PVAs)

Members of the public are not the only drivers who may engage in careless or dangerous driving. Police drivers too are occasionally convicted of these offences, usually following a crash in which a police vehicle was directly or indirectly involved.

The role of pursuits and emergency responses

Because crashes involving police vehicles occur, however, does not mean that bad driving by police officers is necessarily involved, and indeed few officers (2 per cent) were convicted of criminal offences arising from crashes involving death or serious injury in Rix et al.'s (1997) study of PVAs occurring in Britain between 1990 and 1993.[1] Nevertheless, widespread concern has arisen at the number of crashes involving police during pursuits or while responding to emergency calls, and during 1997–8 4,865 PVAs occurred in these situations that resulted in minor to fatal injuries.[2, 3]

Fuelling the concern is the 178 per cent rise in PVA deaths (from 9 to 25 people) noted by the Police Complaints Authority (PCA 2001: 30) in pursuit cases voluntarily referred to them by police forces between 1997 and 2001 (which means virtually all fatal PVAs in practice). It appears that most PVAs occur in pursuit/follow situations, Rix et al. (1997) finding that roughly 40 per cent of the total deaths and serious injuries arose from this type of incident. Interestingly, the rather sparse literature suggests that harm arising from responses to emergencies is more likely to involve *direct* police vehicle contact, while harm arising from pursuits is more likely to concern *indirect* police involvement with victims being in the cars being chased (e.g. PCA 2001).

The onus on officers

Police drivers are regulated by various road traffic Acts, which *inter alia* allow them unrestricted power to stop a vehicle, and exemption from many traffic regulations, *providing* they can show they were reacting to an emergency and that the action was justified. Yet ignoring road signs, excessive speed and other dangerous manoeuvres would seem rarely justified except where serious threat to life is posed by the suspect driver, though even this would be questionable if similar risk arose to other road users or police drivers themselves. Certainly most would agree that nobody should be at risk of serious injury or death in defence of property, yet almost 20 per cent of drivers involved in serious PVAs were subsequently reported for taking a vehicle without consent (TWOC) and 1 per cent for other theft offences in Rix *et al.*'s study (1997: 32), indicating that substantial risks with severe consequences can be taken by police drivers to apprehend property offenders.

Conversely, it is fair to note that altogether 48 per cent of (non-police) drivers were reported for offences in the Rix study, including 11 per cent of the total of pursued drivers for no insurance, 7 per cent for dangerous driving, 4 per cent for driving while disqualified, 3 per cent for drink-driving offences and 2 per cent for having no licence. Some of these police reports might have been made to justify the pursuit or emergency, but they do identify a cluster of unregulated drivers of great concern to police who are often found to be linked with mainstream crime (see Rose 2000 in Chapter 8). While these figures only relate to pursuits and emergencies where crashes occurred and give no indication of the proportion with no mishap, pursuits of possible offenders such as in the Rix study surely should not be at the expense of police or others' lives.

Behind the statistics

Several reasons have been proffered to account for the recent rise in PVAs including the setting by government of performance targets relating to police response times to emergencies. Such is the concern for road danger that at least one police force has declined to record response times to emergency calls to discourage inappropriate speed by police drivers (e.g. *The Independent* 5.11.01). Another explanation concerns the attraction of traffic policing with its car-type culture to inappropriately suited young men who may relish the prospect of a car chase undertaken within a macho context 'as part of the job'. In these circumstances, the determination to catch a suspect can become compelling (evoking a 'red mist' scenario) despite considerable risks.

The commonest accounts, however, relate to claims of insufficient training and expertise such that police drivers are sometimes deployed in high performance vehicles for pursuits and emergencies beyond the limits of their skill. Her Majesty's Inspectorate of Constabulary noted this in their thematic inspection on roads policing (HMIC 1998: 31), urging forces to carry out an urgent review of training provision, while the Police Complaints Authority (2001: 30) welcomed the decision by the Association of Chief Police Officers to introduce a universal standard for police drivers in their training to raise skill levels of all drivers. In the meantime, PVAs are hardly good for public relations and do not enhance the public's confidence in the police or provide good road safety examples to be followed by the mass of ordinary drivers.

The perspectives of victims and the bereaved

The chaos and bewilderment caused by the everyday horror of 'ordinary' road traffic collisions rarely attract media attention, and the voices of the crash-involved and their relatives go mostly unheard except through the campaigning of pressure groups set up for support and self-help (e.g. Campaign Against Drinking and Driving (CADD) and RoadPeace). Yet hidden distress is pervasive and severe, as will be outlined in this section.

Coroners' court proceedings

Coroners' inquests are separate from the criminal justice system and are begun for every road death in England and Wales, although they are rarely completed if criminal proceedings are taken. A key purpose of inquests is to ascertain by inquisitorial means how the deceased met his or her death, rather than to apportion blame by adversarial means, but this rarely fulfils the expectations of the bereaved, who hope to gain insight into the social circumstances of the crash (e.g. Pearce *et al.* 2002: 64).

In addition, the legal procedure in practice is often at variance with theory. This concerns the continuing 'good law' contained in *Beresford* [1952] which states that normally an inquest will be completed *before* any charge less than manslaughter is heard in a criminal court.[4] RoadPeace (2002), among others, state that frequently cases are heard in magistrates' courts before the coroner completes the inquest, which can be distressing to the bereaved if additional evidence or an 'unlawful killing' inquest verdict is thought to have warranted a more serious criminal charge. Because of 'double jeopardy' rules, drivers cannot be charged with other offences relating to the same event once a trial begins.

Howarth's (1997) study of coroners' courts also confirmed the dissatisfaction of bereaved relatives. 'Accidents' were largely constructed as blameless, chance and unlucky events, where the medical and legal discourses used in court contradicted the social discourse that was desired and meaningful to the families. In particular, the default verdict of 'accidental death' rather than 'unlawful killing' in road fatalities (Matthews and Foreman 1993: 250, cited by Howarth 1997: 148; see also RoadPeace 2002) was strongly objectionable to those who believed another was to blame, especially where illegal driving behaviour was involved. Relatives often felt deeply cheated that no-one was held responsible at the inquest.[5]

Criminal court proceedings

The levels of dissatisfaction found in a nine-nation European survey of 1,364 crash victims and their relatives undertaken by the European Federation of Road Traffic Victims (FEVR 1995) were highest in respect of their perception of the legal process. Eighty-nine per cent of the bereaved and 69 per cent of disabled survivors felt that justice had not been done in their specific case, with 97 per cent of British bereaved experiencing most dissatisfaction with the court procedure and nearly all believing the sentence was unjust (RoadPeace 1997: 8–9).

Other complaints emerging in the Pearce study (2002) included the speed at which proceedings for careless driving were typically dealt with in magistrates' courts, which was experienced as an insult to the memory of relatives (ibid.: 58), and distress over the omission that a death had occurred in 'careless driving' hearings.

Downgrading charges from dangerous to careless driving at the last moment before the case was heard caused considerable distress to many bereaved, leaving them with no time to take advice on how best to proceed, and a lack of information generally on progress in the criminal process led to the perception that the system was biased towards the offender. Lack of information was also a key complaint among the injured and bereaved at European level (FEVR 1995). In the Pearce study, relatives were sometimes not told of the trial date until informed by reporters after the trial, and impediments preventing access to the investigation file to decide if civil action might be appropriate were frustrating and distressing (2002: 68). In sum, the impression arising from both studies was that there was no proper role for victims and the bereaved in the legal aftermath.

Police investigations

Police resources available to investigate traffic crashes have also been hampered by the gradual dwindling of traffic police numbers. For example, most witness statements were formerly taken at the scene, or as soon as possible afterwards, but are now made on proformas sent by post. They may be completed some while after the event, when memories have faded, and may have no help from probes and prompted recall. The closure of some specialist Accident Investigation Units, operated within each police force, has been considered, which is surprising since many serious traffic cases collapse without scientific evidence (Pearce *et al.* 2002: 31–2).

Officers at a crash scene have a number of conflicting objectives – to get traffic moving again, to promote the safety of survivors and other road users, and to preserve evidence. The upshot is dissatisfaction among police and others that road deaths are not treated as seriously as violent deaths off the road (ibid.: 30) where much effort is made to preserve the crime scene. Certainly, the FEVR survey (1995) confirmed a strong European-wide desire among relatives and survivors for better-quality investigations and prosecutions similar to the standard found in murder cases (see also Pearce *et al.* 2002: 58).

'Secondary victimisation' by insurance companies

Poor treatment by insurances companies was one of two main reasons for ongoing distress reported among families affected by injury or bereavement in the FEVR survey (1995: 8). Financial hardship is an extremely common consequence of traffic crashes, considerably reducing quality and enjoyment of life among survivors, their families and the bereaved in the short and long term, and delays by insurance companies to cover funeral costs and other immediate expenses added to their suffering. Such complaints were strongest in Britain (RoadPeace 1997: 2). FEVR recommended advance payments to those who have lost breadwinners and regular revision of compensation tailored to the effects suffered (1995: 8).

Support for victims and bereaved

Victim Support (VS) is an independent charitable organisation comprising a national network of affiliated local schemes (partly funded by government) that offers an outreach service to mainstream crime victims. It is largely operated by a volunteer workforce who send letters, telephone or visit victims in their homes to offer practical help, advice and emotional support. By 2002, around seven in ten of its schemes offered a limited service to road crash victims and their families, perhaps helping to arrange a funeral or advising of access to benefits.[6] One scheme with separate local funding (in Bedfordshire) provided specialist bereavement support from trained counsellors, but this was an exception. All others, including the three in ten schemes unable to offer direct help because of limited resources, referred road crash victims to other organisations for specialist support.

Ironically, the self-help organisations to which those seeking support are referred are largely unfunded themselves. Consisting mainly of bereaved relatives and victims, it is thought they may provide the most beneficial resource to others trying to cope with their own tragedies. Mutual support arising from shared experience is not available from uninvolved others and such help can promote healing through giving strength, solidarity, empowerment and specialist advice. Self-help groups in Britain include CADD, RoadPeace and Compassionate Friends, while other support organisations include Cruse and the Samaritans.

Despite the tremendous work of these organisations it is curious that help for victims has largely been left to volunteers and unfunded groups, even where criminal charges have been brought. The minimal sponsorship or absence of it for self-help groups has effectively treated crime on the road as less important and serious than mainstream crime and arguably has discriminated against its victims and bereaved.

Yet the winds of change are blowing, and an independent working party to investigate road deaths and the needs of relatives and survivors was set up by Victim Support (1994) to produce proposals for improvements. Further, a Home Office Road Deaths Working Group was convened early in the millennium consequent to the government's revised Victims' Charter to consider a collaborative national service to cater for the needs of road crash victims. Improvements are likely in the provision of information to victims and bereaved under the terms of a European Union directive requiring that adequate information about their legal rights be given.

Psychological and physical effects of road trauma

More help is often needed than that offered by volunteer groups and health care professionals. For survivors there may be long-term difficulties arising from whiplash and head injury that can cause impaired neurological and cognitive functioning, and other physical injuries may completely transform lives of the accident-involved and their relatives (e.g. FEVR 1995: 9).

Crash victims can suffer serious psychological and psychiatric effects. For instance, Norris (1992), who surveyed adults in four US cities, concluded that road crashes were probably the commonest cause of post-traumatic stress disorder (PTSD), and that they alone would yield 28 seriously distressed persons for every 1,000 US adult citizens.

Mayou (1997), reporting on two longitudinal studies of road crash survivors, concluded that PTSD and phobic travel anxiety were persistent and had a continuing disabling impact on up to one in five survivors at a five-year follow-up. Limiting or avoiding travel, changing to a safer vehicle, giving up driving altogether and considerable concern about travel by close relatives characterised travel anxiety, and anger at the lack of recognition of their suffering – by the legal system, those thought responsible for the crash and others – prevented normal recovery.

Being unable to work and loss of income are among the most devastating effects for injured survivors (e.g. Bryant 1997; Mayou 1997), while leisure, social life and relationships can suffer considerably from depression, frustration, anger, loss of independence and self-esteem (Bryant 1997). Such symptoms can worsen or persist over time, FEVR finding that over a quarter of relatives still experienced suicidal feelings at least three years later (1995: 10). Together with sleeping problems, headaches and distressing nightmares, long-term general health problems were suffered by around half the survivors and relatives (ibid.: 9).

PTSD also affects emergency service workers. Hetherington *et al.* (1997) found that police in particular can be more affected by the horror of these everyday events than some survivors, and they have added difficulties through their own self-image as helpers and the public's assumption that they can cope because it is their job. These researchers suggested that routine intervention should be offered to all officers at the scene to avoid anyone standing out as in need of help.

In sum, the impact of road crashes can be severe and long term, and negative effects are wide ranging and largely hidden. Pervasive dissatisfactions with legal, court and insurance procedures can be compounded by physical and physiological injuries and psychiatric and psychological disorders, and the capacity to enjoy life permanently disappears for many (FEVR 1995: 11). The default practice of treating crashes as accidents (rather than crimes) when illegal driving behaviour has been involved understandably aggravates survivors, who may see their losses treated disrespectfully or ignored by wider society. Unsurprisingly they may feel themselves treated as the unwanted by-product of car culture and dismissed as part of the price paid for the mobility and convenience of the masses.

Crime control efforts

There may be limited deterrent potential in changing the structure of penalties for bad driving, yet discourse around the control of this behaviour frequently centres on what sanctions are most appropriate to meet other sentencing aims like incapacitation and just deserts. This will be considered first, after which re-education with the aim of reducing instances of minor bad driving will be discussed.

Length of imprisonment

One key task of the Home Office Road Traffic Penalty Review (2000b) was to reconsider penalty and offence structures for bad driving offences, which effectively acknowledged that considerable disquiet was felt despite changes introduced by the RTA 1991. One consideration was to review imprisonment maxima where several anomalies had been noted. One of these was the peculiar position whereby the maximum for burglary is 14 years' imprisonment while that for CDDD is 10 years. As the judge remarked in his summing-up of a case where a man had run down and killed a police officer manning a speed check and failed to stop, '[T]hat might strike the public as an odd approach to the value placed on human life' (*Sunday Telegraph* 2.1.00).

Even in that very serious case, a penalty of seven years' imprisonment was given, reduced to recognise the guilty plea entered (ibid.). Indeed, the maxima are rarely if ever used for CDDD, as found by the Pearce study (2002: 6) and as pointed out by the Traffic Penalty Review consultation which showed that between 1996 and 1998[7] only 66 drivers were imprisoned for 5½ years or more, and none for more than 8 years in CDDD cases (Home Office 2000b: 15, Figure 1). As the review noted: 'It would be an empty gesture to raise a maximum penalty when the present maximum is clearly not preventing the courts from sentencing at a level which they regard as right for the cases which come before them' (ibid.: 15).

Such a stance hardly challenges perceptions of the low seriousness of fatal traffic crashes even when caused by highly dangerous repeat offenders who, some would emphasise, are at least restrained from reoffending while in prison. It is noteworthy that the government's response to the report on the Traffic Penalty Review (Home Office 2002a: 6) indicated its intention to raise the maximum penalty to 14 years for causing death offences. While the Pearce study showed little deterrent value in longer sentences of imprisonment imposed on dangerous drivers generally, and found that reconviction rates differed little whether or not convicted dangerous drivers had been imprisoned (2002: 82–3), arguably the denunciatory function of a higher maximum sentence for CDDD would signal society's disapproval of such behaviour and underline its seriousness.

Disqualification, retesting, reoffending and community penalties

Licence disqualification is obligatory for any dangerous driving conviction and discretionary for careless offences. There is a requirement to take an extended driving retest (about twice as long) at the end of a ban for dangerous driving before driving legally recommences, and ordinary or extended retests are discretionary for other traffic convictions where penalty points are awarded.

Whether the experience of disqualification is effective at reducing the risk of reoffending dangerously is rather unclear, this seeming to depend on the driver's previous motoring convictions. For instance, the Pearce study found that those with few previous motoring convictions appeared to observe their ban, passed a retest and reoffended far less once relicensed than disqualified dangerous drivers with a worse record (2002: 82–3). Among those with 10+ motoring convictions, more were reconvicted of dangerous driving (9–11 per cent), of other traffic convictions (about 60 per cent) and driving whilst disqualified (percentage not reported) within two years than drivers with fewer convictions (ibid.). This reinforces the seminal finding of Philpotts and Lancucki (1979) that past criminal behaviour is the best predictor of future criminal behaviour.

Although those who passed a retest offended less than those who did not pass one, this did not necessarily mean that retests 'work'. This is because those who passed a retest appeared not to reoffend *during* their disqualification period while those who did not pass one did reoffend during their ban (Pearce *et al.* 2002: 83). In other words, those who passed a retest were a self-selecting group less inclined to reoffend anyway, in contrast to the retest desisters/fails who continued to drive and break other traffic laws during their disqualification period. Such retest desisters are likely to feature among a key group of dangerous drivers identified by Rose (2000: x) who accumulated frequent convictions for mainstream and other serious driving offences.

Interestingly, retesting appeared to fare best as a deterrent for disqualified dangerous drivers with 5–9 motoring convictions. This group was significantly less likely to be reconvicted than similar offenders who had not passed a retest (ibid.: 82). Those with the fewest previous convictions were very unlikely to reoffend anyway within two years of sentence, whether or not they were sentenced to a retest, so the effectiveness of retesting could not properly be explored. These findings are somewhat equivocal, and further research could explore whether offending is reduced among those sitting the retests.

Most worryingly, the Pearce study found that the *majority* of those required to pass a retest to regain their licence did not do so within three years of being banned (2002: 83), suggesting – in light of the proportion who were convicted of driving whilst disqualified – that many dangerous drivers, especially those with the worst records, continue to drive unlicensed and unconcerned for the consequences. Whatever the re-educative value of extended and ordinary retests, it is surely imperative to find better ways to ensure disqualified dangerous drivers either get relicensed or desist from driving.

As well as inviting comments on retesting, licence disqualification and vehicle forfeiture (see Chapter 8 for the latter), the Road Traffic Penalty Review consultation welcomed views on its proposal to introduce community penalties for motoring offenders convicted of non-imprisonable offences (Home Office 2000b: 14). Although these were not then applicable to bad driving offences (which are imprisonable), they might be welcomed by the bereaved more than small fines but would have resource implications for the National Probation Service (Pearce *et al.* 2002: 60–1). The government's response to the review indicated that the idea would be considered further (Home Office 2002a: 5).

National Driver Improvement Scheme

The main thrust of alternative sanctions for bad drivers has come from the rapid growth of Driver Improvement Schemes. These schemes are operated by county councils in conjunction with local police forces and co-ordinated by the Association of National Driver Improvement Schemes. Together with ACPO, this association is responsible for standardising courses offered. Attendance at a course is available for drivers facing prosecution for a s. 3 'careless driving' offence, and is at the driver's own expense in place of prosecution. In practice, attendance is offered to offenders where minor lapses of attention or errors of judgement and low seriousness is involved. Not only might some benefit accrue to the driver and other road users, offenders are diverted from the courts which helps to explain the fall in careless driving prosecutions and convictions in recent years (see Table 7.1). Schemes are operational in most British police force areas, and driver attitudes and behaviour are assessed by professional trainers during the short duration of the course. Failure to attend or to co-operate with the course leads to reassessment for prosecution.

An evaluation study by Burgess (1999) examined whether attitudes improved towards four common traffic violations (drink-driving, close-following, dangerous overtaking and speeding) and whether self-reported offending of this nature decreased. Attitudes were assessed pre-course, immediately afterwards and three months after course completion. More than half registered a significant increase in the perceived seriousness of speeding immediately post-course and three months later, although only 41 per cent of the original participants responded at the later follow-up. As non-respondents may hold less socially responsible attitudes than respondents, it is possible that the findings might not have been so positive had all participants replied.

Nevertheless, those who responded reported significant decreases in all four driving behaviours in the three months after the course, compared with a similar pre-course period, indicating that at least a short-term improvement can be achieved for some 'careless' offenders. Over two thirds of clients (70 per cent) perceived the course as a means to avoid prosecution, although 90 per cent accepted it was an opportunity to consider some areas of their driving that might need attention. Thus generally encouraging results emerged from the evaluation, and further research is awaited on whether driving convictions are lowered following course attendance.

Certainly, training that helps with weaknesses in driving skills would seem useful for those prone to errors of judgement and lapses of attention whether or not they have been detected for such an offence, and some courses are available to drivers who self-refer. Whether such courses would impact usefully on the worst dangerous drivers with many motoring convictions remains to be seen. Yet in light of unimpressive findings regarding the impact of imprisonment and disqualification on such drivers, and the reasonable successes of, and enthusiasm for, cognitive-behavioural programmes for mainstream offenders (e.g. Home Office 1998), this possibility deserves consideration.

Concluding comments

The Road Traffic Act 1991 introduced several changes to bad driving offences, partly to help the court make objective assessments rather than subjective ones about the defendant's state of mind. Yet only partial success might be expected since deciding what a careful and competent driver would do and how far the alleged behaviour fell short of this standard requires subjective evaluation. Pearce *et al.* (2002) found that convictions for CDDD and DD offences did not increase as a consequence of the RTA 1991 as had been expected, and victims and bereaved self-help groups continue to express great disaffection with the criminal justice system's response to the consequences of injury and fatal crashes, which implies that bad driving is rarely perceived and treated seriously. For instance, little or no central funding for self-help survivor and bereaved groups has been given, dwindling traffic police numbers limit enforcement capability and administrative resources to process these cases, crash scenes have been cleared as fast as possible by police especially if no fatality is expected or happened and courts are reluctant to impose more than half the maximum sentences allowed for the worst instances of CDDD.

Another illustration of how society has marginalised the consequences of bad driving is the continuing widespread use of careless driving for serious breaches of traffic laws where death is caused. A consequence of such a charge is that the occurrence of someone's death does not even need acknowledgement in court and can remain hidden. Unsurprisingly, calls have been made for an intermediate offence of 'causing death by negligent driving' to be explored which would denote negligence or serious failure to take sufficient care while driving (e.g. Pearce *et al.* 2002: 98). This would go some way towards meeting relatives' and survivors' distress, even if little deterrent value were realised.

Interestingly, the hitherto marginalised position of road traffic victims provides a sharp contrast to how mainstream crime victims have come in from the cold in recent years and now occupy a central position on the criminal justice stage where their concerns and needs are taken more seriously and their role has become more functional (e.g. Zedner 2002).

While there are indications that the marginalised position of road crash victims may start to improve, the short shrift paid until now to the victims and bereaved relatives of others' bad driving underlines a underpinning theme of this book. The dominant ideology of 'the car is king' helps explain how deliberate risky manoeuvres are treated as accidental and not necessarily as crime, how inappropriate speed for the conditions that causes a fatality may be charged as careless rather than dangerous driving, and how victims and bereaved relatives may feel like the unwanted outcomes of car culture.

'Car supremacy', according to Davis (1992: 258), has suffused our culture with the ideology that the car is master and demands respect, that road safety education is learning that one must get out of the car's way, and that hapless pedestrians and cyclists who fail to heed this warning must accept the consequences. Davis's position may be uncomfortable to some and largely focuses on the car's hegemony in relation to the car-less. Yet as he points out (ibid.), until a genuine commitment is made to treat the capacity to hurt others as the central problem of driving, rather than an inconvenient by-product, little progress in 'improving road safety' will be made because the cause of the problem is sidestepped.

Summary of main points

- Lack of guidelines leads to inconsistencies in charging, with some overlap between careless and dangerous charges.
- The objective assessment of bad driving required by the RTA 1991 is partly based on subjective interpretation of evidence about which there can be much ambiguity (e.g. what are inappropriate speeds, what would a careful and competent driver do?).
- Sentencing in English law is largely based on culpability not consequences, but most imprisonment terms for causing death by dangerous driving are for less than half the maxima provided.
- The perceived big gap between 'careless' and 'dangerous' offences needs filling.
- In the Pearce *et al.* (2002) fatal crash sample, half as many drivers were reported for causing death by dangerous driving as for careless driving, and it was easier to secure convictions for the latter. Around 1 in 5 fatality cases ended in convictions, mostly for careless driving.
- Dangerous drivers are mainly young males with either few/no previous motoring convictions or a comprehensive criminal career encompassing mainstream offending.
- There may be a common aetiology between dangerous driving, other risky or deviant behaviour and accidents of many kinds. If so, there are policy implications for health, accident and crime prevention agencies who will tend to deal with the same people.
- While much research situates the causes of road rage within the individual, the phenomenon could reflect society's growing levels of aggression and violence.
- Hand-held and hands-free mobile phone usage is more distracting than conversations with passengers and causes slower reactions.
- Several factors contribute to the current rise in police vehicle accidents, including insufficient training for the tasks of pursuit and emergency responses.

- For many victims and bereaved, dissatisfactions with court, legal and insurance procedures, compounded by physical, psychological and psychiatric disorders and financial distress can cause enjoyment of life to disappear for ever.
- Over a quarter of survivors and relatives feel suicidal three years after the crash.
- Survivors of crashes caused by dangerous drivers may feel the inconvenient by-product of car culture, dismissed as the unfortunate price paid for the convenience of the masses.
- Most dangerous drivers do not take the required retest to regain their licence within three years of being sentenced, suggesting that many continue to drive unlicensed.
- Imprisonment and disqualification seem ineffective in deterring the worst dangerous drivers, though early results from Driver Improvement Schemes for careless drivers are more encouraging.

Notes

1 Despite the small proportion of convictions (2 per cent), of the total drivers 27 per cent were referred to the Crown Prosecution Service and 5 per cent were acquitted, suggesting that roughly 20 per cent of cases were not proceeded with (Rix *et al.* 1997: 35).
2 Calculated from written government reply by Mr Boateng (18.1.99, *Hansard*: Cols 333–35).
3 Between 1993 and 1997–8, 27,721 PVA incidents occurred (ibid.).
4 Beresford was reinforced in 1999 by Smith *v.* DPP (*The Times* 28.7.99, QB Div Ct).
5 See also Green (1997) and Davis (1992) for powerful discourses around the social construction of road accidents.
6 Personal communication, Peter Dunn, Victim Support, 2002.
7 Some 10,618 were killed between 1996 and 1998 (DTLR 2001c: Table 4.15).

Chapter 8

Unlicensed driving

Introduction

Before operating a vehicle, a person must hold a valid driving licence and be insured against third-party risks. The registered keeper must also ensure that the vehicle has a current excise licence and is properly registered. No part of the vehicle should be in a dangerous or defective condition, and vehicles over three years old must have a valid Ministry of Transport (MOT) test certificate. But many people do not comply with these requirements. Excluding speed limit, failures to comply with traffic signs, and parking and obstruction breaches, they are the most common motoring offences dealt with by official police action in Great Britain (Ayres and Hayward 2001b: Table 1). In 2000, driving licence, insurance, excise licence and registration, test certificate and vehicle condition offences together comprised almost a third (32 per cent) of all motoring offences proceeded against (ibid.).

Although drivers are often charged simultaneously with more than one of these breaches, this chapter will mainly focus on licence-related offending. More is known about these offences and they are arguably the most serious. They comprise three main types:

1 Driving whilst disqualified having previously held a valid licence.
2 Failing to observe the terms of a provisional licence.
3 Driving having never held any form of licence (offenders commonly referred to as NELIs).

A serious consequence of driving without a valid licence is that any insurance cover held is most likely invalidated (e.g. Gordon *et al.* 1998: 59). Those involved in a crash with an unlicensed driver can rarely claim against that person's insurance and, in Britain, their only recourse could be limited compensation through the Motor Insurers' Bureau. All drivers pay for this through a small levy automatically added to insurance premiums (Home Office 2000c). Also, unlicensed driving is associated with higher-than-average crash risk (Forsyth and Silcock 1987: 25–6; de Young *et al.* 1997). Unlicensed drivers are likely to be inexperienced drivers (Home Office 2000b: 20) and yet they have great faith in their superior driving skills (Silcock *et al.* 1999a: 11).

Despite the large numbers apprehended, unlicensed drivers are difficult to detect. Prosecutions usually result from attracting police attention by committing another vehicle-related offence or crash-involvement, and most unlicensed driving is likely to occur outside these categories. Unless a person is suspected of an arrestable offence, such as driving whilst disqualified, unlicensed drivers can continue on their journeys after being stopped. Also, as licence-carrying is not compulsory in Britain, there are many ways for drivers to circumvent prosecution. By law, drivers normally have seven days to produce the missing documents at a police station, or prosecution will follow. However, this presumes that those stopped give a correct name and address, and even where this is done, drivers anticipating disqualification can apply for a licence to replace the 'lost' one, which is later surrendered to the court when the disqualification is imposed, allowing the driver to continue until the deception is discovered. Police in some areas do not follow up those who fail to produce their documents within the allotted period since this task may be futile where false information has been given. The net effect is that only a minority of unlicensed drivers are likely to be prosecuted. The same is true for uninsured drivers, those with irregular vehicle documentation and those who drive defective vehicles as these offences often occur together (e.g. Forsyth and Silcock 1987: Table 17).

Disqualification orders are sometimes imposed on those who drive while already disqualified and on those who have never gained a full licence, but this may be no deterrent to those who already drive illegally (e.g. PACTS 1999: 72). Maximum fines are rarely imposed since courts need to impose realistic financial penalties (ibid.: 57–61), so more severe penalties may not be needed. While courts could feel hamstrung, current penalty levels may convey the message that unlicensed driving is not taken very seriously. Indeed, some groups of young offenders find the behaviour acceptable within their social environment (Silcock *et al.* 1999a: 17). Interestingly, driving whilst disqualified was reduced to summary status under the Road Traffic Offenders Act 1988, suggesting this was not seen by the state as a serious breach, although the Magistrates' Association subsequently made efforts to change the breach's status to a triable-either-way indictable offence (e.g. PACTS 1999: 61). In 1996 it became a standard list offence, which means that convictions for disqualified driving are now recorded within the Home Office Offenders' Index.

In sum it appears that unlicensed driving is common, difficult to detect and enforce, is closely linked with other traffic offending and raised crash risk, and is not severely penalised.

Historical and legal context of unlicensed driving

Since 1999, all new drivers in Britain take a two-stage test – a theory test followed by a practical test – in order to obtain a full licence to drive unsupervised. Drivers must be at least 17 to apply for a provisional licence to drive a car, and once they have reached 70 a licence must be renewed every three years. Changes in fitness to drive must be notified to the Secretary of State, in which case restrictions or a revocation of licence may follow. Since 1998, British drivers applying for licences receive a new photocard licence which was introduced for more European standardisation. Paper licences are gradually being phased out.

The principal regulations concerning driver licensing have been amended many times and were consolidated under the Motor Vehicles (Driving Licences) Regulations 1996, which incorporated an EC directive on driving licensing. Most infringements are charged under the Road Traffic Offenders Act 1988, including offences relating to driving whilst disqualified under s. 103. The New Drivers Act 1995 provides for the licence revocation of new drivers who have acquired six penalty points in the first two years of holding a full licence. Such drivers revert to provisional status until the two-stage test is retaken and passed.

For driving without a valid licence the offence is usually endorsable and the maximum penalty is a fine on level 3 (currently at £1,000), and there are no specific powers of arrest. By contrast, driving whilst disqualified is an arrestable offence punishable by up to a level 5 fine (maximum £5,000) and/or 6 months' imprisonment. However, the average fine imposed by magistrates' courts for driving licence-related offences in 2000 was £59 (Ayres and Hayward 2001b: Table 6).

Extent and trends in unlicensed driving

Assessing the extent of the various kinds of unlicensed driving is not straightforward because few prevalence surveys are in the public domain and Home Office statistical data relate only to detected offences. Nevertheless, some idea of the extent of unlicensed driving can be gathered from Table 8.1. The largest category is for driving, causing or permitting another person to drive other than in accordance with the licence (Table 8.1). Provisional licence offences are included in this category although their proportion cannot be accurately assessed after counting rules were changed in 1992. Nevertheless, should 1992 offence proportions still apply, then the two main provisional licence offences – driving without 'L' plates and driving unaccompanied – comprise by far the two largest single offences of unlicensed driving, closely followed by failing to produce a licence (which includes NELIs). In contrast, Table 8.1 shows that driving while disqualified comprises a much smaller percentage of total licence offences proceeded with (12 per cent) and total convictions (18 per cent).

Of course these figures tell us only about the extent of *discovered* licence offences. Two data sources can help in gauging the real incidence of unlicensed driving among the British motoring population. First, by virtue of the close links between uninsured, untaxed and unlicensed driving (e.g. Silcock *et al.* 1999a: 6), a rough figure can be estimated. Extrapolating from a Motor Insurance Bureau report (1998), which

Table 8.1: Driving licence offences proceeded against and findings of guilt – England and Wales 2000

Offence category	Total proceedings	Total findings of guilt
Driving while disqualified	49,000	41,468
Driving, or causing or permitting another person to drive other than in accordance with the licence	254,077	148,630
Failing to produce driving licence	95,543	43,555
Driving after false declaration as to physical fitness, etc.	36	21
Other driving licence-related offences (excluding fraud and forgery)	1,877	1,054
Totals	400,533	234,728

From Ayres and Hayward (2001b: Table 2).

calculated a ratio of licence breaches per police stop and suggested that between 4 per cent and 6 per cent of the driving public drove whilst uninsured, Silcock et al. estimated that similar proportions were also unlicensed on British roads. This converts into around 1.5 million people who drive without a valid licence.

Secondly, the nationally representative Young People and Crime (YPAC) survey of around 2,500 young people in Britain, which included a booster sample of ethnic minorities, confirmed that licence and insurance offences were more common than drink-driving and dangerous driving offences among young men and women (reported in Rose 2000: 15). Indeed 13 per cent of young males admitted committing at least one licence or insurance offence 'in the previous year' (1992–3), and 30 per cent admitted 'ever' committing such an offence (ibid.: 14). Unfortunately, these offences cannot be disaggregated and the licence offences could be of any type.

With regard to driving while disqualified in Britain, Home Office figures for 2000 show that about 153,000 disqualification orders were imposed (Ayres and Hayward 2001b: Tables 13 and 14). In the same year, there were over 41,000 convictions for driving while disqualified (DWD) (Table 8.1). These figures are not directly comparable because not all DWD drivers convicted in 2000 would have been disqualified in the same year. Nevertheless, the actual proportion of disqualified drivers who continue to drive is likely to be higher than the approximate 1 in 4 ratio suggested, as only a proportion of those driving illegally will be discovered. In England, Kinchin (1990) and Corbett and Simon (1992a: 50) found that 26 per cent and 27 per cent respectively of disqualified drivers completing self-report questionnaires admitted to some driving, and 44 per cent of Mirrlees-Black's (1993) sample admitted driving during the current or a previous disqualification.

Some western countries are very concerned about the high incidence of unlicensed and disqualified driving. In Australia, Robinson (1979) found over a third of 1,500 banned drivers revealed some disqualified driving, and Smith and Maisey (1994) reported that 36 per cent of a sample of banned drivers continued to drive. In California, a study by de Young and colleagues (1997) used crash and licensing data to estimate a prevalence rate of 3.3 per cent for unlicensed motorists driving on Californian roads, and 8.8 per cent for those whose licences had been suspended or revoked.

In Britain, there is little information on trends in unlicensed driving. The total number of licence, insurance and record-keeping offences dealt with by official police action shows a year-on-year decline since a peak in 1994. In that year 1,395,000 offences were dealt with compared with a total of 1,201,200 in 2000 (Ayres and Hayward 2001a: Table 2). However, all other offence categories listed in the official motoring statistics also show a decline in numbers proceeded with since 1997, except for speed limit offences which have risen because of speed camera operations (ibid.). Thus the fall may reflect reduced police enforcement activity rather than greater compliance with road traffic law (see Rose 2000: Ch. 6).

Crash risk and offending links

While these prevalence estimates and findings are worrying, the real problem of unlicensed and disqualified driving is the safety risk. A comprehensive US analysis revealed that 20 per cent of fatal crashes involved one or more drivers who were invalidly licensed (AAA 2000). Similar studies in Sweden (Goldberg 1997) and Australia (Harrison 1997) show that many deaths are caused by unlicensed and banned drivers, who are often alcohol impaired. The de Young *et al.* (1997) study estimated that, compared with validly licensed drivers, unlicensed drivers may be 4.9 times as likely to be involved in fatal crashes than valid licence holders, while those with suspended or revoked licences may be 3.7 times more likely. In Britain, Forsyth and Silcock (1987) explored the relationship between road crashes and traffic offence prosecutions in Northumbria. They found that 25 per cent of all police accident reports led to one or more traffic prosecutions and, of these, driving licence offences were the third most common type (after careless driving and drink/drug offences), prosecuted in 25 per cent of serious injury and 17 per cent of slight injury cases.

Moreover, several analyses reveal that unlicensed driving is closely linked with other serious traffic offending. Forsyth and Silcock (ibid.: Table 17) showed that licence offences were often prosecuted alongside careless driving, drink/drug-driving, vehicle insurance, MOT test certificate and reckless driving offences. Broughton (1999), in a study of DVLA records between 1988 and 1997, showed that (excluding provisional licence holders) unlicensed drivers committed 24.5 per cent of all insurance offences, 13 per cent of drink/drug offences, 26 per cent of reckless or dangerous driving offences, and 49.9 per cent of all theft or unauthorised taking offences.

In aggregate, therefore, the claim by some disqualified and unlicensed drivers to drive more safely and cautiously than would otherwise be the case (e.g. Mirrlees-Black 1993: 21) could just mean that as a group they are less safe than average drivers in the first place. Certainly, Silcock *et al.* (1999a: 11) found that unlicensed drivers were more aggressive on the road and had higher opinions of their driving skills than others.

Who does it?

Most early evidence on the characteristics of unlicensed drivers came from unrepresentative or small-scale studies. Even now, because many offenders remain undetected, it is unwise to rely solely on data from convicted offenders. Analysis of the Home Office Offenders Index (OI) by Rose (2000) provides much valuable data on the criminal histories of a large sample of offenders who were convicted in 1996 of a range of mainstream (non-vehicle) offences, car theft and serious traffic offences (including disqualified driving). These OI data have been compared and augmented by self-report data on offending provided by the YPAC survey (ibid.).

Classifying offenders by the principal offence for which they were convicted in 1996, this analysis showed that 97 per cent of the OI driving while disqualified (DWD) sample were male, and that almost three times as many males admitted a licence or insurance offence in the last year in the YPAC survey (13 v. 5 per cent females). OI data revealed that 72 per cent of the DWD offenders were aged between 18 and 32 with the peak age between 21 and 25 (ibid.: Table 3.1) compared with 62 per cent of mainstream offenders with a similar age profile. Controlling for access to a vehicle, the YPAC found that white young people admitted more serious traffic offences 'ever' and 'in the last year' than either Asian or black young people (male and female), suggesting that, in 1992, when the survey was conducted, serious traffic offending was mainly a white preoccupation. Interestingly, those in the YPAC ever committing a licence/insurance offence were more numerous among the lower socioeconomic groups (C2 and DE), which contrasts sharply with the profile of young drink-drivers who were found mainly to come from the higher A/B socioeconomic groups.

OI criminal history data revealed that 78 per cent of the DWD group had previous convictions compared with 70 per cent of mainstream offenders (Rose 2000: 31). Table 8.2 shows that 73 per cent of the DWD drivers had previous convictions for mainstream offences compared with 67 per cent of mainstream offenders, and that more DWD offenders had convictions for vehicle theft than the mainstream group. Almost half the DWD group (46 per cent) but only 34 per cent of the mainstream offenders had convictions within the previous 10 months (ibid.: 36), and there was a tendency for the DWD group to repeat the offence although this was mainly in the context of generalised offending. In all, DWD

Table 8.2: Prevalence of previous convictions among disqualified drivers and mainstream offenders (%)

Previous convictions (type of offence)	Disqualified drivers	Mainstream offenders
Mainstream offences	73	67
Other standard list offences	42	30
Bail breaks or breaches	52	38
Vehicle theft offences	51	31
Valid *n*	1,608	23,026

From Rose (2000: 32, Table 4.2).

drivers had slightly higher levels of previous criminality than mainstream offenders, which tends to destroy any notion that the detected disqualified driving incident was exceptional.

Unfortunately, little is known of the characteristics of unlicensed drivers other than DWD offenders, except for the suggestion from Silcock *et al.'s* (1999a: 10) exploratory study of 50 unlicensed drivers that young people may be over-represented, most are male and that offenders may come from many social and cultural backgrounds, as indicated in the next section.

Explanations for unlicensed driving

Those who have never held a licence

The YPAC included questions on family life, school experiences and peers, and an 'adverse factor' score was constructed for each respondent. This score was strongly related to mainstream offending for both males and females (Graham and Bowling 1995: 47–8), and further analysis by Rose revealed that this association was repeated for serious traffic offending, highlighting the importance of social factors related to delinquent peers, school and family.

Social factors also emerged as important in Silcock *et al.'s* study (1999a). Many viewed driving without a valid licence as a routine, acceptable behaviour in which peers engaged. There appeared little social stigma attached to admitting the behaviour to a skilled interviewer. Such a picture fits with subcultural explanations for crime (e.g. Cohen 1955), whereby membership of a subculture confers identity, status and belonging, and conduct, rules and values are frequently opposed to those of mainstream society but seen as normative. Similarly, Matza's techniques of neutralisation might also fit these findings since it seems unlicensed drivers may minimise their wrongdoing by excusing it as routine and normative.

Strain theory too might account for unlicensed driving, as noted in Chapter 1. This proposes that when people cannot achieve what they want legally, some may bypass the blockages to reach their objectives by unlawful means – especially those in marginalised, disadvantaged and excluded groups who may experience the mismatch more acutely (e.g. Merton 1938; Agnew 1992). Where the costs of driver training, taking the two-part test and subsequent vehicle insurance are beyond the means of intending new drivers, it seems they may accept the risk of being detected without a valid licence. Silcock *et al.* (1999a: 13) found evidence that some unlicensed drivers thought the likely penalty a cheaper option than paying to drive legally.

Blocked opportunities may also be perceived by those with literacy problems and by non-English-speaking groups such as minority ethnic groups and immigrants, because the theory component of the driving test requires English comprehension. Cultural differences may explain a further portion of unlicensed driving as some unused to the bureaucracy of driver licensing systems in their native country may not appreciate the salience of the licensing rules in the adopted country.

Disqualified drivers
Studies on driving while disqualified are notoriously difficult to conduct owing to the obvious difficulties of obtaining representative samples of such drivers. Research in this field has been more concerned with exploring the effects of disqualification among those receiving the penalty and their motivations for ignoring it. Mirrlees-Black (1993) interviewed 70 drivers who had been disqualified (for different reasons and for different periods of time). Almost half admitted driving while disqualified during the present or a previous ban. Their various strategies to avoid detection included wearing disguises, not parking at home, using other people's vehicles and allegedly driving more safely (ibid.: 21). In addition, one third of those who broke their ban kept the disqualification secret from friends, relatives and employers, but details published in local newspapers prompted one in five who did not keep it secret to say that concealment would have been impossible even had they wanted this (ibid.: 34).

The most common reason for driving while banned was the need to continue normal routines, with curtailment of employment seen as the most serious consequence of not driving. Indeed, the jobs of over three quarters of those previously employed were lost or negatively affected by the disqualification (ibid.: 10).

While this suggests seemingly compelling motivations for breaching disqualifications, Rose (2000), as noted, showed that disqualified driving is merely one behaviour resulting from an intertwined history of traffic and mainstream offending where criminal careers are often well established. On the other hand, the widespread nature of unlicensed and uninsured driving among the young in the YPAC survey, and the drift into unlicensed driving noted by Silcock, suggests that not all such offenders have mature offending histories.

Yet whatever their characteristics and motivations, the urgency among unentitled drivers to become or to continue as participants in car culture, and their preparedness to do so illegally, emphasises the increasing dependence on personal, private transportation to enable and facilitate the smooth functioning of lives.

Crime control efforts

For a long time government initiatives to control the prevalence of unlicensed driving were not high priority. Average fines were much lower than the cost of driving lessons and taking the test, and a disqualification from driving may be thought odd where such an order is already in operation or where the lack of a valid licence has not discouraged the offender previously. Further, a comparison of the penalty types and maxima available for disqualified driving, licence and other motoring offences with the averages imposed in 1996 prompted PACTS (1999: 58–9) to remark that the British courts and the Crown Prosecution Service were missing existing opportunities to signal society's disapproval of such offending. Even if evidence is equivocal that more severe sanctions help to reduce casualties or to improve driver behaviour, the failure to show society's disapproval of such behaviour does not help (ibid.: 60–1).

Vehicle forfeiture

By 2000, more attention was focused on the various licence offences, and research, consultation, legislation and brainstorming were organised in attempts to reduce their incidence. Some key suggestions will be considered here. The government's Road Traffic Penalty Review (Home Office 2000b: 21) included a proposal to promote vehicle confiscation for licence offences. This was already permitted by the Powers of Criminal

Courts Act 1973 but was virtually unused for motoring offences (PACTS 1999: 74). Although Mirrlees-Black (1993: 23) found that the majority of her disqualified driver sample thought that forfeiture would be an effective obstacle against breaching a ban as the temptation would be removed, the remainder thought the opposite because of the ease of acquiring another vehicle. In California, de Young (1997) found that while vehicle forfeiture for 30 days significantly reduced convictions and crashes during that period and the following 11 months, many continued to drive while suspended and/or became crash-involved. Whether such a strategy works may depend on the personal and financial circumstances of the offender and his or her determination to bypass the disqualification.

Moreover, since other family members could be penalised by the forfeiture of a vehicle, it has been suggested that this penalty be kept for repeat DWD offenders (after an earlier court warning). Temporary or permanent forfeiture of a vehicle lent by a parent or friend to an unlicensed person could be a severe deterrent penalty.

Educational initiatives

A common research finding is the lack of awareness among motoring offenders and other drivers of the implications of driving while disqualified or otherwise unlicensed. For instance, drivers do not always know that insurance cover (if held) is usually invalidated by an invalid licence, and that a disqualification order takes immediate effect (e.g. Mirrlees-Black 1993; Harland and Lester 1997). Anecdotal evidence also suggests that provisional licence holders are not always aware of the restrictions of their licence, especially where the full licences of young drivers have been revoked and substituted by provisional licences. More publicity, and warnings of the consequences of unlicensed driving and driving while disqualified, may prevent some offending.

Educational campaigns to underline the anti-social nature of unlicensed driving may take considerable time to yield results, especially given its prevalence and routine nature, as found with drink-driving and speeding. However, making perpetrators, their peer groups and families more aware of the harmful implications may be a useful policy, as Mirrlees-Black (1993) found that families provided the best restraining influence on potential DWD offenders.

Closing administrative loopholes

Unlicensed driving is aided by various procedural loopholes. As noted above, the naming and shaming in local newspapers of disqualified drivers may inform the general public and family members, but employers of those who drive as part of their job are not routinely told of any disqualification from driving, allowing concealment to occur. Although challenge could arise under the Human Rights Act if courts were permitted to notify employers, a utilitarian view would argue that withholding this information could be more harmful to potential victims than releasing it could be for the employee. Less controversial measures under consideration include formalising a requirement for employers to check employees' licences when recruiting (where driving is part of the job) and regularly to check the licences of drivers who are already employed (HSE 2001).

Increasing the difficulty of obtaining false or duplicate driving licences and insurance documents and of using other people's driving licences are other impending preventive strategies, as is the provision of insurance and licence databases to patrolling police cars to enable online checking. Meanwhile, in the USA, the adoption of electronic driving licences is under consideration (e.g. AAA 2000).

Mandatory carrying of driving licences?

The non-mandatory carrying of driving licences in Britain is doubtless a key barrier preventing the apprehension of unlicensed drivers. Although some believe that those with nothing to hide have nothing to fear from carrying mandatory identification cards, such a move is likely to be opposed by civil liberty lobby groups; and criminologists note the tightening grip of state surveillance of citizens (e.g. Ericson and Haggerty 1997; Norris et al. 1999). While traffic police are empowered to check only who drivers say they are (rather than who they actually are), the detection of unlicensed driving could remain haphazard.

Abandoned and untaxed vehicles (AUVs)

Scope of the problem

Driving an untaxed vehicle, having failed to pay the excise duty, is a very common summary motoring offence, often prosecuted alongside other documentation offences like unlicensed driving, uninsured driving and not having a valid MOT certificate. In 2000, almost 133,000 people were found guilty of driving without a valid vehicle excise licence (Ayres and Hayward 2001b: Table 3), which makes it one of the most numerous single offence categories. The 1999 DVLA roadside survey showed 5 per cent of all vehicles on the road were untaxed, suggesting a widespread problem (Ledger 2001: Table G.2). Another is that untaxed vehicles are abandoned when they become unroadworthy This section briefly considers the implications of both problems.

Wrecked and burnt-out vehicles are not only an eyesore but they can block parking spaces, obstruct roads and cause other difficulties. Vehicle abandonment is a crime linked with a sense of decline and decay that detracts from the quality of life, as sharply characterised in Wilson and Kelling's seminal (1982) article on 'broken windows'. AUVs also present a danger to children who play in wrecked cars, and a considerable proportion of fire service time is spent dealing with AUVs set alight by arsonists, vandals and joyriders (e.g. Jacobson *et al.* 2002). Little investigation has been undertaken into this murky world of criminal activity although anecdotal evidence suggests that driving untaxed vehicles is meshed with a subculture of widespread unregulated vehicle use at best and with serious traffic offending and mainstream crime at worst. Indeed with regard to the latter, police reports indicate that some groups of offenders regularly commit crimes by using untaxed and unregistered 'pool vehicles' whose existence is officially unknown (ibid.).

Strangely, the official extent of the problem has been unknown because national statistics on abandoned vehicles were not gathered before April 1999.[1] Instead, reliance has been placed on police and local authority estimates that varied widely. One in 2000 was of 350,000 abandoned vehicles and up to two million scrapped cars (*The Times* 1.11.01). Certainly, commentators accept that the problem is growing rapidly and is exacerbated by a combination of factors.

Probable causes and potential solutions

A prime cause is the sharp fall in the cost of scrap metal throughout Europe, which means that instead of scrapyards paying to collect old vehicles, disposal costs are now higher than the value of the recoverable materials that can be salvaged, giving old vehicles a negative value. In addition, used car parts have lost value in tandem with falling vehicle prices, while repair costs have risen sharply, partly to meet more stringent MOT test requirements. At the same time, an EU End of Vehicle Life Directive that Britain agreed to though arguably did not make adequate provision for (e.g. *Guardian* 2.2.02), means that from 2002 there are higher costs associated with environmentally friendly disposal regulations for hazardous vehicle waste. The need to drain all harmful oils, gases and metals – including lead, cadmium and mercury – before scrapping, to prevent effluents from seeping into the water table, has reportedly added up to another £100 to disposal costs (*The Times* 1.11.01), with the net effect that it is now more economical for an owner to dump a useless vehicle than to dispose of it legally.

While the legal responsibility for disposing safely of a vehicle rests with its registered keeper, in practice inadequate licensing and registration regulations mean it has been relatively easy in the UK to evade prosecution for dumping a vehicle. Despite the inclusion in the Vehicle (Crime) Act 2001 of tentative first steps to close some of the registration loopholes, few keepers are prosecuted for abandonment as it is difficult to prove. In other words, last owners are protected from paying disposal costs and it is easy to claim that a vehicle has been sold on. Even where sellers are sometimes required to advise the DVLA of the identity of a new keeper, false information might be given to the seller for which the seller cannot be held responsible.

Interestingly, the fall in scrap metal prices has affected all EU countries similarly yet the problem of AUVs is much less acute outside Britain. This may possibly be attributed to stricter and more formal vehicle registration procedures in European countries (Jacobson *et al.* 2002: 4, 48), and hints that the problem may be a cultural one specific to Britain (ibid.: 47–8). In Holland, seller and buyer must go to a post office together to register a change of ownership which firmly links the vehicle's identity with the transfer of keepers (ibid.). Certainly it is clear that existing regulations are inadequate, and primary legislation is planned to place greater responsibility on the last registered keeper to tax and license a vehicle.

In addition, under the Removal and Disposal of Vehicles (England) (Amendment) Regulations 2002, the removal process has been accelerated with local councils empowered to remove unlicensed vehicles after 24 hours and to hold them only for seven rather than the previous 35 days. Although removal costs are shared with police under the Refuse Disposal Act 1978, these along with storage costs have been a major expense for local authorities that are inevitably passed on to council tax payers, and these remedial measures could help to cut costs.

The problem could partly be resolved in 2007 when the cost of vehicle disposal becomes the responsibility of motor manufacturers rather than owners under the EU directive, but until more keepers decide that legitimate disposal is better than dumping and possible detection, abandoned vehicle numbers could rise.

Roadworthy vehicles that are driven untaxed could also increase as owners face the combined economic pressure of increasing MOT repairs and insurance costs, and as more take to the roads without a valid licence for the reasons discussed above. Indeed, the link between the use of untaxed vehicles and wider criminal activity by disqualified drivers and mainstream offenders requires further examination in light of preliminary evidence that suggests considerable overlap (Jacobson *et al.* 2002: 32–3).

Concluding comments

Unlicensed driving is hardly a new problem but only now is it attracting serious attention. Hopes are that the selected combination of situational measures will have the desired effect of reducing this behaviour, and the closure of administrative loopholes would certainly help as would mandatory driving licence-carrying if that were ever countenanced.

Currently, however, detection is largely dependent on proactive police vehicle stops (Rose 2000: xi), and the low prioritisation of roads policing in recent years by government means that enforcement effectiveness has been compromised by the depletion of traffic officers. This situation is more likely to explain the gradual reduction in offenders proceeded against in nearly all categories except speeding between 1997 and 2000 than better driver behaviour or improved vehicle roadworthiness. This is a recurring theme considered more fully in Chapter 10.

That said, it needs emphasising here that a good opportunity is being missed to capitalise on the close links found by Rose (2000) between mainstream and serious traffic offending – including disqualified driving – and by Broughton (1999) between unlicensed driving and other kinds of car crime. These studies chime with Chenery *et al.*'s (1999) study which found that drivers who parked illegally in disabled bays were significantly far more likely to have criminal records for serious traffic and mainstream offences than others: 21 per cent of their vehicles warranted immediate police action – e.g. the registered keeper was wanted, the car was stolen, the registration number 'did not exist', and 11 per cent cars were 'illegal' in some way (e.g. defective tyres, no vehicle tax disk). Together, the suggestion is that far more could be made of the potential in police vehicle stops and illegal parking for intelligence-led offender targeting and intelligence gathering.

Yet situational measures and more resourcing of roads policing have their limitations, and any control efforts should be set against the tightening grip of car culture on our lives and the seemingly unstoppable growth of drivers and vehicles on our roads. They must also be located within the context of the continuing structural, social and economic marginalisation of some vulnerable groups in society, whose transport and mobility problems may be less likely to respond to situational efforts to prevent unlicensed driving.

Summary of main points

- Unlicensed driving is widespread, and seemingly common among young people.
- It is difficult for police to enforce and easy for perpetrators to commit undetected.
- Unlicensed offenders have a higher crash risk, and costs of their uninsured driving are passed to all other drivers.
- Those who drive while disqualified tend to have more mature criminal histories than those of mainstream offenders.
- Unlicensed driving may be linked with vehicle document offences, serious traffic and mainstream offending, all of which activity may unfold within a broad subculture of unregulated vehicle use.
- Various control strategies are under consideration, but the low prioritisation of roads policing means opportunities for intelligence-led offender targeting are missed.
- Abandoned, untaxed vehicles represent a worrying economic and environmental problem for local authorities and communities.

Note

1   Government reply by Mr Meacher (14.3.02), *Hansard* (42242, col. 1233W).

Chapter 9

Car crime in wider society

Introduction

Much of the research used for this book has been constructed around the notion that deviant acts are perpetrated by individual deviant drivers, and that all would be well if we could control them. Yet a theme has been highlighted noting the broader involvement of society in creating a car culture in which transgressions may flourish largely unchecked, where some breaches are fairly consensual (e.g. speeding), and where the disciplinary stance taken by governments can sometimes be described as lukewarm. In other words, it is inaccurate to lay the blame solely on individuals; wider society is also implicated.

This chapter takes this theme further, focusing on motor manufacturers, companies and the state with examples of half-hearted or minimal efforts to prevent breaches of the law. In some circumstances, either civil or criminal liability, for example, tort liability in negligence might be concluded. This topic is broad and deep, and these examples only scratch the surface. It is akin to mainstream white-collar and corporate crime, where investigations into irregular activities and 'omissions to act' have also been piecemeal (e.g. Tombs 1999).

The concerns highlighted in this chapter are selective, and several mentioned in earlier chapters are as important. They include the following:

- The marketing of 'alcopops' as fun drinks with 'cool' status that could encourage a dismissive attitude to alcohol rather than something to be taken seriously, and where the strongly flavoured mixers used may confuse consumers as to the actual alcohol content imbibed.

- The marketing of in-vehicle navigational products as 'driver aids' that may help journey time and directions, but could raise distraction levels and promote failures of attention to the road. Similarly, ever more sophisticated gadgetry and dashboard displays could also facilitate driver inattention.

- The failure by pharmaceutical manufacturers always to label their products so that consumers are informed about the potential sedating or other side-effects of certain over-the-counter medicines (Horne and Barrett 2001), which could unwittingly impair driving more than the symptoms for which the medicine is taken.

- The self-regulation by drivers of their eyesight which means up to 1 in 10 drivers would 'fail a driving test if retaken today' (Eyecare Trust 2002; HSA 2002). While drivers of large vehicles or minibuses/buses are subject to more stringent eyesight requirements and must have medical and eyesight checks every five years from age 45 (as part of licence renewal), this is not the case for others who are tested only during their practical driving test. 'Looked but failed to see' is a common recorded reason for road crashes (e.g. Pearce *et al.* 2002: 45), and the proportion of such drivers with defective vision is unknown.

- The additional deaths, estimated as between 104 and 138 per year by government researchers, resulting from Britain's practice of putting clocks forward and back each year. These deaths are attributed to the loss of one hour's sleep in spring and to darker afternoons in autumn when visibility is more dependent on car and street lighting and children are less attentive when leaving school (Broughton and Stone 1998).

This chapter will be divided into two main sections, each highlighting areas where a lack of appropriate action might be described as negligent or even criminal. The first section focuses on motor manufacturers and their reluctance to act (for reasons of corporate profit and convenience). The second looks at the responsibilities (and shortcomings) of organisations employing drivers. Although the spotlight falls on the car industry and the commercial sector, the government has a central role in regulating business activities, and any inadequacies in the extent, nature and enforcement of regulatory processes connected with occupational road safety inevitably implicate government.

The power of motor manufacturers

Product recall: the Ford Pinto and other examples

It has been said that there is probably not a car in the world without a safety hazard known to the car's manufacturer (Dowie 1987: 28). This may be tolerable if the fault is put right at source (on the production line) and any vehicles already on the road are effectively recalled and modified. However, as the following examples illustrate, these conditions are not always met. This leads to many preventable deaths and injuries.

One of the biggest global motor manufacturers, Ford Motors, has courted controversy on various occasions in relation to vehicle safety. The worst example of these is probably the Pinto affair which spanned the 1970s. Dowie (1987) admirably documented and researched this matter, which was essentially a case of Ford valuing corporate profit above the expense of injuries and deaths because it made economic sense.

To fight off competition in the lucrative small-car market, Ford began production of the Pinto in record time in 1970 despite pre-production tests indicating weaknesses in the fuel system. These weaknesses meant that rear-end collisions would easily rupture the petrol tank, causing burn deaths and injuries at relatively low impact speeds. Correcting the defect was estimated to cost $11 per vehicle, but the assembly-line machinery was already set up and making the change was not considered advantageous, especially since 'safety doesn't sell' and it was believed that the extra cost would price the new car out of the market (ibid.: 17).

According to Dowie's research, the next eight years saw vigorous lobbying by Ford against a key US government safety standard that would have required the company to redesign the fire-prone gas tank. These attempts included 'some blatant lies' (ibid.: 14), cover-ups of safety tests (ibid.: 15) and the decision to settle damage suits out of court in order to minimise bad publicity. In addition, because of the custom of consulting interested parties before new standards were introduced, Ford began many stalling procedures. The main US regulatory body, the National Highway Traffic Safety Administration (NHTSA) had to test Ford's claims that vehicle fires were a rare problem (ibid.: 23), that rear-end collisions were relatively rare (ibid.: 24) and that most car occupant fatalities would have died anyway from their injuries rather than fire (ibid.).

As a consequence of Dowie's exposé, the US Department of Transportation asked Ford to recall 1.5 million Pintos, which was followed by many high-cost lawsuits for burn deaths and injuries, and the landmark State of Indiana *v.* Ford Motor Co. (1979), where Ford became the first American corporation prosecuted for criminal homicide. Although Ford was acquitted of reckless homicide, its reputation was tarnished and the Pinto soon ceased production (Larsen 1998).

More recently, Ford was involved in a legal wrangle with Bridgestone/Firestone tyres, where the motor manufacturer insisted Firestone tyres were to blame for a series of around 100 fatal crashes in which Ford's best-selling Explorer sports utility vehicle (SUV) rolled over. For its part, Firestone alleged that many Explorers were 'defectively designed' and dangerous with a greater tendency to roll over when tyres burst than other vehicles (*The Sunday Times* 10.6.01). In the first of many expected cases, Bridgestone/Firestone was ordered to pay $7.5 billion compensation to the husband of a paralysed victim whose Explorer rolled over following a puncture (e.g. Public Citizen 2001). Although Ford had been aware of the defect and risks much earlier – ordering tyre replacements in Saudi Arabia, Venezuela and other markets – it did not warn Americans until dealers refused to sell the Firestone tyres (Hartenfels 2001). Millions of tyres were then recalled by Ford in 2000 and 2001, costing the company dearly in financial and loyalty terms, with sales of Explorers plunging in 2001 (ibid.).

Echoing the Pinto tale, where engineers were strongly discouraged from raising safety issues with management (Dowie 1987: 16–17), evidence in the Explorer story suggested that Ford engineers warned of the danger of fitting inappropriate Firestone tyres but were overruled by executives who were concerned more with the commercial need to produce an SUV (e.g. *The Sunday Times* 10.6.01). Indeed, expense is also a prime reason why manufacturers resist recalling vehicles, yet internationally recalls are rising annually (e.g. Car Care Clinic 2001 for Britain; Hartenfels 2001 for elsewhere).

On the one hand, increasing recalls indicate that safety is considered paramount but conversely these figures raise concerns that so many defects occur. Reasons include ever shorter production cycles, more electronically sensitive components, non-compliance with legal standards and increasingly critical consumers (Hartenfels 2001). Faster production means that some new vehicles may be technically immature; the Ford Focus 2000 was recalled six times in the USA in its first year for faulty brakes, defective seats and accelerator problems (ibid.).

However, in some countries (e.g. Germany) there is no legal

requirement to inform the public that recalls have been made, and 'silent' recall campaigns require only that garages are informed so that defective parts can be exchanged at the vehicle's next servicing (ibid.). This means that vehicle owners may never know a defect existed.

Volvo, the Swedish motor manufacturer famed for its symbolisation of safety and reliability, found itself in an awkward position when a dangerous brake defect in its 850 TDi diesel model was alerted to Volvo dealers worldwide for rectification at routine servicing but no public announcement was made to owners (*The Sunday Times* 27.5.01). This meant that owners who took their cars to non-Volvo garages would be unlikely to have the defect rectified, and owners using Volvo garages might not have their vehicles routinely serviced as recommended. The matter came to light because a fatal crash in France implicated brake failure and manslaughter charges were threatened (ibid.). Although a key legal issue appeared to be the vagueness of Volvo's repair instructions, since a garage had attempted the repairs (*The Independent* 20.5.01), the alleged cover-up of a potentially grave defect may have dented the company's image of trustworthiness.

Mitsubishi is another manufacturer whose public reputation was tarnished. This followed criminal charges for a 30-year failure to notify Japanese authorities of complaints lodged by consumers about leaky fuel caps, faulty clutches and defective brakes in various Mitsubishi models (e.g. *Guardian* 30.8.00; Knight Ridder Inc. 2000). A surprise inspection of its headquarters had revealed employee lockers stuffed full of consumer complaints. Mitsubishi's policy was to repair vehicles quietly to avoid costly recalls, but the publicity led to urgent inspection of more than 800,000 vehicles worldwide, a relatively minor fine ($37,000) and the resignation of the company's chief executive.

Reducing injury risk: bumpers and bonnets

Motor manufacturers have also resisted ways of improving pedestrian safety. While drivers and vehicle occupants are now more likely to avoid serious crash injuries because of better seatbelts, airbags and crumple zones designed to reduce impact on the inside, little has been done by way of less rigid bonnets and bumpers to lower the injury risk to others. Most fatally injured pedestrians in urban areas – the bulk of which are children and the elderly – are hit by the front of cars (e.g. PACTS 2001). Yet four well validated, internationally supported car crash performance tests that could lead to better protection for vulnerable road users, and would save up to 1,550 deaths and serious injuries in Britain (ibid.) and 20,000 in Europe annually (European Transport Safety Council (ETSC) 2001), had been resisted by the motor industry for a decade.

Acting on behalf of European manufacturers, Ford claimed that design changes to existing models could raise risk to vehicle occupants, and that the proposed European directive which would have made the four pedestrian protection tests compulsory would take longer to implement than a voluntary scheme where all new models would have to pass several less stringent tests (e.g. PACTS 2001; *The Times* 13.8.01). In addition, it was claimed that the changes would not be cost-effective (estimated as 30 euros per car! ETSC 2001). These industry claims were disputed by PACTS (2001), and the European Public Health Alliance pointed out that the voluntary agreement tests would provide 75 per cent less protection against fatal injury than the four proven crash performance tests (ETSC 2002).

At bottom of this matter is a familiar tale of the lobbying power of the car industry, which persuaded first the European Commission to co-operate with a voluntary agreement and then the European Parliament to vote to accept only a slightly amended version. As opined by Jeanne Breen (ETSC executive director) before an earlier European Parliament vote on furtherance of the proposed agreement: 'We hope that the European Parliament will not be taken in by the extensive lobbying of the car industry which has blocked progress on this issue for over a decade' (ETSC 2001). When Britain followed the European lead, PACTS attributed this to the advantage taken by motor manufacturers of the then Transport Secretary's previous links to the car industry where much time was spent saving jobs and preventing the collapse of Rover (*The Times* 23.10.01). Efforts to cosy up to British MPs by offering cut-price cars to 'opinion-formers' may also be a means by which manufacturers encourage favourable outcomes (*The Sunday Times* 30.5.99).

While safety campaigners talk of 'missed opportunities' to save thousands of European pedestrians' lives (e.g. ETSC 2001), this might be put more forcefully by others. In view of proven scientific tests supported by national research laboratories which if implemented could prevent these deaths, resistance by motor manufacturers assisted by acquiescence from European and national officials and parliamentarians might be considered negligent. Yet because of the way organisational and corporate crime gets constructed and defined (e.g. Box 1983; Croall 1998a, 1998b), such a legal label on this slowness to act is unlikely ever to be applied.[1]

Advertising and self-regulation

Motor manufacturers place great store in advertising their products, and self-regulation of advertising – which has been a common international standard – could help. Provided that local rules are adhered to, such as those in the USA where false, unfair or misleading advertising is prohibited (e.g. Burt 2002), self-policing allows much latitude for free commercial speech. Moreover, transgressions of the agreed codes are typically followed by no more than a 'wrist slap' (usually a small fine and an admonishment) after the offending advertisement has appeared and corporate advantage has been gained.

The problem has been that high speed, combined with high performance and good handling ability at speed have frequently been emphasised in advertisements. This is hardly a responsible stance by manufacturers. The message that high speed is desirable and valued, and manufacturers' failure to link speed with breaches of speed limits and increased crash risk, means that complaints from a concerned public are a recurring feature (e.g. Advertising Standards Authority 2000a, 2000b, 2000c). Some people wonder why manufacturers continue to produce vehicles that easily travel at illegal speeds, and how much this depends on economic factors. It is likely that a relaxed attitude on this matter prevails because the vehicle industry remains a key barometer of a nation's health; governments try to attract and maintain motor manufacturing plants (e.g. *Guardian* 24.6.99) without great concern for what is produced.

Although some governments (including Britain) have considered a regulatory approach to advertising, the influence of the car lobby has successfully long defended what it sees as the superiority of a self-regulatory approach (e.g Burt, 2002). But countries like Belgium and Brazil decided to take a closer interest, ruling that safety warnings must accompany all or most car advertisements, including a warning that motorists are responsible for safe driving, and that breaches will incur heavy fines or even imprisonment (ibid.; SMMT 2002). Manufacturers feel threatened by erosion of their freedom in such countries, where past efforts carefully to dissociate products from risk must give way to a situation where this risk must be openly acknowledged in any advertising campaign.

Governments may wish to court motor manufacturers, rather than alienate them, because of economic pressures and many would say this hands too much power to carmakers. Yet when this means that traffic breaches become more likely (through advertising that tends to legitimate high speeds), that more pedestrian deaths are caused (through reluctance to soften crash impact), and that more crashes occur through delayed or no public recall of defective vehicles, the 'hands-off' approach adopted by many governments becomes questionable. It is unlikely that this approach by states will ever be legally constructed as criminal in any country, though by contrast on rare occasions glaring misdemeanours by manufacturers are weakly criminalised (see Mitsubishi above). For the most part, however, the car industry's more dubious activities and profit-motivated stances have escaped construction as criminal, though arguably this in no way reduces their responsibility or that of governments.

Work-related road risk

Driving as a dangerous occupation

Over 1.8 million people in Britain are estimated to drive each day as part of their job (Trades Union Congress 2001) and some of these will be killed or seriously injured in road traffic crashes. Casualty estimates vary because specific statistics on work-related traffic deaths are not kept, but the Royal Society for Prevention of Accidents (RoSPA 1998: 7) and the TUC (2001: 4) both agree that more people at work are killed on the road each year than in other workplaces, which makes traffic crashes the single biggest cause of sudden death at work. Indeed, RoSPA (1998) calculate that those who drive 25,000 miles per annum (a fairly average distance for those who drive as part of their employment) have a risk of death at work similar to construction workers and coal miners.

Naturally, vehicle occupants comprise only part of the casualty toll since all other road users are put at risk from working drivers, and the total extent of harm is vast. The Health and Safety Executive (HSE 2001a) estimate that 7–8 per cent of all traffic fatalities and serious injuries are likely to involve a car at work and 21–3 per cent a commercial vehicle, which together would account for around 850 traffic deaths and 11,000 seriously injured annually in recent years with estimated costs to society at £4.4 billion in terms of lost output, damage and medical costs, plus human costs to reflect grief, pain and suffering (ibid.; see also HSE 2001b).

Are working drivers to blame?

At first glance it may seem reasonable to blame working drivers for the crashes and risks they create, and indeed all workers have legal obligations to behave safely and not to endanger themselves and others. Certainly, recent research has investigated whether extra risks are generated by company car drivers – and if so what kinds – with the purpose of devising interventions such as training, incentives and risk management programmes that may help to reduce occupational crash liability. Thus we know that those who drive a company-owned car are on average around 50 per cent more likely to become crash-involved than the general population of car drivers, even when controlling for higher mileage and demographic variables (Lynn and Lockwood 1998; Chapman *et al.* 2001). Grayson (1999) calls this the 'fleet driver effect'. However, this increased risk varies according to the type of vehicle driven and the purpose for which it is used. Chapman *et al.* (2001) found that sales staff and those who owned company vehicles often as part of remuneration packages (mainly senior managers) – termed 'perk car drivers' by the researchers – were at higher crash risk than other working drivers who had a level of risk similar to the general population of drivers.

Initial investigations have shown that those who drive as part of their work drive faster than others (Stradling 2001), and higher mileage company-car drivers are more likely to use a mobile phone when driving than others (BRAKE 2001) and to fall asleep at the wheel than others (RAC 2001), all behaviours which raise crash risk. These findings are supported by analyses of a representative sample of 1,200 drivers, including a booster sample of 310 company-car drivers, which concluded that the latter regularly broke speed limits and drove in a potentially dangerous way (Lex 1997).

Yet behind these headline figures and casualty estimates several points deserve emphasis.

Underlying problems with regulation

Inadequate statistics
As noted, accurate statistics are not kept, so occupational casualty figures are estimates. Police accident pro formas do not record information on whether casualties were working or not; coroners' inquests are not obliged to record the deceased's employment status when the crash occurred (Matthews and Foreman 1993: 289–90); and only under limited circumstances are employers required to report the deaths of employees killed on the road – unlike the situation where deaths occur in other workplaces.[2] The DfT collect some figures for light goods vehicle and heavy goods vehicle drivers who may be assumed to have been working when killed (e.g. DTLR 2001c: Table 4.15), but there are no rigorous statistics. As underlined by the TUC, this means that occupational road risk cannot be adequately controlled and regulated because its extent is unknown. This is discussed by criminologists (e.g. Croall 1998a; Tombs 1999) as many kinds of health and safety crimes by employers are invisible, not just those that can occur on the road.

Focus on immediate rather than root causes

Research findings show that company-car drivers break traffic laws more than others and have a higher crash risk but the underlying causes can include a number of other factors: failures to maintain employees' vehicles in roadworthy condition; failures to supply vehicles with adequate safety features; and lack of specialist training for workers expected to drive at work. Other concealed reasons for work-related crashes are the setting of schedules, journey times and distances likely to promote unsafe speeds and fatigued driving, and distracted driving, if employees are expected to conduct business by phone (TUC 2001). Similarly, Stradling (2001) notes the stark contrast between those employed to drive vehicles and others employed to operate large and dangerous equipment in terms of selection procedures, training, supervision, feedback, appraisal and remediation. Although safeguards are routine in regard to operating machinery, most employers provide few for drivers, which reinforces the 'picture of complacency' concerning employers' safety policies and practices that emerged from the Lex (1997) survey of company-car drivers.

Yet this complacency is rarely punished. To date, responsibility for road safety falls primarily on drivers, other road users and vehicle owners who are governed by the various statutes of road traffic law. Employers of commercial drivers have duties of care under s. 2 and s. 3 of the Health and Safety at Work Act (HSWA) to ensure 'so far as is practicable' that 'safe systems of work' are in place to reduce work-related risks to employees and others. However, as RoSPA pointed out, the Health and Safety Commission have failed to offer any specific advice on the implications of the HSWA on the public highway, and 'government ministers have agreed that, for enforcement purposes, road traffic law should take precedence over the HSWA' (RoSPA 1998: 12). This means that the focus of enforcement primarily falls on those subject to road traffic law rather than on those responsible for their safety (i.e. drivers not their employers) and so it is the immediate causes of crashes not the latent ones that are punished. The corollary is that employers who are in breach of their duty in tort and/or contract to employees – perhaps offering tacit approval to employees to drive long hours when tired, to exceed speed limits and to conduct business by phone while driving – have rarely been held directly responsible to their employees or injured third parties, even though far more work-related deaths occur on the road as elsewhere (e.g. ibid.: 7; TUC 2001: 4).

Defective vehicles and a consumerist discourse

Despite the efforts of some companies to instil a safety culture such practices do not seem widespread, and a particular problem is the extent of defective vehicles on the road. For instance, one annual report of a traffic commissioner, whose role includes reporting on roadside enforcement (or 'spot checks') undertaken by other government agencies, noted that in his area 10 per cent of *goods vehicles* were found to have faults so serious that they were not allowed to continue on the road without repairs being effected, and 25 per cent had some less serious defects (Heaps 2001: Ch. 3). A major roadside operation involving 40 police forces in 1999 revealed that 1 in 20 *coaches* and *buses* were immediately ordered off the road as dangerous with police reporting 'almost 4,000 people travelling in coaches not fit to be on the road' (*The Times* 26.7.99).

Such figures reveal that many companies are seriously failing to protect employees and the public from the dangers of unroadworthy vehicles. Also 28,032 people complained to the Office of Fair Trading (OFT) in 2000 about unsatisfactory garage servicing and repairs (OFT 2001). An OFT investigation found that 40 per cent of 31,000 garages offered a 'critically poor service', with its Director General wondering 'how many of the 40,000 serious injuries and 3,000 deaths every year in Britain may be due to poor servicing and repair?' (OFT 2000: 2). In similar vein, the Consumers Association found that 21 per cent of 48 garages did a 'very poor job, missing safety-related items' in routine car servicing (Consumers' Association 1999: 8).

These figures and facts show the disregard of companies for the safety of employees (and the public) through supplying or failing to rectify unroadworthy vehicles. However, any shortcomings revealed tend to be constructed by the media and government agencies in terms of servicing, repair standards and consumer dissatisfaction rather than as a danger to all road users or as health and safety crimes. Likewise, reducing the scale of these defects tends to be cast in terms of 'raising low standards' and 'rebuilding consumer confidence' (e.g. OFT 2000; *Daily Mail* 19.9.01; *The Sunday Times* 3.2.02) rather than cutting number of crimes. This type of language deflects attention away from any wrongdoing. Thus the underpinning discourse has been one of consumer law not health and safety or road traffic/criminal law.

The absence of comprehensive statistics on the extent of at-work road crashes inevitably means that occupational road risk cannot be adequately controlled and regulated. This situation is compounded by a focus on the immediate rather than underlying causes of crashes that can conceal poor safety culture among employers, and usually means that drivers not employers are punished. Where some transparency exists, as in the investigation of defective vehicles and repairs, sanctions like the withdrawal of a coach operator's licence may be applied in certain situations, but mostly such negligence is constructed in discourses of consumer issues rather than criminal or health and safety law despite their danger to others.

Concluding comments

A considerable slice of this book has focused on the illegal driving behaviours of individual drivers, but this chapter has shown that it is important to consider the role played by industry and commerce in failing to prevent kinds of 'car crime'.

As the examples indicate, the car industry appears to act largely in its own corporate interest within a self-regulatory approach that it has vigorously defended against only mild rebukes. An erosion of its freedom may be in prospect concerning self-regulation in advertising, but its lobbying powers in other respects seem strong. This has much to do with economic pressures on governments, though in acceding to the influence of the car industry through delay or inaction in pressing for improvements, governments may be failing in their responsibilities to citizens.

In regard to occupational road safety, the disquiet felt in various quarters finally galvanised the British government to appoint a task force to consult and investigate ways of reducing at-work road traffic incidents (DETR 2000c). Their recommendations could lead to legislation which brings responsibility and accountability of employers for drivers within the jurisdiction of the HSE, improving road safety for all. Alternatively, in view of a probable backlash from employers who would have to bear the economic brunt of new regulations (e.g. *The Times* 1.3.01) guidance may become the short-term choice, which could mean 'business as usual' for many employers.

Lastly, in noting that negligence in commercial road safety tends to be constructed as a consumer issue not a health and safety or criminal one, it is interesting to consider that consumer power may become more important than the law in some instances. Consumers could demand changes that public officials seem reluctant to insist upon. For instance, the car industry may have believed that pedestrian safety does not have the same marketing potential as features protecting occupants, but purchasers may seek this as an important new criterion obliging manufacturers to respond (*The Times* 13.8.01). Even so, until the fruits of any vehicle redesign are realised, many more unnecessary and preventable deaths will occur.

Summary of main points

- The power of the car lobby has advanced through economic pressures on governments and is partly manifested by a self-regulatory approach defended by motor manufacturers.
- Motor manufacturers can be resistant to recalling faulty vehicles and improving pedestrian safety for reasons of corporate profit and convenience, putting customers and the public at risk.
- There is a tendency to blame working drivers for crashes rather than to seek root causes that may be connected with the safety culture of organisations.
- Any inadequacies in the extent, nature and enforcement of regulatory processes inevitably implicate government.
- Organisational negligence that creates road risk for employees, consumers and the public tends to be constructed in the language of consumer law rather than health and safety or criminal law. It is rarely constructed as crime.
- Whether delay in acting swiftly or decisively in matters of occupational road risk constitutes a failure by government of its responsibility is arguable.

Notes

1 Unless it were tested under Article 2 of the European Convention on Human Rights, which places positive obligations on states to protect the right to life and to suppress offences against the person and life-threatening activities.
2 Statutory Instrument 3163 (1995), para. 10(2) applies.

Chapter 10

Past, present and future directions

Introduction

The prime purpose of this book has been to bring together diverse information on many topics that constitute (or are closely connected with) car crime in order to provide a sound basis for further exploration. In so doing, the term 'car crime', which has been traditionally constructed to reflect the dominant discourse of 'theft of and from vehicles', has been extended to encompass behaviours not usually considered within its ambit. Incidence and trends of key kinds of car crime have been mapped as far as known and inadequacies in how some offences are measured have been noted. Explanations and theories put forward by others to account for the occurrence of some kinds of car crime have been discussed, and recent means for their control have been assessed.

Several recurring themes have emerged: a lack of seriousness that characterises the way car crime is perceived and treated; an underlying emphasis on the responsibility of individuals for car crime, obscuring the wider role of society, its agents and industry; a realisation that most car crime is perpetuated by males; and a consideration of how car crime is itself constructed. The main underpinning theme, however, is that car crime is a product of car culture, the twentieth-century phenomenon that now dominates lives in western society and threatens to envelop those in developing countries.

In the next section a summary is given on how the legacy of the motor car's short sociolegal history provides the context for car crime. In the penultimate section some of the more pressing and uncomfortable issues identified are listed. Finally, in the last section prospects for the future control of car crime are assessed. Given the anticipated problems ahead - congestion, environmental pollution and more casualties as global vehicle sales, vehicle thefts and driver numbers escalate – control of car crime in its broadest sense will become even more important and urgent.

Ultimately, as long as car culture is central to everyday lives and national infrastructures, then car crime will continue to pose persistent problems and dilemmas.

Legacy of the past

Out of our recent social history we have created a monster that now governs how most lives are lived. On the one hand, car culture confers benefits and advantages to aid mobility, convenience and independence, while on the other, various difficulties and dilemmas have been created for car users and the car-less.

From the car's inception, an elite of drivers welcomed the freedom to explore extended horizons; controls were not especially appreciated, and the criminal labels arising from enforcement of the few existing driving laws were vociferously rejected (Emsley 1993: 374). Pleas of 'unfair treatment' were treated seriously in Parliament and by senior police (ibid.), and what emerged was a sense that drivers were being victimised by an overzealous criminal justice system. Traffic penalties, however, were hardly onerous for the well-to-do (ibid.: 366). Rejecting criminalisation for their own 'minor' infractions, the well-off instead perceived car criminals as 'other drivers' such as 'foreign born chauffeurs' (ibid.: 369) and those who stole their cars.

Interestingly, little has changed over the intervening decades. Dangerous drivers are still 'other drivers' (never ourselves), and inappropriate speeds are never our own. Driving 'infractions' are rarely treated as crime, and powerful newspapers, purporting to represent all drivers, still portray 'the poor victimised motorist' (e.g. *Daily Mail* 15.9.99; *Daily Express* 5.3.02). Theft of vehicles, their parts and contents still represents the traditional view of car crime. The main difference is that a small car-owning elite has grown into a mass of drivers consisting of most adults. Yet importantly, elitist attitudes still prevail, boosted by the erstwhile stewardship of Mrs Thatcher, who supported a car economy and encouraged autonomy and self-responsibility under neoliberal colours, all of which may have helped legitimate drivers' wishes to decide for themselves how to drive and to use laws as guidelines if they desired. Moreover, drivers – as a large proportion of the electorate – need careful handling so that any move to criminalise them, as might occur if a 30 mph speed limit was strictly and widely enforced, could be an injudicious political step.

Elitist attitudes are so deeply rooted that we hardly question the dominant ideology of the 'car as master' (e.g. Davis 1992). Pedestrians have to avoid the car rather than the other way around, pedestrians have to use unpleasant underpasses to facilitate traffic flow. The widely perceived sacrosanct 'right to drive' has been described by Coward (2001) as 'synonymous with individual freedoms' and 'challenging them is akin to violating human rights'. Objections to cars and traffic offending can be considered prudish (ibid.). This 'car as master' attitude is epitomised by the cult appeal, political incorrectness and machismo of media pundits who regularly derogate 'bad' or 'slow' drivers (those who adhere to speed limits) and applaud high speed (e.g. Clarkson 2000, 2002a, 2002b).

Legal arguments about lack of intention to cause harm while driving, and the greater focus on culpability not consequences of driving actions add fuel to the hegemony of the car and car drivers. This has been helped by the normative discourse (at last changing) which sees crashes as blameless accidents that could equally happen to any driver. This discourse, of course, has been used to offset any culpability arising from the human – predominantly male – propensity for the kind of risk that is most glamorously associated with the high speed and daring skills of Formula One racing.

It is not surprising that so many want to be part of this culture (whether they have licences or not) because drivers are treated – and treat themselves – as superior to other road users. Moreover, since the car-less find themselves with poor travel alternatives, even more wish to be part of the driving community, despite the growing problems of congestion and pollution.

Nowadays, excluded categories from car culture comprise two main groups: those who object to cars on ideological or environmental grounds and the honest underclass who cannot afford to buy into car culture and do not want to defraud or steal.

Another legacy concerns the influence wielded by the car industry through last century. Not only have manufacturers been successful at resisting profit-reducing moves such as installing safer vehicle parts and acknowledging driving risk in their product advertisements, but somehow defects in vehicle design, repairs and servicing have been constructed as consumer issues rather than as offences in health and safety or criminal law, so that we do not consider such matters as crime.

Further, part of the current situation seems driven by economic forces whereby states are loathe to restrict motor manufacturers from building cars that go twice as fast as the permitted maximum for fear of losing their business and revenue to other countries. Some would say this has handed too much power to carmakers and results in mixed messages for drivers. Thus there is an official keenness for citizens to buy new, fast cars for economic reasons, but less enthusiasm for drivers to travel fast in them for safety reasons. At its extreme, the delay and inaction by states to regulate more firmly the activities of motor corporations might be thought a failure in their responsibilities to citizens, though such an official construction is almost inconceivable.

In all, the car's social history contributes significantly to the present landscape of car culture and prevalence of car crimes of all kinds, especially to breaches of traffic laws. The roots of car crime thus arise from a cocktail that includes the following: the initial ownership of cars limited to the elite which paved the way for the hegemony of the car and the elitism connected with it; the early lack of seriousness linked with driving offences that set the scene for the commonly perceived minor nature of car crime generally, which perception also characterises the hitherto lukewarm response of states to deal adequately with associated escalating problems; the ability of cars to transform and expand lives through the mobility, convenience and status they confer which led to mass appeal, mass ownership and mass theft; and the failure of individual drivers for many reasons to perceive a need to adhere rigidly to the traffic laws. These reasons include social, cultural and gendered ones and the tendency of drivers to perceive their own skills as superior precluding the need to stick to the rules.

Concerns and dilemmas of the present

The following difficult and important issues raise much concern:

- As better vehicle security devices protect against vehicle theft, a worrying consequence is increased *carjackings* where drivers are attacked for their ignition keys, which ironically makes drivers of luxury, new cars more vulnerable than drivers of old cars. While carjackings heighten the seriousness of vehicle theft, they are classified as robberies so do not appear in vehicle theft figures.
- *International crime rings* operating in global markets are likely to commit some carjack thefts to order. Other innovative vehicle thefts underline the worldwide demand for the lifestyle enhancing power of luxury cars whether legally or illegally supplied, helping to make vehicle theft the world's third most numerous crime behind domestic

burglary and violent crime (Barclay *et al.* 2001: Tables 1.3, 1.4, 1.5).

- *Drink-driving*, probably on the increase again after an earlier reduction, remains unacceptably high. Worryingly, drink-driving often occurs with illegal drug-taking and by disqualified drivers. Driving above the blood-alcohol limit is not helped by the popularity of alcopops with their 'cool' image that could encourage a dismissive attitude to alcohol and drink-driving.

- The reclassification of *cannabis* in Britain from a Class B to Class C drug – meaning that police may give users warnings only – could encourage more to drive while ingesting or shortly after. As the effects of cannabis can be unpredictable for the individual and their interaction with driving performance is not well established, reclassification is not necessarily a good road safety move and its impact should be closely monitored.

- Similarly, the effects of prescribed *legal drugs* on driving ability are not well known, but could cause unwitting impairment when first taken while tolerance develops with dosing or when drugs are withdrawn. Issues remain, however, about how fit drivers should be (with or without medication), and how and where the balance should be drawn between the loss of personal mobility and the maintenance of public safety given an ageing driving population.

- Since labels and warnings accompanying *over-the-counter medicines* can be inconsistent, inaccurate and misleading (Horne and Barratt 2001), and as consumers may unwittingly drive impaired as a consequence, is it appropriate to leave the matter to the consciences of pharmaceutical manufacturers or should more than discretionary warning labels be required?

- It may soon be possible to measure *tiredness*, but if and when this happens would we really wish to ban fatigued driving, because of its established links with crashes, and how tired would be 'too tired'? What would the implications be for an increasingly 24-hour society which is dependent on night workers for its smooth functioning, where many people think that driving when fatigued is a routine matter, and where few people always get enough sleep?

- *Exceeding speed limits* and *driving too fast for the conditions* have become the problem of 'the other driver'. When most think they are better and more skilful than the average, and that their chosen speeds are never dangerous or inappropriate for the conditions, how do we get drivers to acknowledge that their own crash risk is raised at higher speeds?

- It is difficult to engender an *attitude change towards speed* among ordinary individuals while road speed is so prized and endemic in society, affording glamour, status and power and when royalty, celebrities and politicians get caught for speeding. Until greater technological controls become acceptable or higher penalties are coupled with greater detection risk, drivers' appetite for speed is unlikely to change.

- There are worrying indications that *road rage* incidents are increasing. It is especially ironic that many women have purchased cars to escape fear of crime on public transport or when out walking, and yet driving attracts its own fear of violence, including fear of carjacking.
- In view of research that reveals much slower reactions and distraction among drivers talking on hand-held or hands-free *mobile phones,* which both raise crash risk, are we content with 'strong advice' in the *Highway code* against this activity, or would provision of such a law simply be too difficult to enforce?
- The wide-ranging physical, practical and psychological impacts of road crashes on *survivors and the bereaved* deserve more attention and support, particularly given that the bereaved in Britain have the greatest dissatisfaction with court procedures of nine European nations (FEVR 1995). Initiatives like the planned British memorial to road victims (*The Times* 7.6.02) to highlight the extent of road casualties might help raise awareness of the real consequences of poor driving.
- *Unlicensed driving* is now recognised as a big problem, comprising a huge 'dark figure' of car crime, which could affect large subcultures of disaffected young people, ethnic groups with language problems and the socially excluded.
- A linked problem exists with *convicted dangerous drivers*, most of whom do not get retested when expected, suggesting that many continue to drive unlicensed. More efficient ways are needed to ensure disqualified drivers either get relicensed or refrain from driving. Further, since many convicted *dangerous and disqualified drivers* have substantial records for serious traffic and conventional crime, insufficient traffic policing resources mean a failure to capitalise on good intelligence and detection opportunities, and increased road dangers for everyone.
- The lack of a safety culture among many *companies employing drivers* is greatly concerning, especially where speeding and driving when fatigued are not discouraged or are even indirectly rewarded in employee incentive schemes. It is hoped that inadequate regulation and controls will be superseded by a new approach, though 'guidance' to industry may prove less incisive than tighter regulatory controls. Meanwhile, many more will die in at-work road crashes.

Future prospects

As enthusiasm for car culture shows little sign of diminishing there is an even greater need to regulate and control its escalating symptoms. These symptoms include the diverse range of car crimes outlined in this book, and in this section some key means are summarised that are used or being considered to curb car crime together with some recurring themes.

Usual strategies for controlling car crime, traditionally cast as 'theft of and from vehicles', have focused on the '3Es' – enforcement, engineering and education – and efforts to reduce moving traffic violations have followed a similar format (e.g. Corbett 2000a). The focus of such control mechanisms has been on the individual deviant. Rarely have the perpetrators of car crime been framed as companies, corporations, industry or the state, though the '3Es' have loosely been applied to address their 'irregularities', 'breaches', 'delays' and 'inaction'. In the current criminological context, however, 'opportunity reduction' is a more appropriate generic heading than 'engineering', which is narrower in scope.

Enforcement

Roads policing
It is ironic that as numbers of registered vehicles in Britain rapidly rise, numbers of traffic police to deal with driver transgressions are falling. This has coincided with and probably led to a trend of falling conviction rates for nearly all moving traffic offences except those enforced by cameras, which have risen. Other causes may contribute to the drop in convictions such as police process departments rationing traffic prosecutions and dropping them to make way for 'real' crime (HMIC 1998: 22), though both together indicate that traffic offending is not taken that seriously at the top. As noted earlier, roads policing has never been accorded core objective status by the Home Office, which means that senior police have not channelled scarce resources to it since no financial benefits to forces would directly accrue.

The failure to target roads policing as a core task could be a short-sighted policy. Some of the worst traffic offenders have mature records for conventional crime, including violence (e.g. Rose 2000; Pearce *et al.* 2002; Soothill *et al.* 2002), and offenders who commit a range of 'minor' document offences, such as having no insurance, no MOT, no licence or failing to register their vehicle, can be more likely to commit serious driving offences such as driving while disqualified, drink-driving or dangerous driving (Forsyth and Silcock 1988; Broughton 1999). Thus good intelligence opportunities are being missed to target some of the worst offenders on the road and perhaps off it (see also Chenery *et al.* 1999).

Moreover, a reduced likelihood of seeing police traffic patrols sends the wrong message to the driving public – or perhaps it is the right one – that offending by ordinary drivers appears not of great concern to police and the state. Further, if ordinary drivers think there is little objective threat of being detected for anything other than speeding past cameras, failing to observe red traffic lights and driving in bus lanes, they will offend more in other ways especially as most believe they are good and safe drivers whom others would do well to emulate (Corbett and Simon 1992a: 41). There is already a strong tendency for drivers to want to decide for themselves how to drive and to use speed limits as guidelines (Corbett *et al.* 1998: Ch. 3), and further cuts in visible traffic police patrols may serve only to reinforce the view that the government condones such personal decision-making.

Conversely, even trebling police presence on the roads would not necessarily prevent road crashes directly. Such a resource increase would symbolically show that government has started to take traffic offending seriously, and it would serve to remind drivers that some objective chance of detection exists, which could encourage wider general adherence to the laws. In addition, there would be greater opportunities to remove from the roads the riskiest offenders who may be disproportionately responsible for crashes (e.g. Junger *et al.* 2001).

Automatic enforcement 'safety' cameras

Although automatic enforcement cameras – often termed 'safety' cameras – are unpopular among some sections of the driving community (e.g. *Daily Mail* 21.5.02), most drivers in Britain were in favour of them for speed detection purposes (Corbett and Simon 1999: 75; Mori Financial Services 2001). Their main advantages are round-the-clock deterrence and an enforcement capacity when deterrence fails. Importantly, they have the potential to detect a broader range of moving traffic and document offences, such as out-of-date vehicle tax disks, or valid insurance certification (if windscreen display was a requirement).

Naturally, strong resistance to a wider surveillance and enforcement role for cameras would be expected from civil liberty groups as well an unknown percentage of drivers. Such drivers would believe their own road behaviour posed no danger to others; they would resist further surveillance of themselves while cameras were detecting the poor driving of others. Yet such opposition could change if the social climate switched to one where car crime was treated as important and serious.

This could happen, for example, if further links between 'minor' vehicle document offences and road crashes were found and publicised, or between major violence and serious traffic offending. In this scenario, the camera-shy might be won over by realising that some drivers unconcerned about appropriate documentation also committed serious traffic and mainstream crimes that jeopardise everyone's safety, and that cameras and related administrative procedures could be developed to assist in their detection.

Other technology

Though questions may remain over a wider role for cameras, the use of technology generally to detect vehicle document and driving licence offences is being promulgated by police and could be more effective. One concern is the non-mandatory carrying of driving licences, said to illustrate the view that Britain's vehicle registration and driver licensing procedures are lax in comparison with the rest of Europe (Jacobson *et al.* 2002: 3, 47–8), facilitating fraud and deception while impeding offence detection. This chimes with debates about the British government's consultation on entitlement cards (HMSO 2002) to prevent unauthorised access to benefits and services by the unentitled, and the outcome could have repercussions for the carrying of driving licences. Yet while police are empowered only to make roadside checks on a driver's stated identity rather than on that indicated by a mandatorily carried photolicence, the upshot will probably be more unlicensed, unregulated and unlawful driving.

Opportunity reduction

In contrast to the law-enforcement emphasis on detecting offences that have already happened, opportunity reduction is primarily concerned with preventing future offences. It is based on the premise that less crime will happen where it is made more difficult, more risky or less rewarding. Various strategies have been used: the fitting of steering column locks and electronic immobilisers to vehicles; the installation of CCTV in public car parks to prevent opportunist vehicle theft; the strengthening of regulations concerning the purchase and sale of used vehicles to prevent fraud and 'ringing'; and traffic-calming measures such as road humps, chicanes and bollards to prevent inappropriate speed.

Despite concerns over displacement effects, the straightforward effectiveness of various situational measures, and the growing tentacles of state surveillance represented by CCTV (e.g. Norris *et al.* 1999), opportunity reduction techniques are currently a preferred antidote to some car crimes since they do not directly require offender motivation to change. As the demand for lawfully and unlawfully obtained vehicles is unlikely to diminish in the short-term, crime prevention based on non-motivational principles is needed.

Some developing technologies for opportunity reduction may, however, exceed public acceptance. For instance, most people recognise the dangers of drink-driving, though it would go far beyond public tolerance to fit compulsorily breath-alcohol interlock ignition devices (BAIIDs) to all new (or registered) vehicles even if this could prevent alcohol-impaired driving. Difficulties might still be experienced with tampering or breath samples being given by sober accomplices, yet BAIID developments could largely eliminate drink-driving if a consensus approved. Use of such technology with previously disqualified drink-drivers, as a half-way stage towards restoration of a full driving licence, may be more acceptable.

Smart speed limiters, used in conjunction with satellite technology, are being developed and tested (e.g. Carsten and Comte 2001) and could be made dynamically responsive to prevailing road conditions or vehicle type (Carsten 2002). Many drivers appear in favour of them for voluntary use (SWOV 1998: 78), though mandatory use of limiters would probably be fiercely opposed by a large proportion of drivers as this would curb free choice of top speeds. Nevertheless, limiters are compulsorily installed in some kinds of vehicle (e.g. passenger coaches) and some drivers, such as those previously disqualified for speeding, may be thought to have forfeited their 'right' to decide maximum speeds for themselves. Wider usage may be further away.

Education

Efforts to educate drivers out of bad habits have mostly relied on publicity campaigns warning drivers of the dangers and repercussions of driving while fatigued, drugged or drunk. This keeps these issues in the foreground for 'ordinary' drivers, some of whom may heed the advice. For those who have been prosecuted or who face prosecution, various cognitive-behavioural programmes, such as those offered by Britain's National Driver Improvement Scheme, are coming on-stream to help with driver aggression, poor attitudes and ignorance about the effects of behaviours like drink-driving, speeding and close following.

A difficulty with publicity campaigns targeted at specific groups is that most think their own driving behaviour is not a problem as their skills are superior. It is only 'other drivers' who would do well to heed the campaign advice given. Somehow the means must be found to penetrate the shield of invulnerability that promotes risky behaviour. This shield arises not only from insufficient knowledge but also from faulty logic, such as the impossibility of most drivers being better than average (e.g. Svenson 1981) and of more crashes thought likely to occur as a passenger than as a driver (e.g. Horswill and McKenna 1999).

The elitism of individual drivers' beliefs in the superiority of their own driving may prove difficult to tackle, as may the elitism of drivers who see themselves as superior to other road users. The attitude shifts required to appreciate that a driving licence is a privilege and not a right, that road safety is for drivers to respect pedestrians as much as it is for pedestrians to respect vehicles, and that lack of intention to do harm when deliberately breaking a traffic law does not absolve all responsibility, may prove elusive in a social climate where victims of car culture and car crime are treated as inconvenient rather than as a major problem. Until the effects of car culture really become intolerable for societies internationally, the political will needed to challenge drivers' existing attitudes to road safety and their perceived rights and position may not be forthcoming.

A start could be made by giving victims of car culture and car crime more opportunity to raise awareness of their existence and of drivers' capacity to harm others. This could lead to improved treatment in the aftermath of road crashes. At a national level it would help to bring road crash survivors into line with mainstream crime victims, who are now at the forefront in British criminal justice ideology and policy, and could encourage attitude and behavioural changes towards greater road safety generally.

Whatever reformative efforts are made to reduce individuals' risky driving actions, there will always be some who are 'untouchable' by education. These could include the disaffected young, the deprived and disadvantaged, and those unknown to the authorities, where the legal or illegal use of cars provides status and power otherwise unobtainable, and where scant regard is given to the formalities of driving, such as being properly licensed and insured. As the forces of social exclusion gather pace in Britain (e.g. Young 1999), creating more people who are unable or uncommitted to uphold the social bonds of society, unregulated drivers may be distanced from the attitudinal and behavioural changes invited by publicity campaigns. Moreover, difficulties in identifying such drivers means that they cannot participate in reformative efforts like cognitive-behavioural programmes.

Ironically, because of the close links suggested between those who engage in risky driving, those prone to accidents on and off the road, and involvement in conventional crime (Junger *et al.* 1995, 2001), there appear several avenues through which unregulated drivers and dangerous drivers may come to light. As Junger and colleagues have observed (1995: 52), this situation raises big policy implications for health, crime prevention and social service agencies since they may share the same clients, although good opportunities for closer and more effective inter-agency working are simultaneously presented.

Back to the centre

Finally, all roads lead back to the centre and some fast introspection by the British and other states is needed to tackle the negative ramifications of car culture encompassing car crime.

The scale of the global problem concerning theft of vehicles, their parts and contents should not be underestimated, and has no easy or foreseeable solution, but the tendency to view car crime as crime *to vehicles* rather than *by drivers* and *by the vehicle industry* is one which deserves far more scrutiny. As well as considering fresh ways to deal with individual deviants – which may of course include most drivers – it is important to tackle crime linked with the vehicle industry, companies and corporations. Immediate concerns are organisations lacking a safety culture that puts employee drivers (and the public) at risk of at-work crashes, inadequacies in regulatory oversight, vehicle defects that are cast as consumer issues rather than matters of health and safety or crime, the resistance of manufacturers to improve pedestrian safety through vehicle design and their staunch defence of self-regulation.

The quandary facing governments is that their hands are tied to a considerable extent by the power of their increasingly motorised electorates who may resist further curbs on the driving choices of the 'oppressed' motorist as voiced through their respective populist media. They are also hamstrung by the power wielded by the international motor lobby which has benefited through economic pressures on states to promote the car industry and thus car culture. Yet the inertia, delay and prevarication often linked with official responses must give way to more positive, decisive action to deal with these dilemmas. Doubtless, solutions will need tailoring to the sociocultural templates of individual democracies, and these may be hard fought for in view of increasing global embeddedness in car culture. The volume of preventable injuries and deaths caused by car crimes of all kinds means there can be no shirking from this task.

References

AA (Automobile Association) Public Policy Group (1998) *Drugs and driving: notes of a meeting of a panel of experts.* Basingstoke: AA.

AA (1999) *The Great British motorist 2000.* Basingstoke: AA.

AAA (American Automobile Association) (2000) *Unlicensed to kill.* Washington, DC: AAA Foundation.

Äberg, L. (1997) 'The role of perceived risk of detection'. In *Traffic and transport psychology: theory and application,* 395-402, (eds T. Rothengatter and E. Carbonell Vaya). Oxford: Pergamon.

Äberg, L., Larsen, L., Glad, A. and Beilinsson, L. (1997) 'Observed vehicle speed and drivers' perceived speed of others'. *Applied Psychology: An International Review,* 46(3): 287–302.

Adams, J. (1988) 'Risk homeostasis and the purpose of safety regulation'. *Ergonomics,* 31(4): 407–28.

Agnew, R. (1992) 'Foundation for a general strain theory of crime and delinquency'. *Criminology,* 30: 47–87.

Allen, T. (1999) *Coffins on wheels.* Hadleigh: Trading Standards Institute.

Alpert, G. (1987) 'Questioning police pursuits in urban areas'. *Journal of Police Science and Administration,* 15: 298–306.

Alvarez, F. and Del Rio, M. (1994) 'Drugs and driving'. *The Lancet,* 344: 282.

ASA (Advertising Standards Authority) (2000a) 'Adjudication regarding Peugeot motor company plc', 13.10.99. London: ASA.

ASA (2000b) 'Adjudication regarding Jaguar motor company plc', 9.2.00. London: ASA.

ASA (2000c) 'Self-regulation: background briefings: motoring', 21.12.00 (www.asa.org.uk/issues/background/show_briefing.asp?briefing_id=23).

Ashton, S. and Mackay, G. (1979) 'Some characteristics of the population who suffer trauma as pedestrians when hit by cars and some resulting implications'. Paper presented at the Fourth IRCOBI International Conference, Gothenberg.

Assailly, J.-P. (1999) 'Drink driving and young road users: epidemiology and prevention'. In *Behavioural research in road safety IX*, 179–87, (ed. G. Grayson). Crowthorne: Transport Research Laboratory (TRL).

Association of British Drivers (2002a) 'The truth about speed' (www.abd.org.ujk/speed_truth.htm).

Association of British Drivers (2002b) 'Rigging the evidence' (www.abd.org.uk/rigging_the_evidence.htm).

Ayres, M. and Hayward, P. (2001a) *Motoring offences and breath test statistics, England and Wales 2000. Statistical Bulletin*, 24/01. London: Home Office.

Ayres, M. and Hayward, P. (2001b) *Offences relating to motor vehicles England and Wales 2000: supplementary tables.* London: Home Office

Barbone, F., McMahon, A., Davey, P., Morris, A., Reid, I., McDevitt, D. and MacDonald, T. (1998) 'Association of road-traffic accidents with benzo-diazepine use'. *The Lancet*, 152: 1331–135.

Barclay, G., Tavares, C. and Siddique, A. (2001) *International comparisons of criminal justice statistics 1999. Statistical Bulletin*, 5/01. London: Home Office.

Barjonet, P. (1988) 'Sex differences in risk exposure and risk perception'. In *Road user behaviour: theory and research*, 133–8, (eds J. Rothengatter and A. de Bruin). Assen: Van Gorcum.

Barty-King, H. (1980) *A history of the first 75 years of the Automobile Association.* Basingstoke: AA.

BBC News Online (1999) 'UK drivers "arming against road rage"' (issued 6.4.99) (www.news.bbc.co.uk/hi/english/uk/newsid_312000/312908.htm).

BBC News Online (2002) 'Car-jacking law change urged' (issued 17.3.02) (http://news.bbc.co.uk/1/hi/uk/1877272.stm).

Beck, U. (1992) *Risk society: towards a new modernity.* London: Sage.

Black, J. (1993) *Drinking and driving: a decade of development.* Winchester: Waterside Press.

Bonnet, M. and Moore, S. (1982) 'The threshold of sleep: perception of sleep as a function of time asleep and auditory threshold'. *Sleep*, 65: 267–76.

Bottoms, A. (1999) Keynote address to British Criminology Conference, Liverpool.

Box, S. (1983) *Power, crime and mystification.* London: Tavistock.

BRAKE (2001) *The green flag report on safe driving.* Huddersfield: Brake.

Brennan, W. (1995) 'Driven to the edge'. *Nursing Standard*, 9(42): 41.

Brody, S. (1976) *The effectiveness of sentencing.* HORS, 35. London: HMSO.

Brookes, I. (1999) 'Local crime and disorder strategies and their contributions to reducing casualties and improving road safety'. Paper presented to the Association of Chief Police Officers Traffic Committee.

Broughton, J. (1993) *The actual number of non-fatal drink-drive accidents. TRL Project Report 40.* Crowthorne: TRL.

Broughton, J. (1999) *Analyses of driver licence records from DVLA. TRL Report* 403. Crowthorne: TRL.

Broughton, J. and Stone, M. (1998) *A new assessment of the likely effects on road accidents of adopting SDST. Project Report* TRL 368. Crowthorne: TRL.

Brown, I., Tickner, A. and Simmonds, D. (1969). 'Interference between concurrent tasks of driving and telephoning'. *Journal of Applied Psychology*, 53: 419–24.

Brown, R. (1995) *The nature and extent of heavy goods vehicle theft. Crime Detection and Prevention Series* Paper 66. London: Home Office.

Brown, R. and Saliba, J. (1998) *The nature and extent of light commercial vehicle theft. Crime Detection and Prevention Series*, Paper 88. London: Home Office.

Bryant, B. (1997) 'Road accidents: the impact on everyday life'. In *The aftermath of accidents*, 199–204, (ed. M. Mitchell). London: Routledge.

Buchanan, C. (1963) *Traffic in towns: a study of the long term problems of traffic in urban areas.* London: HMSO.

Bucks County Council (1992) *Internal memorandum on the effect of speed limit reductions in Buckinghamshire, May/June 1992.*

Burgess, C. (1999) *The National Driver Improvement Scheme – a psychological evaluation.* Devon and Cornwall Constabulary.

Burt, T. (2002) 'Move to safety warnings in car adverts dismays industry' (10.3.02). All-Ukrainian Advertising Coalition site (www.adcoalition.org.ua/coalition/at.html).

Campbell, B. (1993) *Goliath: Britain's dangerous places.* London: Methuen.

Car Care Clinic (2001) 'Vehicle recalls' (www.carcareclinic.com/newsarchive. asp).

Carsten, O. (2002) 'The effect of new technologies on speed distributions'. Paper presented at the Department for Transport Behavioural Studies Seminar, Dublin.

Carsten, O. and Comte, S. (2001) 'User trials with intelligent speed limiters'. In *Behavioural research in road safety: X*, 29–39 (ed. G. Grayson). London: DETR.

Carter, T. (2001) 'Fitness standards for the transport industries'. *Journal of the Royal Society of Medicine*, 94: 534–5.

Carter, T. (2002) 'Medical aspects of fitness to drive'. Paper presented at the Department for Transport Behavioural Studies Seminar, Dublin.

Chapman, P., Roberts, K. and Underwood, G. (2001) 'A study of the accidents and behaviours of company car drivers'. In *Behavioural research in road safety: X*, 61–73 (ed. G. Grayson). London: DETR.

Chapman, T. (1994) 'Toys for the boys, gender and car crime'. In *Proceedings from Masculinity and Crime conference, Brunel University, September 1993.*

Chapman, T. (1995) 'Creating a culture of change: a case study of a car crime project in Belfast'. In *What works: reducing reoffending: guidelines from research and practice*, 127–38, (ed. J. McGuire). Chichester: Wiley.

Chen, G., Meckle, W. and Wilson, J. (2002) 'Speed and safety effect of photo radar enforcement on a highway corridor in British Columbia'. *Accident Analysis and Prevention*, 34(2): 129–38.

Chenery, S., Henshaw, C. and Pease, K. (1999) *Illegal parking in disabled bays: a means of offender targeting. Briefing Note 1/99, HORS.* London: Home Office.

Clarke, R.V. (1999) *Hot products: understanding, anticipating and reducing demand for stolen goods. PRS Paper 112.* London: Home Office.

Clarke, R.V. and Cornish, D. (1985) 'Modeling offenders' decisions: a framework for research and policy'. In *Annual review of crime and justice. Vol. 6*, 147–85, (eds M. Tonry and N. Morris). Chicago, IL.: University of Chicago Press.

Clarke, R.V. and Harris, P. (1992) 'Auto theft and its prevention'. In *Crime and justice: a review of research. Vol. 16*, 1–54, (ed. M. Tonry). Chicago, IL: University of Chicago Press.

Clarke, R.V. and Mayhew, P. (1996) 'Preventing crime in parking lots: what we know and need to know'. In *Crime prevention through real estate management and development*. Washington, DC: Urban Land Institute.

Clarkson, J. (2000) 'My plan to cut congestion: ban all the bad drivers'. *The Sunday Times*, 14.5.00: 28, Motoring Section.

Clarkson, J. (2002a) 'Please keep the motorways clear for dads on a deadline'. *The Sunday Times*, 28.7.02: 22, Motoring Section.

Clarkson, J. (2002b) 'If you've got speed like this Audi's, nothing else matters'. *The Sunday Times*, 25.8.02: 26, Motoring Section.

Cohen, A. (1955) *Delinquent boys*. New York: Free Press.

Connell, D. and Joint, M. (1996) *Driver aggression*. Basingstoke: AA, Group Public Policy Road Safety Unit.

Connor, J., Whitlock, G., Norton, R. and Jackson, R. (2001) 'The role of driver sleepiness in car crashes: a systematic review of epidemiological studies'. *Accident Analysis and Prevention, 33*(1): 31–41.

Consumers' Association (1999) *Secret service: special report on garage servicing*. Caerphilly: Consumers Association.

Corbett, C. (1993) 'Discretion in practice: speed limit enforcement'. In *Behavioural research in road safety: III*, 38–48, (ed. G. Grayson). Crowthorne: TRRL.

Corbett, C. (1995) 'Road traffic offending and the introduction of speed cameras in England: the first self-report survey'. *Accident Analysis and Prevention*, 27(3): 345–54.

Corbett, C. (2000a) 'A typology of drivers' responses to speed cameras: implications for speed limit enforcement and road safety'. *Psychology, Crime and Law*, 6: 305–30.

Corbett, C. (2000b) 'The social construction of speeding as not "real" crime'. *Crime Prevention and Community Safety: An International Journal*, 2(4): 33–46.

Corbett, C. (2001) 'Explanations for "understating" in self-reported speeding behaviour'. *Transportation Research Part F: Psychology and Behaviour*, 4(2): 133–50.

Corbett, C. and Simon, F. (1991a). 'Unlawful driving behaviour: a criminological perspective'. Unpublished report submitted to TRL.

Corbett, C. and Simon, F. (1991b) 'Police and public perceptions of the seriousness of road traffic offences'. *British Journal of Criminology*, 31(2): 153–64.

Corbett, C. and Simon, F. (1992a) *Unlawful driving behaviour: a criminological perspective. Contractor Report* 310. Crowthorne: TRL.

Corbett, C. and Simon, F. (1992b) 'Decisions to break or adhere to the rules of the road, viewed from the rational choice perspective'. *British Journal of Criminology*, 32(4): 537–49.

Corbett, C. and Simon, F. (1999) *The effects of speed cameras: how drivers respond. Road Safety Research Report* 11. London: DETR.

Corbett, C., Simon, F. and Hyde, G. (1991) 'Driving with excess alcohol: why some drivers do and why some don't'. In *Behavioural research in road safety: II*, 108–117, (eds G. Grayson and J. Lester). Crowthorne: TRRL.

Corbett, C., Simon, F. and O'Connell, M. (1998) *The deterrence of high-speed driving: a criminological perspective. Contractor Report* 296. Crowthorne: TRL.

Coward, R. (2001) 'Males and motors'. *Guardian*, 9.5.01: 20.

CPS (Crown Prosecution Service) (1996) *Driving offences charging standard.* London: CPS.

CPS (2000) *The code for crown prosecutors.* London: CPS.

Croall, H. (1998a) *Crime and society in Britain.* London: Longman.

Croall, H. (1998b) 'Business, crime and the community'. *International Journal of Risk, Security and Crime Prevention*, 3(4): 281–92.

Croall, H. (2001) 'The victims of white collar crime'. In *White-collar crime research: old views and future potentials. Lectures and papers from a Scandinavian seminar, National Council for Crime Prevention. Sweden Bra-Report* 2001:1.

Daily Express (2000) 'Drivers facing speed limits purge'. 24.7.00: 1, 8 (Harrabin, R. and Swift G.).

Daily Express (2002) 'Why do they victimise motorists?'. 5.3.02: 1 (Marsh, G.).

Daily Mail (1999) 'Why do the police hate the middle classes?'. 15.9.99: 4.

Daily Mail (1999) 'War on the motorist'. 18.11.99: 1 (Hughes, D. and Massey, R.).

Daily Mail (1999) 'Blair puts a stop to lowering speed limit'. 27.11.99 (Eastham, P.).

Daily Mail (1999) 'Now Labour wants more motorists'. 18.12.99: 2.

Daily Mail (2001) 'Garage crackdown'. 19.9.01: 28.

Daily Mail (2002) 'Hundreds of speed cameras to be scrapped'. 21.5.02: 1 (Massey, R.).

Daily Telegraph (1993) 'Unit fines abolished in Clarke U-turn'. 14.5.93: 1–2.

Daily Telegraph (2000) 'Credit card crime'. 11.11.00. Motoring Section: 3 (Foxall, J.).

Davies, G., Broughton, J., Clayton, A. and Tunbridge, R. (1999b) *The High Risk Offender Scheme for drink-drivers. TRL Report* 394. Crowthorne: TRL.

Davies, G., Harland, G. and Broughton, J. (1999a) *Drink-driver rehabilitation courses in England and Wales. TRL Report* 426. Crowthrone: TRL.

Davis, G. (2002) 'Is the claim that "variance kills" an ecological fallacy?' *Accident Analysis and Prevention*, 34(3): 343–6.

Davis, R. (1992) *Death on the street: cars and the mythology of road safety.* Hawes: Leading Edge Press.

de Gier, J. (1993) *Driving licences and known use of licit or illicit drugs* (IHP 93–39). Maastricht: University of Limburg, Institute for Human Psycho-pharmacology.

de Gier, J. (1998) *Road traffic and illicit drugs: review of investigations of prevalence of illicit drugs in road traffic in different European countries* (P-PG/Circroit (98)1.1998). Strasbourg: Council of Europe, Pompidou Group.

de Haan, W. (1991) 'Abolitionism and crime control: a contradiction in terms'. In *The politics of crime control*, 203–17, (eds K. Stenson and D. Cowell). London: Sage.

Department of Health (1998) *The quantification of the effects of air pollution on health in the United Kingdom*. London: HMSO.

Department of Transport and Home Office (1988) *Road traffic law review report*. London: HMSO.

DETR (Department of the Environment, Transport and the Regions) (1998) *Combatting drink-driving – next steps*. London: DETR.

DETR (1999) *Transport statistics Great Britain 1999*. London: HMSO.

DETR (2000a) *Tomorrow's roads: safer for everyone*. London: DETR.

DETR (2000b) *New directions in speed management: a review of policy*. London: DETR.

DETR (2000c) *Work related road safety*. London: DETR.

DETR (2000d) *Summary of public response to the government's proposals in 'Combatting drink driving: next steps'*. London: DETR.

DETR (2000e) *Road accidents Great Britain 1999: the casualty report*. London: HMSO.

de Waard, D. and Rooijers, T. (1994) 'An experimental study to evaluate the effectiveness of different methods and intensities of law enforcement on driving speed on motorways'. *Accident Analysis and Prevention*, 26(6): 751–65.

de Young, D. (1997) *Evaluation of the specific deterrent effect of vehicle impoundment on suspended, revoked and unlicensed drivers in California* (RSS-97-171). Sacramento, CA: California State Deptartment of Motor Vehicles.

de Young, D., Peck, R. and Helander, C. (1997) 'Estimating the exposure and fatal crash rates of suspended/revoked and unlicensed drivers in California'. *Accident Analysis and Prevention*, 29(1): 17–23.

DfT (Department for Transport) (2001) '25 years of drink drive campaigns but the work goes on – Jamieson 20,000 lives saved since 1976'. News release 2001/0519: 4.12.01.

DfT (2002) *Road accidents Great Britain 2001: the casualty report*. London: HMSO.

Direct Line Insurance (2002) *A report on the effects of using a 'hand-held' and 'hands-free' mobile phone on road safety*. London: Direct Line Insurance.

Dowie, M. (1987) 'Pinto madness'. In *Corporate violence: injury and profit for death*, 13–29, (ed. S. Hills). Totowa, NJ: Rowman & Littlefield.

DTLR (Department for Transport, Local Government and the Regions) (2001a) *Road accidents Great Britain 2000: the casualty report*. London: HMSO.

DTLR (2001b) *A survey of public education literature regarding driver sleepiness*. London: HMSO (www.roads.dtlr.gov.uk/roadsafety/sleepiness/12.htm).

DTLR (2001c) *Transport statistics Great Britain 2001*. London: HMSO.

Elvik, R. (1997) *Status report* Vol. 32(3), 22 March. Oslo: Insurance Institute for Highway Safety.

Emsley, C. (1993) '"Mother, what *did* policemen do when there weren't any motors?" The law, the police and the regulation of motor traffic in England, 1900–1939'. *The Historical Journal*, 36(2): 357–31.

Emsley, C. (1997) 'The regulation of motor traffic in Britain'. In *Le Controle de la Circulation routiere dan les Pays de la CEE*, 77–89, (eds G. Kellens and C. Perez-Diaz). Paris: L'Harmattan.

Ericson, R. and Haggerty, K. (1997) *Policing the risk society.* Toronto: Toronto University Press.

ETSC (European Transport Safety Council) (1999) *Police enforcement strategies to reduce traffic casualties in Europe.* Brussels: ETSC.

ETSC (2001) 'ETSC urges MEPs to insist on pedestrian protection legislation to save 2000 lives'. Press release 22.11.01. Brussels: ETSC.

ETSC (2002) 'MEPS' decision on pedestrian protection: 2000 lives annually at stake'. Press release 16.4.02. Brussels: ETSC.

Everest, J., Davies, C. and Banks, S. (1990) *Roadside surveys of drinking and driving: England and Wales 1990.* TRL Report 319. Crowthorne: TRL.

Everest, J., Tunbridge, R. and Widdop, B. (1989) *The incidence of drugs in road accident fatalities. TRRL Report* RR202. Crowthorne: TRRL.

Eyecare Trust (2002) 'Millions of British drivers have poor vision' (www.eyecare-information-service.org.uk/pages/news/news1.htm).

Faith , N. (1998) *Crash.* London: Boxtree.

Farmer, C., Retting, R. and Lund, A. (1999) 'Changes in motor vehicle occupant fatalities after repeal of the national maximum speed limit'. *Accident Analysis and Prevention*, 31: 537–43.

Felson, M. and Clarke, R.V. (1998) *Opportunity makes the thief.* PRS Paper 98. London: Home Office.

FEVR (Federation Européene des Victims de la Route) (1995) *Executive summary: impact of road death and injury: proposals for improvements.* Geneva: FEVR.

Finch, D., Kompfner, P., Lockwood, C. and Maycock, G. (1994) *Speed, speed limits and accidents.* Project Report PR58. Crowthorne: TRL.

Finn, P. and Bragg, B. (1986) 'Perception of the risk of an accident by young and older drivers'. *Accident Analysis and Prevention,* 18: 289–98.

Flood-Page, C., Campbell, S., Harrington, V. and Miller, J. (2000) *Youth crime: findings from the 1998/99 Youth Lifestyles Survey.* HORS 209. London: Home Office.

Forensic Science Service (2000) 'DNA profiles on National Database top one million'. Press release 14.11.00 (www.forensic.gov.uk/forensic/news/press_releases/2000/131100.htm).

Forsyth, E. and Silcock, D. (1987) *The association of traffic offences with road accidents in the Northumbria police area.* TOSG Research Report 71. Newcastle: University of Newcastle upon Tyne.

Gallup (1990) *Car drivers' survey: company drivers versus ordinary drivers.* London: Social Surveys (Gallup Polls).

Garland, D. (2001) *The culture of control.* Oxford: Oxford University Press.

George, C. (2001) 'Reduction in motor vehicle collisions following treatment of sleep apnoea with nasal CPAP'. *Thorax*, 56(7): 508–12.

Gibbens, T. (1958) 'Car thieves'. *British Journal of Delinquency*, 8(4): 257–65.

Gibson, B. (1994) 'Crime and the motor car'. Paper presented at the conference 'Dealing with traffic offenders: current issues and future directions', Brunel University.

Goldberg, F. (1997) 'Swedish government is now field-testing the electronic driving licence'. In *Proceedings of the 14th International Conference on Alcohol, Drugs and Traffic Safety*, Annecy.

Gordon, W., Cuddy, P. and Wesson, A. (1998) *Introduction to road traffic offences*. Winchester: Waterside Press.

Gottfredson, M. and Hirschi, T. (1990) *A general theory of crime*. Stanford, CA: Stanford University Press.

Graham, J. and Bowling, B. (1995) *Young people and crime*. HORS 145. London: Home Office.

Grayson, G. (1999) 'Company cars and road safety'. In *Behavioural research in road safety IX*, 65–70, (ed. G. Grayson). Crowthorne: TRL.

Green, J. (1997) *Risk and misfortune: a social construction of accidents*. London: UCL Press.

Groombridge, N. (1994) 'The car and crime: is joyriding a male driving disorder?' In *Proceedings from Masculinity and Crime conference, Brunel University, September 1993*.

Groombridge, N. (1998) 'Masculinities and crimes against the environment'. *Theoretical Criminology*, 2 (2): 249–68.

Guardian (1999) 'BMW to invest £3.3bn in Rover over six years'. 24.6.99. Business Section: 21.

Guardian (1999) 'Transport now Labour's weak link'. 13.7.99: 21 (MacAskill, E.).

Guardian (1999) 'Judge admits drink driving'. 28.7.99: 6.

Guardian (1999) 'Motorway madness'. 19.10.99. G2: 2 (Glancey, J.).

Guardian (1999) 'Prescott thinks again on air traffic'. 2.12.99: 1 (Harper, K.).

Guardian (1999) 'Jams tomorrow'. 21.12.99: 17 (Probert, A.).

Guardian (2000) 'Police outline leeway on speeding'. 5.2.00: 5.

Guardian (2000) 'Crime targets cannot be met, say police'. 15.2.00: 13 (Travis, A.).

Guardian (2000) 'Policy and politics: road safety moves dismay campaigners'. 2.3.00: 12 (Harper, K.).

Guardian (2000) 'Cash for crime, drugs and asylum backlog'. 19.7.00: 5 (Travis, A.).

Guardian (2000) 'Tougher police line on speeding'. 25.7.00: 7 (Press Association).

Guardian (2000) 'Adventure that ended in coach crash tragedy: EU rules lay down driving hours and rest periods'. 8.8.00 (Ward, D.).

Guardian (2000) 'Mitsubishi admits 30-year cover-up of vehicle defects'. 30.8.00: 26 (Watts, J.).

Guardian (2000) 'OFT "too soft" on rogue car dealers'. 30.8.00: 8 (Watt, N.).

Guardian (2001) 'Selby crash driver faces lengthy prison sentence'. 14.12.00: 1 (Ward, D.).

Guardian (2002) 'Illegal dumping fear over scrap cars'. 2.2.02: 5 (Brown, P.).

Gulliver, N. (1991) Unpublished questionnaire survey. Northumbria Probation Service.

Gusfield, H., Kotarba, J. and Rasmussen, P. (1981) 'Managing competence: an ethnographic study of drinking-driving and the context of bars'. In *Social drinking contexts. Research Monograph 7*, 155–72, (eds T. Harford and L. Gaines). Washington, DC: US Government Printing Office.

Haglund, M. and Äberg, L. (2000). 'Speed choice in relation to speed limit and influences from other drivers'. *Transportation Research: Part F*, 3: 39–51.

Haigney, D. and Taylor, R. (1998). 'Mobile phone use whilst driving: phone operation vs vehicle transmission'. Birmingham: ROSPA (www.rospa.co.uk/pdfs/mobiles/studies.pdf).

Harland, G. and Lester, J. (1997) *Does retesting deter dangerous driving?* TRL Report 252. Crowthorne: TRL.

Harrison, W. (1997) 'An exploratory investigation of the crash involvement of disqualified drivers and motorcyclists'. *Journal of Safety Research*, 28(3): 213–19.

Hartenfels, M. (2001) 'Product recalls – current developments and trends'. FORUM (www.erc-frankona.com/forum/forum08_en/e05_rueckruf.html).

Heaps, C. (2001) *Traffic Commissioners' annual report 2000–2001: Chapter 3 for South Eastern and Metropolitan Traffic Area*. London: DTLR.

Heaton, R. (1997) *Criminal law*. London: Blackstone Press.

Hedderman, C. and Sugg, D. (1997) *Changing offenders' attitudes and behaviour: what works*. HORS 171. London: Home Office.

Hetherington, A., Munro, A. and Mitchell, M. (1997) 'At the scene: road accidents and the police'. In *The aftermath of accidents*, 113–22, (ed. M. Mitchell). London: Routledge.

Hillman, M. (1993) *Time for change*. London: Policy Studies Institute.

Hinchliffe, M. (1994) *Professional car thieves: their knowledge and social structure*. London: Home Office.

Hindmarch, I. (1986) 'The effects of psychoactive drugs on car handling and related psychomotor ability: a review'. In *Drugs and driving*, 71–82, (eds J. O'Hanlon and J. Grier). Philadelphia, PA: Taylor & Francis.

Hirschi, T. (1969) *Causes of delinquency*. Berkeley, CA: University of California Press.

HMIC (Her Majesty's Inspector of Constabulary) (1998) *Road policing and traffic. HMIC thematic inspection report 1998*. London: Home Office.

Hobbs, C. and Mills, P. (1984) *Injury probability for car occupants in frontal and side impacts. TRRL Report* 1124. Crowthorne: TRL.

Holdaway, S. (1983) *Inside the British police: a force at work*. Oxford: Blackwell.

Home Office (1998) *Reducing offending: an assessment of research evidence on ways of dealing with offending behaviour*. HORS 187. London: Home Office.

Home Office (2000a) *Car theft index*. London: Home Office.

Home Office (2000b) *Road traffic penalties: a consultation paper*. London: Home Office.

Home Office (2000c) 'Regulatory impact assessment' (www.Homeoffice.gov.uk/vcb/vcb1.htm).

Home Office (2000d) 'Regulatory impact assessment. regulating the supply of number plates' (www.Homeoffice.gov.uk/vcb/vcb4.htm).

Home Office (2000e) 'Regulation of the motor salvage industry' (www.Homeoffice.gov.uk/vcb/vcb2.htm).

Home Office (2000f) 'Proposal to introduce the vehicle identity check (VIC) scheme' (www.Homeoffice.gov.uk/vcb/vcb3.htm).

Home Office (2002a) *Report on the review of road traffic penalties.* London: Home Office.

Home Office (2002b) *Entitlement cards and identity fraud – consultation paper.* CM 5557. London: HMSO.

Homel, R. (1988) *Policing and punishing the drinking driver.* New York, NY: Springer Verlag.

Homel, R. (1993) 'Drivers who drink and rational choice: random breath testing and the process of deterrence'. In *Routine activity and rational choice. Advances in criminological theory. Vol. 5,* 59–84, (eds R.V. Clarke and M. Felson). New Brunswick, NJ: Transaction.

Hood, R. (1972) *Sentencing the motoring offender.* London: Heinemann.

Hooke, A., Knox, J. and Portas, D. (1996) *Cost benefit analysis of traffic light and speed cameras. PRS Paper* 20, Police Research Group. London: Home Office.

Hopkins Burke, R. (2001) *An introduction to criminological theory.* Cullompton: Willan.

Horne, J. and Barrett, P. (2001) *Over-the-counter medicines and the potential for unwanted sleepiness in drivers: a review. Road Safety Research Report* 24. London: DTLR.

Horne, J. and Reyner, L. (1995) 'Sleep-related vehicle accidents'. *British Medical Journal,* 6979: 565–7.

Horne, J. and Reyner, L. (1997) 'Driver sleepiness'. In *Behavioural research in road safety VII,* 82–9, (ed. G. Grayson). Crowthorne: TRL.

Horne, J. and Reyner, L. (2001) *Driver sleepiness: overview of findings from phase 3 of DETR research programme.* London: DTLR.

Horswill, M. and McKenna, F. (1999) 'The effect of perceived control on risk-taking'. *Journal of Applied Social Psychology,* 29(2): 337–91.

Hotten, R. (1999) *Formula One: the business of winning.* London: Orion.

Houghton, G. (1992) *Car theft in England and Wales: the Home Office car theft index. CPU Paper* 33. London: Home Office.

Howarth, G. (1997) 'Death on the road: the role of the English coroner's court in the social construction of an accident'. In *The aftermath of accidents,* 144–58, (ed. M. Mitchell). London: Routledge.

HSA (Hospital Savings Association) (2002) 'Eye tests could cut road accidents' (www.hsa.co.uk/news/020131.1.asp).

HSE (Health and Safety Executive) (2001a) *Work related road safety: initial regulatory impact assessment* (www.hse.gov.uk/road/content/ria.pdf).

HSE (2001b) 'Work-related road safety task group: preventing at-work road traffic incidents' (www.hse.gov.uk/disdocs/closed/dde16.htm).

Illustrated London News Supplement (1986) *Century of the motor car 1986–96.* April issue.

The Independent (1997) 'Forget about Swampy. All they want is their own car'. 19.11.97: 5 (Veash, N. and O'Sullivan, J.).

The Independent (1999) 'Compulsory car immobilisers plan is attacked'. 23.9.99: 3 (Judd, T.).

The Independent (1999) 'Prescott makes a U-turn to woo drivers'. 28.11.99: 1 (Carr-Brown, J.).

The Independent (2000) 'Faking crash to shock joyriders is too "traumatic"'. 10.3.00 (Bennetto, J.)

The Independent (2000) 'Labour's eight-year poll lead ends as Blair is blamed for crisis'. 17.9.00: 4 (Brown, C. and Dillon, J.).

The Independent (2001) 'Volvo in "killer brakes" inquiry'. 20.5.01: 4 (Lichfield, J.).

The Independent (2001) 'Police tell death-chase inquiry of "red mist" risk'. 5.11.01: 2 (Bennetto, J.).

The Independent (2001) 'One-armed driver was over limit and talking on mobile'. 24.11.01: 16 (Peachey, P.).

Ingram, D., Lancaster, B. and Hope, S. (2001) *Recreational drugs and driving: prevalence survey.* Scottish Executive (www.scotland.gov.uk/cru/kd01/blue/prevalence-00.htm).

Institute of Transportation Engineers (1999) *Automated enforcement in transportation.* Victoria: Institute of Transportation Engineers.

Jackson, D. (1992) 'Riding for joy'. *Achilles Heel,* summer issue.

Jacobs, G., Aeron-Thomas, A. and Astrop, A. (2000) *Estimating global road fatalities.* TRL Report 445. Crowthorne: TRL.

Jacobson, J., Davison, T. and Tarling, R. (2002) *Tackling abandoned and untaxed vehicles: an evaluation of operation Cubit.* RDS On-line Report 11/02. London: Home Office (www.homeoffice.gov.uk/rds/pdfs2/rdsolr1102.pdf).

Joint, M. (1995) *Road rage.* Basingstoke: Automobile Association Group Public Policy Road Safety Unit.

Jones, E. and Nisbitt, R. (1972) 'The actor and the observer: divergent perceptions of the causes of behaviour'. In *Attributing: perceiving the causes of behaviour,* (ed. E. Jones). Morristown, NJ: General Learning Press.

Jones, S. (1998) *Criminology.* London: Butterworths.

Junger, M. (1994) 'Accidents'. In *The generality of deviance* (eds T. Hirschi and M. Gottfredson). New Brunswick, NJ: Transaction.

Junger, M., Terlouw, G.-J. and van der Heijden, P. (1995) 'Crime and accident involvement in young road users'. In *Behavioural research in road safety V,* 35–54, (ed. G. Grayson). Crowthorne: TRL.

Junger, M., West, R. and Timman, R. (2001) 'Crime and risky behavior in traffic: an example of cross-situational consistency'. *Journal of Research in Crime and Delinquency,* 38(4): 439–59.

Keane, C., Maxim, P. and Teevan, J. (1993) 'Drinking and driving, self-control and gender: testing a general theory of crime'. *Journal of Research in Crime and Delinquency*, 30(1): 30–46.

Kershaw, C., Budd, T., Kinshott, G., Mattinson, J., Mayhew, M. and Myhill, A. (2000) *The 2000 British Crime Survey: England and Wales*. Issue 18/00. London: Home Office.

Kilpatrick, R. (1997) 'Joy-riding: an addictive behaviour?'. In *Addicted to crime*, 165–90, (eds J. Hodge, M. McMurran and C. Hollin). Chichester: Wiley.

Kinchin, D. (1990) *Drivers on the banned wagon: a research project into disqualified drivers living in Oxfordshire*. Thames Valley Police.

Kinshott, G. (2001) *Vehicle related thefts: practice messages from the British Crime Survey. PRCU Briefing Note* 6/01. London: Home Office.

Knight Ridder Inc. (2000) 'Mitsubishi Motors gets expected slap on wrist in cover-up case' (www.auto.com/autonews/cwira3_20001003.htm).

Kunzli, H., Kaiser, R., Medina, S., Studnicka, M., Chanel, O., Filliger, P., Herry, M., Horak, F., Puybonnieux-Texier, V., Quenel, P., Schneider, J., Seethaler, R., Vergnand, J.-C. and Sommer, H. (2000) 'Public health impact of outdoor and traffic-related air pollution: a European assessment'. *The Lancet*, 356 (9232): 795.

LAAU (London Accident Analysis Unit) (1997) *West London speed camera demonstration project*. London: Highways Agency.

Lajunen, T. and Parker, D. (2001) 'Are aggressive people aggressive drivers? A study of the relationship between self-reported general aggressiveness, driver anger and aggressive driving'. *Accident Analysis and Prevention*, 33(2): 243–55.

Lajunen, T., Parker, D. and Summala, H. (1999) 'Does traffic congestion increase driver aggression?'. *Transportation Research Part F: Traffic Psychology and Behaviour*, 2(4): 225–36.

Larsen, S. (1998) 'Safety last'. Mother Jones (17.2.98) (www.motherjones.com/mother_jones/SO77/larsen.html).

Leaseplan (2001) 'Leaseplan organises 3d European drivers survey' (www.leaseplan.be/LP/LP.nsf.e44bc0).

Ledger, A. (2001) *The use and characteristics of vehicle stock data. Transport Trends*. London: DETR.

Lennox, R. and Quimby, A. (1990) *A survey of drink-driving behaviour, knowledge and attitudes. TRL Contractor Report* 147. Crowthorne: TRL.

Levelt, P. (1998) *Aggressive behaviour in traffic*. Leidschendam: SWOV.

Lex (1989) *The 1989 Lex report on motoring*. London: Lex.

Lex (1997) *The 1997 Lex report on motoring*. London: Lex.

Lex (1999) *The 1999 Lex report on motoring*. London: Lex.

Light, R. (1988) 'Drinking, driving, and the legal profession'. *Howard Journal*, 27(3): 188–97.

Light, R., Nee, C. and Ingham, H. (1993) *Car theft: the offender's perspective*. HORS 130. London: Home Office.

Lombroso, C. (1876) *L'Uomo delinquente* (5th edn). Turin: Bocca (first published Milan: Hoepli).

London Research Centre (1998) *Women's travel in London.* London: LRC.

Lynn, P. and Lockwood, C. (1998) *The accident liability of company car drivers.* TRL Report 317. Crowthorne: TRL.

Mackie, A. (1998) *Urban speed management methods.* TRL Report 363. Crowthorne: TRL.

Mannheim, H. (1960) 'Review of Wootton: social science and social pathology'. *Jewish Journal of Sociology*, II: 57.

Marks, J. and Cross, G. (1992) *An evaluation of the Turas project.* Belfast: The Extern Organisation.

Marsh, P. and Collett, P. (1986) *Driving passion: the psychology of the car.* London: Cape.

Marshall, E. and Thomas, N. (2000) *Traffic calming: the reality of 'road rage'. Briefing Note* 12/00. London: Home Office.

Marshall, S. (1986) 'Motoring into the future'. *Illustrated London News Supplement*, April.

Matthews, G., Desmond, P., Joyner, L., Carcary, B. and Gilliland, K. (1997) 'A comprehensive questionnaire measure of driver stress and affect'. In *Traffic and transport psychology*, 317–24, (eds J. Rothengatter and V. Carbonnell). Oxford: Pergamon.

Matthews, P. and Foreman, J. (1993) *Jervis on the office and duties of coroners* (11th edn). London: Sweet & Maxwell.

Maxwell, R. (2000) 'Going . . . going . . . gone'. *Canadian Insurance*, 105(3): 18–20.

Maycock, G. (1996) 'Sleepiness and driving: the experience of UK car drivers'. *Journal of Sleep Research*, 5: 229–37.

Maycock, G. (1997) *Drinking and driving in Great Britain – a review. TRL Report* 232. Crowthorne: TRL.

Maycock, G., Brocklebank, P. and Hall, R. (1998) *Road layout design standards and driver behaviour. TRL Report* 332. Crowthorne: TRL.

Mayhew, P. (1990) 'Opportunity and vehicle crime'. In *Policy and theory in criminal justice: contributions in honour of Leslie T. Wilkins*, 29–50, (eds D. Gottfredson and R.V. Clarke). Aldershot: Gower.

Mayhew, P., Clarke, R. and Elliot, D. (1989) 'Motorcycle theft, helmet legislation and displacement'. *Howard Journal of Criminal Justice*, 28: 1–8.

Mayhew, P. and van Dijk, J. (1997) *Criminal victimisation in eleven industrialised countries.* Netherlands: Wetenschappelijk Onderzoek- en Documentatiecentrum.

Mayou, R. (1997) 'The psychiatry of road traffic accidents'. In *The aftermath of accidents*, 33–48, (ed. M. Mitchell). London: Routledge.

McCullough, D., Schmidt, T. and Lockhart, B. (1990) *Car theft in Northern Ireland. Cirac Paper* 2. Belfast: The Extern Organisation.

McKenna, F. (1993) 'It won't happen to me: unrealistic optimism or illusion of control?' *British Journal of Psychology*, 84: 39–50.

McKenna, F., Waylen, A. and Burkes, M. (1998) *Male and female drivers: how different are they?* Basingstoke: AA Foundation for Road Safety Research.

Merton, R. (1938) 'Social structure and anomie'. *American Sociological Review*, 3: 672–82.

Messerschmidt, J. (1993) *Masculinities and crime: critique and reconceptualization of theory.* Lanham, MD: Rowman & Littlefield.

Mirrlees-Black, C. (1993) *Disqualification from driving: an effective penalty?* HORPU 74. London: HMSO.

Mirrlees-Black, C., Budd, T., Partridge, S. and Mayhew, P. (1998) *The 1998 British Crime Survey: England and Wales. Statistical Bulletin* 21/98. London: Home Office.

Mitchell, M. (ed.) (1997a) *The aftermath of accidents.* London: Routledge.

Mitchell, M. (1997b) 'Death and injury on the road'. In *The aftermath of accidents*, 3–14, (ed. M. Mitchell). London: Routledge.

Mizell, L. (1997) *Aggressive driving.* Washington, DC: AAA Foundation for Traffic Safety.

Montagu of Beaulieu (1986) 'Pioneers of the motoring age'. *Illustrated London News Supplement*, April.

Mori Financial Services (2001) 'Direct Line survey reveals drivers approve of speed cameras' (2.8.01) (www.mori.com/polls/2001/dl-01720.shtml).

Motor Insurers Bureau (1998) *Motor Insurers Bureau Newsletter*, 1. Milton Keynes: MIB.

Muncie, J. (2001) 'The construction and deconstruction of crime'. In *The problem of crime*, 8–70, (2nd edn) (eds J. Muncie and E. McLaughlin). London: Sage.

Muncie, J. and McLaughlin, E. (eds) (2001) *The problem of crime.* (2nd edn). London: Sage.

NHTSA (National Highway Traffic Safety Administration) (1998) *Auto theft and recovery: effects of the Anti Car Theft Act of 1992 and the Motor Vehicle Theft Law Enforcement Act of 1984. Report to the Congress.* DOT HS 808 761. Washington, DC: NHTSA.

Norris, C., Moran, J. and Armstrong, G. (eds) (1999) *Surveillance, closed circuit television and social control.* Aldershot: Ashgate.

Norris, F. (1992) 'Epidemiology of trauma: frequency and impact of different potentially traumatic events on different demographic groups'. *Journal of Consulting and Clinical Psychology,* 60(3): 409–18.

O'Connell, M. and Whelan, A. (1996) 'Taking wrongs seriously: public perceptions of crime seriousness'. *British Journal of Criminology*, 36(2): 299–318.

OFT (Office of Fair Trading) (2000) 'Car servicing and repair industry should clean up its act, says Bridgeman' (10.8.00) (www.oft.gov.uk/News/Press+release/2000/PN+32-00.htm).

OFT (2001) 'Annexe E: consumer complaints' (www.oft.gov.uk/NR/rdonlyres.htm OFT).

O'Malley, P. (1992) 'Risk, power and crime prevention'. *Economy and Society*, 21 (3): 252–75.

PACTS (Parliamentary Advisory Council for Transport Safety) (1999) *Road traffic law and enforcement*. London: PACTS.

PACTS (2001) 'Safer car fronts for vulnerable users' (www.pacts.org.uk/ pedprotectionMPbrief.htm).

Parker, D., Lajunen, T. and Summala, H. (2002) 'Anger and aggression among drivers in three European countries'. *Accident Analysis and Prevention*, 34(2): 229–35.

Parker, H. (1974) *View from the boys: a sociology of Down Town adolescents*. Aldershot: Gregg Revivals.

Partridge, E. (1984) *Dictionary of slang and unconventional English* (8th edn). London: Routledge & Kegan Paul.

Paternoster, R. (1987) 'The deterrent effect of the perceived certainty and severity of punishment: a review of the evidence and issues'. *Justice Quarterly*, 4: 173–217.

PCA (Police Complaints Authority) (2001) *The 2000/2001 annual report*. London: HMSO.

Pearce, L., Knowles, J., Davies, G. and Buttress, S. (2002) *Dangerous driving and the law*. Road Safety Research Report 26. London: DTLR.

Pease, K. (2001) 'Rational choice theory'. In *The Sage dictionary of criminology*, 235–6, (eds E. McLaughlin and J. Muncie). London: Sage.

Pettifer, J. (1986) 'Engine of social change'. *Illustrated London News Supplement*, April.

Philip, P., Vervialle, F., Le Breton, P., Taillard, J. and Horne, J. (2001) 'Fatigue, alcohol, and serious road crashes in France: factorial study of national data'. *British Medical Journal*, 322: 829–30.

Philpotts, G. and Lancucki, L. (1979) *Previous convictions, sentence and reconviction*. HORS 53. London: HMSO.

Porter, J. (1999) 'Driving and musculoskeletal health'. *Ergonomics*, 17(7): 8–11.

Porterfield, A. (1960) 'Traffic fatalities, suicide, and homicide'. *American Sociological Review*, 25: 897–901.

Public Citizen (2001) 'Chronology of Firestone/Ford knowledge of tire safety defect' (www.citizen.org/autosafety/articles.cfm?ID=5336).

Quimby, A., Maycock, G., Palmer, C. and Grayson, G. (1999) *Drivers' speed choice: an in-depth study*. TRL Report 326. Crowthorne: TRL.

Rabbit, P. (2001) 'Using lab tests to predict age-related changes in driving competence'. In *Behavioural research in road safety: X*, 179–95, (ed. G. Grayson). London: DETR.

RAC (Royal Automobile Club) (2000) *RAC report on motoring 2000*. Feltham: RAC Motoring Services.

RAC (2001) *RAC report on motoring 2001*. Feltham: RAC Motoring Services.

RAC (2002) *RAC report on motoring 2002*. Feltham: RAC Motoring Services.

RAC Foundation (2001) 'Code breakers: Highway Code proves to be an enigma'. Press release, 20.4.01. London: RAC Foundation.

Reason, J., Manstead, A., Stradling, S., Baxter, J. and Campbell, K. (1990) 'Errors and violations on the road: a real distinction?'. *Ergonomics*, 33(10/11): 1315–32.

Recarte, M. and Nunes, L. (1996) 'Perception of speed in an automobile: estimation and production'. *Journal of Experimental Psychology: Applied*, 2(4): 291–304.

Red Cross and Red Crescent Societies (1998) *World disasters report 1998*. Oxford: Oxford University Press.

Redelmeier, D. and Tibshirani, R. (1997) 'Association between cellular-telephone calls and motor vehicle collisions'. *New England Journal of Medicine*, 336(7): 453.

Reiner, R. (2002) 'Media made criminality: the representation of crime in the mass media'. In *The Oxford handbook of criminology*, 376–416, (eds M. Maguire, R. Morgan and R. Reiner) (3rd edn). Oxford: Clarendon.

Research Services Limited (1994) *Drink driving: a survey of male offenders*. London: The Portman Group.

Retail Motor Industry Federation (2002) 'Facts and figures' (www.epolitix.dev.x-port.net/Data/Companies). London: RMIF.

Reyner, L., Flatley, D. and Horne, J. (2002) *Sleep-related vehicle accidents on sections of selected trunk roads and motorways in the UK (1995–1998)*. Road Safety Research Report 22. London: DfT.

Rix, B., Walker, D. and Brown, R. (1997) *A study of deaths and serious injuries resulting from police vehicle accidents*. PRG Ad Hoc Paper AH312. London: Home Office.

RoadPeace (1997) *Newsletter*, 9: Spring. London: RoadPeace.

RoadPeace (2002) *Inquests and road deaths*. London: RoadPeace.

Robinson, C. (1979) 'Reasons for driving while disqualified'. *Accident Analysis and Prevention*, 11: 307–10.

Rolls, G. and Ingham, R. (1992) *'Safe and 'unsafe' – a comparative study of younger male drivers*. Basingstoke: AA Foundation for Road Safety Research.

Rose, G. (2000) *The criminal histories of serious traffic offenders*. HORS 206. London: Home Office.

RoSPA (Royal Society for the Prevention of Accidents) (1998) *Managing occupational road risk*. Birmingham: RoSPA.

RoSPA (1999) 'New research links mobile phones with road accidents'. Press release, 25.2.99. Birmingham: RoSPA.

Ross, H. (1985) 'Deterring drunken driving: an analysis of current efforts'. *Journal of Studies on Alcohol*, supplement 10: 122–8.

Rothengatter, J. (1988) 'Risk and the absence of pleasure: a motivational approach to modelling road user behaviour'. *Ergonomics*, 31(4): 599–607.

Sabey, B. (1989) 'Road safety: inside the general figures'. In *Drinking to your health*, 118–36, (ed. D. Anderson). London: Social Affairs Unit.

Sabey, B. (1999) *Road safety: back to the future.* Basingstoke: AA Foundation for Road Safety Research.

Sallybanks, J. (2001) *Assessing the police use of decoy vehicles.* Briefing Note Paper 137. London: Home Office.

Sallybanks, J. and Brown, R. (1999) *Vehicle crime reduction: turning the corner.* PRS Paper 119. London: Home Office.

Sallybanks, J. and Thomas, N. (2000) 'Thefts of external vehicle parts: an emerging problem'. *Crime Prevention and Community Safety: An International Journal,* 2(3): 17–22.

Sampson, F. (1999) *Police manual: road traffic, 2000 edition.* London: Blackstone Press.

Scraton, P. and Chadwick, K. (1991) 'The theoretical and political priorities of critical criminology'. In *The politics of crime control,* 161–87, (eds K. Stenson and D. Cowell). London: Sage.

Sexton, B., Tunbridge, R., Brook-Carter, N., Jackson, P., Wright, K., Stark, M. and Englehart, K. (2000) *The influence of cannabis on driving.* TRL Report 477. Crowthorne: TRL.

Sherwood, N. (1998) *A critical review of the effects of drugs other than alcohol on driving.* Report prepared for AA Group Public Policy Drugs and Driving Seminar July.

Shinar, D. (1998) 'Speed and crashes: a controversial topic and an elusive relationship'. In *Managing speed: review of current practice for setting and enforcing speed limits. National Research Council Special Report* 254. Washington, DC: Transportation Research Board.

Shinar, D. and McKnight, A. (1985) 'The effects of enforcement and public information on speed compliance'. In *Human behaviour and traffic safety* (eds L. Evans and R. Schwing). New York, NY: Plenum Press.

Silcock, D., Smith, K., Knox, D. and Beuret, K. (1999b) *What limits speed? Factors that affect how fast we drive.* Basingstoke: AA Foundation for Road Safety Research.

Silcock, D., Sunter, A. and Van Lottum, C. (1999a) *Unlicensed driving: a scoping study to identify potential areas for further research.* Basingstoke: AA Foundation for Road Safety Research.

Simmons, J. (ed.) (2002) *Crime in England and Wales 2001/02. Issue* 07/02. London: Home Office.

Simon, F. and Corbett, C. (1991) 'A small roadside study of drivers caught breaking speed limits'. In *Behavioural research in road safety II,* 25–36, (eds G. Grayson and J. Lester). Crowthorne: TRL.

Simon, F. and Corbett, C. (1996) 'Road traffic offending, stress, age, and accident history among male and female drivers'. *Ergonomics,* 39(5): 757–80.

Sivak, M. (1983) 'Society's aggression level as a predictor of traffic fatality rate'. *Journal of Safety Research,* 14: 93–9.

Smith, A. (1999) *Motor projects reviewed: current knowledge and good practice. PRCU Ad Hoc Paper* 183. London: Home Office.

Smith, D. and Gray, J. (1985) *Police and people in London.* Aldershot: Gower.

Smith, D. and Maisey, G. (1994) *Survey of driving by disqualified and suspended drivers in Western Australia.* Report CR94. Canberra: Office of Road Safety.

SMMT (Society of Motor Manufacturers and Traders) (2002) 'Commission expected to consider tougher car advertising rules'. The Week in Brussels: w/e 15.3.02 (www.smmt.co.uk/downloads/weeklywb/binb150302.doc).

Smyth, G. (1990) Unpublished questionnaire survey. Greater Manchester Probation Service.

Soothill, K., Francis, B. and Fligelstone, R. (2002) *Patterns of offending behaviour: a new approach.* London: Home Office (www.homeoffice.gov.uk/rds/rfpubs1.htm).

Sorenson, D. (1994) 'Motor vehicle accidents'. In *The generality of deviance*, 113–29, (eds T. Hirschi and M. Gottfredson). New Brunswick, NJ: Transaction.

Spencer, E. (1992) *Car crime and young people on a Sunderland housing estate.* CPU Paper 40. London: Home Office.

Stanko, E. and Newburn, T. (eds) (1994) *Just boys doing business.* London: Routledge

Stenson, K. and Sullivan, R. (eds) (2001) *Crime, risk and justice.* Cullompton: Willan.

Stradling, S. (1997) 'Violators as "crash magnets"'. In *Behavioural research in road safety: VII*, 4–9, (ed. G. Grayson). Crowthorne: TRL.

Stradling, S. (1999) 'Why drivers speed'. In *Speed: whose business is it?'*. London: PACTS.

Stradling, S. (2001) 'Driving as part of your work may damage your health'. In *Behavioural research in road safety: X*, 74–83, (ed. G. Grayson). London: DETR.

Strand, G. Jr and Garr, M. (1994) 'Driving under the influence'. In *The generality of deviance*, 131–49, (eds T. Hirschi and M. Gottfredson). New Brunswick, NJ: Transaction.

Stuster, J., Coffman, Z. and Warren, D. (1998) *Synthesis of safety research related to speed and speed management.* FHA-NHTSA publication. Washington, DC: NHTSA (www.tfhrc.gov/safety/speed/spdtoc.htm).

Stutts, J., Reinfurt, D., Staplin, L. and Rodgman, E. (2001) *The role of driver distraction in traffic crashes.* Washington, DC: AAA Foundation for Traffic Safety.

Stutts, J., Wilkins, J., Osberg, J. and Vaughn, B. (in press) 'Driver risk factors for sleep-related crashes'. *Accident Analysis and Prevention*.

Suchman, E. (1970) 'Accidents and social deviance'. *Journal of Health and Social Behaviour,* 11(1): 4–15.

Sugg, D. (1998) *Motor projects in England and Wales: an evaluation.* Research Findings 81. London: Home Office.

Summala, H. and Mikkola, T. (1994) 'Fatal accidents among car and truck drivers: effects of fatigue, age and alcohol consumption'. *Human Factors*, 36: 315–326.

The Sun (2000) 'The great petrol revolt of 2000'. 12.9.00: 1.

Sunday Telegraph (2000) 'Life sentences for dangerous drivers who kill'. 2.1.00: 17 (Bamber, D.).

The Sunday Times (1996) 'Drivers rush for "speed" policies'. 21.1.96. Money Section: 1.

The Sunday Times (1998) 'US puts brake on teen car dreams'. 2.8.98: 19 (Campbell, M.).

The Sunday Times (1998) 'It's a steel: how car gangs beat trackers'. 15.11.98: 9 (Macaskill, M. and Dignan, C.).

The Sunday Times (1999) 'So why aren't we getting enough?'. 17.1.99. Magazine Section: 36 (Martin, P.).

The Sunday Times (1999) 'Motor giants give MPs secret cut-price car deals'. 30.5.99: 1.

The Sunday Times (1999) 'Speed limit will be cut to 50 mph'. 19.9.99: 1 (Prescott, M.).

The Sunday Times (1999) 'Cars that shaped the century'. 26.12.99. Motoring Section: 17 (Hutton, R.).

The Sunday Times (2000) 'Cannabis may make you a safer driver'. 13.8.00: 3 (Carr-Brown, J.).

The Sunday Times (2001) 'Volvo faces death charge on brake fault'. 27.5.01: 7 (Ungoed-Thomas, J. and Bell, S.).

The Sunday Times (2001) 'Ford's feud with Firestone backfires'. 10.6.01. Business Section: 7 (Alexander G.).

The Sunday Times (2002) 'Call that service or just a con?' 3.2.02. Good Car Bad Car Section: 32–3 (Baker, S.).

The Sunday Times (2002) 'Corrugated road to replace humps'. 10.3.02: 5 (Leake, J. and Watt, G.).

The Sunday Times (2002) 'The road with the most speed cameras in England'. 21.4.02 (Dobson, R.).

Sustrans (1997) *Safety on the streets for children. Information Sheet* 10. Bristol: Sustrans.

Sutherland, E. (1949) *White collar crime.* New York, NY: Dryden Press.

Sutton, M. (1998) *Handling stolen goods and theft: a market reduction approach.* HORS 178. London: Home Office.

Svenson, O. (1981) 'Are we all less risky and more skilful than our fellow drivers?' *Acta Psychologica,* 47: 143–8.

SWOV (1998) *SARTRE2: the attitudes and behaviour of European car drivers to road safety. Part 1.* Leidschendam: SWOV.

Sykes, G. and Matza, D. (1957) 'Techniques of neutralisation: a theory of delinquency'. *American Sociological Review,* 22.12.57: 664–70.

Taylor, H. (1999) 'Forging the job: a crisis of "modernization" or redundancy for the police in England and Wales 1900–1939'. *British Journal of Criminology,* (39)1: 113–35.

Taylor, M., Lynam, D. and Baruya, A. (2000) *The effects of drivers' speed on the frequency of road accidents.* Transport Research Laboratory Report 421. Crowthorne: TRL.

Thurston, G. and Krewski, D. (2002) 'Lung cancer, cardiopulmonary mortality, and long-term exposure to fine particulate air pollution'. *Journal of the*

American Medical Association, 287 (9): 1132–41.

Tillmann, W. and Hobbs, G. (1949) 'The accident-prone automobile driver'. *American Journal of Psychiatry*, 106: 321 31.

The Times (1995) 'Police unit fights international car racket gangs'. 26.5.95 (Tendler, S.).

The Times (1997) 'Car theft rivals drugs in world crime earnings'. 17.2.97 (August, O.).

The Times (1998) 'Straw blames lax sentencing for £2bn car crime'. 30.4.98: 9 (Fresco, A.).

The Times (1998) 'Know the limit'. 2.2.98: 21.

The Times (1998) 'New laws will be aimed at the four-pint driver'. 27.4.98: 1 (Leathley, A.).

The Times (1999) 'Driver in fatal crash was on mobile phone'. 4.2.99: 3.

The Times (1999) 'Highway Code attacks in-car gadgets'. 27.2.99: 3 (Leathley A.).

The Times (1999) 'Jury decides 145 mph is not dangerous'. 25.3.99: 13 (Leathley, A.).

The Times (1999) 'One in 20 coaches unsafe to drive'. 26.7.99: 5 (Lawson, A.).

The Times (1999) 'Prescott's slips cost him dear'. 13.12.99: 8 (Leathley, A.).

The Times (2000) 'Advert booked for speeding'. 9.2.00: 9.

The Times (2000) 'Driver fined for 183 mph road death'. 16.6.00: 13.

The Times (2000) 'So crime does pay'. 23.6.00: 27 (Mall, E.).

The Times (2000) 'Widdecombe falls for speed trap'. 5.8.00: 3 (Pierce, A.).

The Times (2000) 'Straw's driver not to be prosecuted'. 25.11.00: 9.

The Times (2001) 'Firms reject driving plans'. 1.3.01: 12 (Studd, H.).

The Times (2001) 'Locked out car gangs resort to hijacking'. 17.4.01: 10 (Fresco, A. and Tendler, S.).

The Times, (2001) 'Thieves target drivers' airbags'. 20.1.01. Motoring Section: 41.

The Times (2001) 'Driver jailed for fatal phone text'. 15.2.01: 3 (Fresco, A.).

The Times (2001) 'Carmakers seek to soften impact of safety rules'. 13.8.01: 6 (Webster, B.).

The Times (2001) 'Byers "caves in" on car safety'. 23.10.01: 12 (Webster, B.).

The Times (2001) 'Crushing blow aimed at dumped car wrecks'. 1.11.01: 15 (Webster, B.).

The Times (2002) 'Driver on drink charge number twelve'. 5.1.02: 9.

The Times (2002) 'Ban on use of mobiles in cars is rejected'. 8.5.02: 9 (Webster, B.).

The Times (2002) 'Memorial to road deaths planned'. 7.6.02: 12 (Ford, R.).

The Times (2002) 'Diabetic is cleared over 100 mph death crash'. 4.7.02 (Studd, H.).

Tombs, S. (1999) 'Health and safety crimes: (in)visibility and the problems of knowing'. In *Invisible crimes: their victims and their regulation*, 77–104, (eds P. Davies, P. Francis and V. Jupp). Basingstoke: Macmillan.

Traffic Safety Village (2000) *Global web conference on aggressive driving issues* (www.aggressive.drivers.com).

Tremblay, P., Clermont, Y. and Cusson, M. (1994) 'Jockeys and joyriders'. *British Journal of Criminology*, 34(3): 307–21.

TRL (Transport Research Laboratory) (1998) *Transport Research Laboratory News.* December: 6. Crowthorne: TRL.

TUC (Trades Union Congress) (2001) 'TUC response to the work-related Road Safety Task Group discussion document on preventing at-work road traffic incidents.' Issued 9.6.01 (www.tuc.org.uk/h_and_s/tuc-3261.f0.cfm).

Tunbridge, R. (2001) 'The influence of cannabis on driving'. In *Behavioural Research in Road Safety: X,* 215–29, (ed. G. Grayson). London: DETR.

Tunbridge, R., Keigan, M. and James, F. (2001) *The incidence of drugs and alcohol in road accident fatalities.* TRL Report 495. Crowthorne: TRL.

Tversky, A. and Kahneman, D. (1981) 'The framing of decisions and the psychology of choice'. *Science,* 211: 453–8.

van Kesteren, J., Mayhew, P. and Nieuwbeerta, P. (2001) *Criminal victimisation in 17 industrialised countries: key findings from the 2000 International Crime Victims Survey.* The Netherlands: Wetenschappelijk Onderzoek- en Documentatie-centrum.

VCRAT (Vehicle Crime Reduction Action Team) (1999) *Tackling vehicle crime: a five year strategy.* London: Home Office.

Victim Support (1994) *Support for the families of road death victims: report of an independent working party convened by Victim Support.* London: Victim Support.

Waddon, A. and Baker, C. (1998) *The driver's view: drivers' opinions and behaviour in connection with motoring and the police.* Bangor: University of Wales Bangor.

Ward, N. and Dye, L. (1999) *Cannabis and driving: a review of the literature and commentary.* Road Safety Research Report 12. London: DETR.

Webb, B. and Laycock, G. (1992) *Tackling car crime: the nature and extent of the problem.* CPU Paper 32. London: Home Office.

Webster, D. and Wells, P. (2000) *The characteristics of speeders.* TRL Report 440. Crowthorne: TRL.

Weglian, S. (1978) 'Testimony'. Mimeographed. New York State, Committees on Transportation and Consumer Protection. Washington, DC: US Department of Justice.

West, R., Elander, J. and French, D. (1992) *Decision making, personality and driving style as correlates of individual accident risk.* Contractor Report 309. Crowthorne: TRL.

Whitlock, F. (1971) *Death on the road: a study in social violence.* London: Tavistock.

Wilde, G. (1986) 'Beyond the concept of risk homeostasis: suggestions for research and application towards the prevention of accidents and lifestyle-related disease'. *Accident Analysis and Prevention,* 18(5): 377–401.

Wilkins, G. and Addicott, C. (1999) *Motoring offences.* Issue 12/99. London: Home Office.

Wilkinson, J. (1997) 'The impact of Ilderton motor project on motor vehicle crime and offending'. *British Journal of Criminology,* 37(4): 568–81.

Willett, T. (1964) *Criminal on the road.* London: Tavistock.

Willett, T. (1973) *Drivers after sentence.* London: Heinemann.

Wilson, J.Q. and Kelling, G. (1982) 'Broken windows: the police and neighbourhood safety'. *The Atlantic Monthly*, March.

Young, J. (1999) *The exclusive society.* London: Sage.

Zedner, L. (2002) 'Victims'. In *The Oxford handbook of criminology*, 419–56, (eds M. Maguire, R. Morgan and R. Reiner) (3rd edn) Oxford: Clarendon.

Index

abandoned and untaxed vehicles
  probable causes and potential
    solutions 173–5
  scope of the problem 172–3
accessibility, of cars 20
accident risks
  company car drivers 185
  delinquency 138–9
  legal drugs 89
  mobile phones 144, 145
  speed 105
  unlicensed driving 162, 166–7
accidental death 150
accidents discourse
  marginalisation of car crime 31
  speeding 118
acquittals, bad driving offences
  134
administrative loopholes, unlicensed
  driving 171–2
adolescent boys, pressure to establish
  masculinity 56–9
advertising 182–4
age
  drink-driving 82
  driving ability 74
agent provocateur tactics 63–4

aggravated vehicle-taking 50–1
Aggravated Vehicle-taking Act (1992)
  40
aggression see road rage
air pollution 2
airbags, theft of 49
alcohol-impaired driving see drink-
  driving
alcopops 99, 177–8
amphetamines 87
antihistamines 89–90
apnoea 101
articulated heavy goods vehicles,
  speeding 110
assessment, driver impairment 75
Association of National Driver
  Improvement Schemes 156
attempted vehicle thefts 42
attrition rates, recorded theft offences
  42–3
Austin Seven 18
automatic enforcement cameras
  197–8
Automobile Association 17, 18, 107
awareness
  of car theft 62–3
  fatigue-impaired driving 98–9

bad driving 128–59
  crime control efforts 154–7
  extent and trends in offences
    133–40
  historical and legal context 131–3
  mobile phones and in-vehicle
    distractions 143–7
  perspectives of victims and
    bereaved 149–53
  police vehicle accidents 147–9
  road rage 141–3
badges, theft of 49
bags, theft of 49
benzodiazepines 88, 89
bereaved
  impacts of road crashes 195
  perspectives, bad driving 149–53
Beresford 1952 149
Blennerhasset Committee of Enquiry
  (1976) 76
blocked opportunities, unlicensed
  driving 169
blood-alcohol concentrations
  drivers discouraged from driving
    85–6
  fatally-injured drivers 80
  international threshold variations
    101
blood-alcohol limit 75–6
  amendments to 95
  male drivers exceeding 119
bonnets 181–2
BRAKE 91
breath testing
  police powers 95–6
  random 94
breath tests
  figures 78–9
  rise in positive 99
breath-alcohol interlock ignition
  devices (BAIDS) 100, 199
breath-alcohol limit, amendments to
  95
breathalysers 76
Bridgestone/Firestone 180
British Crime Surveys

emotional dependence on cars 1,
  37–8
joyriding 51
owner carelessness and car theft
  62
road rage 141
vehicle theft
  comparison with Criminal
    Statistics 42, 43
  extent of 41
  stolen parts 48–9
bumpers 181–2
burnt-out vehicles 173
buses, speeding 110

campaigns
  against road building 21
  see also publicity campaigns
Canada
  crash risk and hands-free phones
    144
  rise in professional theft 46
cannabis
  impaired driving 86–7
  reclassification of 96, 194
car crime
  defined 4–7
  future prospects 196–201
  key themes 11–12
  legacy of the past 191–3
  marginalisation of 25–35
  present concerns and dilemmas
    193–5
  research 4
  as theft of and from a vehicle
    37–70
  theoretical perspectives 8–11
  topical nature of 3
  in wider society 177–89
car culture
  excluded categories 192
  growing up and into 66–7
  our embeddedness within 1–3
  social harm 7
  social history of the car 193
  unchecked transgressions 177

vehicle theft as byproduct of 69
car dealers, unscrupulous 6
'car as master' 192
car parts, loss of value 173
car supremacy 158–9
Car Theft Index 47
car usage 18
career progression, in crime 53, 54
careless driving
    acquittals 134
    contentious issues in discourse
        about 129–30
    convictions 133, 134, 136
    downgrading dangerous driving
        to 150
    driver improvement schemes 156
    established as an offence 19
    fatal crash outcomes 135
    general theory of crime 140
    guilt pleas 134–5
    offences 128
    offenders 136, 137
    penalties 133
    unlicensed driving linked with 166
    use of for breach of law where
        death is concerned 158
carelessness 130
carjackings 62, 193
cars 15–23
    increasing accessibility and road
        casualties 18–19
    a privilege of the elite 16–17
    speeding, observed incidences
        109–10
    towards millennium and the
        challenges ahead 20–3
causing death or bodily harm
    acquittals 134
    convictions 133–4, 136
    fatal crash outcomes 135
    offenders 137
causing death by negligent driving
    158
CCTV cameras, in theft hotspots 64
CDDD see causing death or bodily
    harm

chassis numbers, professional theft
    60–1
children, victims of speed 105
class, joyriding 56–7
clock changes, crashes due to 97–8,
    178
coaches, speeding 110
cognitive processes, speeding 115–16
commercial vehicles, theft of and
    from 41
community penalties 155–6
companies
    disregard for employee safety
        186–8
    lack of safety culture 195
company car drivers
    accident risk 185
    fatigue-impaired driving 97
    road rage 142
    road traffic offences 186
    speeding 113–14
complacency, working drivers' safety
    186
compulsion, car theft as 55, 57
conformers, speed cameras 122, 123
constructions, of car crime 6, 30–1, 69
consumerist discourse 186–8
contents and parts, vehicle theft
    48–50
convictions
    bad driving (1961–2000) 133–4
    drink-driving 79–80
    driving whilst disqualified 165
coroners' figures, illegal drink-
    driving 78
coroners' inquests 149–50
corroboration, speeding offences 108
cost, of vehicle theft 37
crashes
    as blameless accidents 192
    correlation between speed and 105
    death toll see death toll
    due to time changes 97–8, 178
    excessive speed 27
    motorways 74, 91
    police investigations 151

psychological and physical effects
152–3
requirement to stop after 17
sleep-related 92
through human error 116
with tiredness as cause 6
work-related road risk 184–5
see also accident discourse;
accident risks; police vehicle
accidents
crime control
bad driving 154–7
impaired driving 93–100
speeding 120–1
unlicensed driving 170–2
vehicle theft 62–8
Crime and Disorder Act (1998) 27
criminal court proceedings 150
criminal damage, to vehicles 41
Criminal Justice Act (1988) 40
Criminal Justice Act (1991) 107
Criminal Justice Act (1993) 76
criminal justice system, road traffic
offending 27–8
Criminal Law Act (1977) 131
criminal purposes, vehicle theft for
53
Criminal Statistics
joyriding 51
vehicle theft 42, 43
criminality
defining in motoring sphere 7
drink-drivers 83
critical criminology
ideological construction of car
crime 6
marginalisation of car crime
29–31
cross-cultural aspect, road rage 142
culture *see* car culture; safety culture,
masculine culture
custody, impaired driving
convictions 77–8

dangerous 130–1
dangerous drivers, convicted 195

dangerous driving
acquittals 134
aggravated vehicle-taking 51
cases withdrawn 135
contentious issues in discourse
about 129–30
convictions 133, 134
downgrading to careless driving
150
fatal crash outcomes 135
offenders 136–8
dashboard displays 145
death toll
bad driving 135–6
drink-driving 72
drug-impaired driving 86
global statistics 2
police vehicle accidents 147
speeding 27, 104–5
working drivers 184
declining rate, vehicle theft 44
decoy vehicles 63
defective vehicles 186–8
defiers, of speed cameras 122, 123
delinquency, accidents risks 138–9
dementia 74
demographics
drink-drivers 82
joyriding 51
vehicle theft 47
detection, unlicensed vehicles 175
deterred drivers, speed cameras 122,
123
deterrence 8
drink-driving 84, 94
length of imprisonment for
dangerous driving 154
sentencing strategies 65–6
devastated professionals, drink-
drivers 83
deviant drivers, speeding connected
to 125
discretionary disqualifications
impaired driving 77
road traffic offences 26
speeding offences 108–9, 117

displacement, situational prevention 64–5

disposal, useless vehicles 173–4

disqualification orders, driving whilst disqualified 162, 165

disqualifications
bad driving offences 155–6
introduction of 17
unawareness about 98–9
see also discretionary disqualifications

disqualified drivers 169–70, 195

DNA samples, taking of 64

'Don't give them an easy ride' campaign 62–3

double jeopardy rules 150

drink-drivers, sympathy for 72

drink-driving
attempts to control the incidence of 72
enforcement and sanctions 94–6
established as an offence 19
explanations for 84–6
extent and trends 78–81
increase in 194
legislation 75–7
linked to dangerous driving 137
magistrates convicted of 26
masculine constructions of fitness to drive 85
offenders 81–3
speeding 114
unlicensed driving linked with 166

driver impairment, assessment and definition of 75

Driver Improvement Schemes 156–7

drivers
aged over seventy 74
aggressiveness *see* road rage
assessment of mental state 20
belief in superiority of their own driving 200
obligation to report changes in well-being 74
option to plead guilty by post 26
reactions to speed cameras 122–4

screened in roadside breath tests (1990–2000) 78–9

self-confessed speeders 111–12
see also dangerous drivers; disqualified drivers; drink-drivers; offenders; police drivers

driving
as a dangerous occupation 184
offending behaviours 6–7
see also bad driving; drink-driving; impaired driving; joyriding; speeding; unlicensed driving

driving whilst disqualified 162–3, 165, 167–8, 169

driving without due care and attention 7, 132

drug-impaired driving 73
controls on 96–7
established as an offence 19
illegal drugs
explanations for 88
extent and trends 86–7
offenders 88
legal drugs
effect on driving 194
explanations for 90
extent and trends 88–90
measuring 77
unlicensed driving linked with 166

dual carriageways, speeding on 110

dumping, useless vehicles 173–4

duties of care, under the HSWA 186

DWD *see* driving whilst disqualified

education
about speed 124–5
fatigue-impaired driving 77, 98
to eliminate bad habits 199–201
unlicensed driving 171
see also awareness

either-way offence, TWOC 40

electoral power, downgrading of car-related offending 33

electronic immobilisers 65

elite
    cars as a privilege of 16–17
    ideological construction of crime
        6, 30–1
elitist attitudes 192, 200
emergency responses, by police 147
emergency service workers, PTSD
    153
emotional buzz, of thieving 55
emotional dependence, on cars 1–2
employers *see* companies
End of Vehicle Life Directive (EU) 173
enforcement
    car theft laws 63–4
    drink-driving 94–6
    roads policing 196–7
    to deter speeding infractions 121–5
engineering countermeasures,
    speeding 120–1
entitlement cards 198
entry skills, car crime 53
environmental pollution 2, 17
epilepsy 74
ethnicity, vehicle theft 47
European Federation of Road Traffic
    Victims 150, 151, 152, 153
European Public Health Alliance 182
European vehicles, stolen 61
excessive speed
    fatal crashes 27
    as problem of 'the other driver'
        194
Explorer sports utility vehicle 180
exportation, stolen vehicles 60–1
external vehicle parts, theft of 49
eyesight 6–7, 178

family involvement, car crime 53
fatalities *see* death toll
fatigue-impaired driving 74–5
    education about dangers of 77
    explanations for 92–3
    extent and trends 90–1
    measures to reduce 97–8
    offenders 92
    raising awareness of 98–9

fear, of road rage 141
female car thieves 51–2
female drivers
    lapses of attention 136
    relationship with cars 118
fines
    impaired driving 77–8
    speeding 107
    unlicensed driving 162, 170
Firestone tyres 180
fitness to drive
    masculine constructions of 85
    notification of changes in 163
fleet driver effect 185
Ford Motors
    Explorer sports utility vehicle 180
    Model T car 18
    pedestrian protection tests 182
    Pinto 179–80
foreign-made cars, professional theft
    61
four-wheel-drive vehicles 120
fraudulent deals, legislation against
    67–8

garage servicing 187
gender
    downgrading of car-related
        offending 32
    see also males; women
gender-based theories 11
    drink-driving 85
    joyriding 56–9
general theory of crime 9–10
    bad driving 138–40
    drink-driving 85–6
    fatigue-impaired driving 93
    speeding 115
good law, *Beresford 1952* 149
governments
    challenge of appeasing opposing
        interests 2
    'hands-off' approach to car
        manufacturers 183–4
    quandary facing 201
    response to tackling speed 125–6

Great Petrol Revolt (2000) 22
guilt pleas
    by post 26
    careless driving 134–5

hand-eye co-ordination 77, 96
hands-free phones, accident risk 144
Health and Safety at Work Act
    (HSWA) 186
Health and Safety Executive (HSE)
    184
High Risk Offenders, drink-driving
    82–3
high speed, and advertising 183
high-speed police chases 40, 58
Highway Code, ignorance of 73
human error, crashes through 116
hypothecation debate 108

ideological construction, of crime 6,
    30–1
Ilderton motor project 67
illegal drugs, impaired driving 73,
    86–8
impaired driving 72–102
    alcohol-impaired driving 78–86
    crime control efforts 93–100
    drug-impaired driving
        illegal drugs 86–8
        legal drugs 88–90
    fatigue-impaired driving 90–3
    historical and legal context 75–8
imprisonment
    bad driving 154–5
    car theft 40, 65–6
in-vehicle distractions 143–7, 178
in-vehicle smart speed limiters 121
individual level theories 8–9
    drink-driving 84
    fatigue-impaired driving 93
    joyriding 54
    speeding 115–17
injury risk, reducing 181–2
insurance
    compulsory third party 19
    unlicensed driving 162

insurance companies, secondary
    victimisation 151
insurance costs, untaxed vehicles
    174
insurance fraud 60, 67
insurance policies, disqualifications
    for speeding 117
international comparisons
    drink-driving 81
    vehicle theft 46
international crime rings 193–4
intrinsic enjoyment, speeding 116

joyriding 19, 50–9
    explanations 54–9
    offenders 51–3
    police scare tactics stunt 63
juveniles *see* young people

Labour government, transport policy
    21–3
lack of intention 28, 192
lapses of attention 132, 136
legal drugs, impaired driving 73,
    88–90, 194
legal explanations, downgrading of
    traffic offences 28–9
legislation
    against fraudulent deals 67–8
    drink-driving 75–7
    see also individual acts; road traffic
        law
Lex survey 111
licence-carrying 162, 172
limited rationality, drink-driving 86
lobbying power, motor industry
    182
Locomotive Act (1861) 16
Locomotive Act (1865) 16
Locomotive and Highways Act (1896)
    16
long distance journeys 98
loss of income, injured survivors 153
low self-control 9, 140
luxury cars, theft and exportation of
    60–1

M1 19
magistrates, convicted of motor
    offences 26
Magistrates' Court Act (1980) 26
male drivers
    dangerous driving 136, 137
    risk of victimisation, vehicle theft
        46
    speeding 118–19
males
    attraction to risk 59
    drink-driving 82
    involvement in car crime 51
manipulators, speed cameras 122, 123
marginalisation
    of car crime 25–35
    consequences of bad driving 158
masculine constructions, of fitness to
    drive 85
masculine culture, showing of high-
    speed skills 58
masculinity
    perceptions of low seriousness of
        illegal driving 32
    pressure to establish, joyriding
        56–9
    and risk-taking, young drivers 140
media
    hypothecation debate 108
    marginalisation of car crime 33
medication see legal drugs
middle-class youth, joyriding 56–7
Mini Minor 19
Mitsubishi, product recall 181
mobile phones 143–5, 195
mobility restrictions, impaired
    driving 73
Model T car (Ford) 18
model-specific indices, car theft 47
money, theft of 49
MOT repairs, untaxed vehicles 174
Motor Car Act (1903) 17, 131
Motor Car Bill (1902) 17
motor courts 25–6
motor industry
    global economic health 106

influence wielded by 192–3
    lobbying power 182
motor manufacturers
    advertising and self-regulation
        182–4
    car crime 6
    product recall 179–81
    reducing injury risk 181–2
motor projects 66–7
motor salvage businesses 67
motor skill co-ordination 77, 96
Motor Vehicles (Driving Licences)
    Regulations (1996) 163
motorcycles
    speeding 110
    theft of 65
motorways 19
    crashes, fatigue-impaired driving
        74, 91
    speeding on 110t
mummy's boy hypothesis 56
mutual support, victims and
    bereaved 152

National Criminal Recording
    Standard (2002) 41
National Driver Improvement
    Schemes 156–7
National Highway Traffic Safety
    Administration (NHTSA) 179
National Safety-first Association 18
navigational products, as distractions
    145, 146, 178
need to drive fast 116
negligences, commercial road safety
    186–8
neoliberalism 32–3, 62
neurotic family relationships, car
    theft 57
neutralisation 10–11, 55–6, 168–9
New Drivers Act (1995) 163
noise, early objections to 17
normal driving, acceptance of risk
    28–9
normalisation 10–11, 55–6
North report 20–1, 76

number plates *see* registration plates

observed incidence, speeding 109–11
offenders
    bad driving 136–8
    bestialisation of 63
    drink-driving 81–3
    drug-impaired driving 88
    fatigue-impaired driving 92
    joyriders 51–3
    professional theft 60
    speeding 113–14
    unlicensed driving 167–8
Offenders Index 83, 137, 138, 163, 167
older vehicles, attraction to thieves 48
one-offs, drink-drivers 83
opportunity reduction 64, 69, 198–9
outcomes
    bad driving offences 134
    fatal accidents 135–6
over-the-counter medicines, warning
    labels 90, 97, 178, 194
owner carelessness, car theft 62–3
ownership, of cars 17, 19, 21

PACTS 95, 170, 182
Paris to Madrid road race (1903) 18
parking, vehicle theft 47
parts *see* car parts; contents and parts
past, legacy of 191–3
Pearce study 150, 154
pedestrian safety 181–2
penalties
    bad driving offences 154
    careless driving 133
    impaired driving 76
    speeding 108
    unlicensed drivers 162, 163
penalty points
    gender comparison 119
    proposal to increase 122
perceived seriousness
    road traffic offending 25–33
    speeding 117–18
perceptual distortions, speeding
    115–17

performance driving 40, 53, 58
permanent deprivation, theft for
    39, 40, 45–6, 59–62
persistent drink-drivers 83
personality traits
    drink-driving 84
    and speeding 115–17
petrol prices, rising 22
physical effects, road trauma 152–3,
    195
Pinto (Ford) 179–80
police
    breath testing powers 95–6
    brushes with the well-to-do 17
    crash investigations 151
    enforcement and sanctions,
        speeding 121–5
    targeting of drink-drivers 82
    see also traffic police
police chases 40, 57–8
police drivers, training 149
police vehicle accidents
    behind the statistics 148–9
    onus on officers 148
    role of pursuits and emergency
        responses 147
Policy Studies Institute (PSI) 58
political construction, car crime 69
post-traumatic stress disorder (PTSD)
    153
pressure groups 21, 22
pressures *see* social pressure; work
    pressures
privatised prudentialism 62
procurators' fiscal figures, drink-
    driving 78
product recall 179–81
professional theft 39, 45–6, 59–62
prosecutions
    for speeding
        increase in 111, 121
        warning of intended 108
    unlicensed drivers 162
    vehicle abandonment 174
prospect theory, drink-driving 84
protest groups, road humps 120

provisional licences 163
   holders' awareness of restrictions 171
   offences 164
psychological effects, road trauma 152–3, 195
psychotropic drugs 89
PTSD *see* post-traumatic stress disorder
public car parks, vehicle theft 47
publicity campaigns
   car theft 62–3
   impaired driving 98–9, 199–200
pursuits, by police 147

racing cars 18
ramraiding 40
random breath testing 94
rational choice perspective 8–9
   drink-driving 84
   fatigue-impaired driving 93
   joyriding 54
reckless driving 17, 20
recorded offences, vehicle theft 42–3
recovered stolen vehicles 45
red lights, driving through 119
Refuse Disposal Act (1978) 174
refuters, drink-drivers 83
registration plates
   introduction of 17
   removal of 49
   secure system for 67–8
rehabilitative education, impaired driving 100
removal costs, useless vehicles 174
Removal and Disposal of Vehicles (England) (Amendment) Regulations (2002) 174
reoffending
   bad driving offences 155–6
   impaired driving 78
   through neutralisation 10
reported incidences, speeding 111–12
research, car crime 4
rest periods, drivers 97
retesting, bad driving offences 155–6

riders, screened in roadside breath tests 78–9
'right to drive' 192
ringers 60
ringing 60
risk
   acceptance of, in normal driving 28–9
   of injury, reducing 181–2
   of victimisation, vehicle theft 46–7
   see also accident risks; work-related road risk
risk compensation, speeding 116
risk society 62
risk-taking
   joyriders 58, 59
   male drivers 119
Rix study 148
road casualties
   car accessibility 18, 19
   drink-drive accidents 78, 79t
   reductions after Road Safety Act 76
Road Deaths Working Group 152
road humps 120
road races 18
road rage
   definitions and prevalence 141–2
   fatal crashes 140
   increase in 195
   a reflection of our times 143
   unique phenomena 142
   unlicensed drivers 166–7
road safety, commercial disregard for 186–8
Road Safety Act (1967) 20, 75–6, 107
road safety strategy 22
Road Traffic Act (1930) 19, 39, 75, 107, 131
Road Traffic Act (1956) 131
Road Traffic Act (1962) 39
Road Traffic Act (1972) 131
Road Traffic Act (1988) 76, 132
Road Traffic Act (1991) 20, 21, 76, 122, 131, 132, 133, 136, 157
road traffic law

accident avoidance 28
integral to criminal law 108
North report 76
offences 5
Road Traffic Law Review (1985) 20–1, 23, 131
Road Traffic Offenders Act (1988) 76, 108, 163
road traffic offending
company car drivers 186
low perceived seriousness
explanations for 28–33
illustrations of 25–8
Road Traffic Penalty Review 23, 95, 121–2, 154, 156, 170
Road Traffic Regulation Act (1984) 108
Road Transport Act (1934) 19, 107
road type, vehicle speeds 110
RoadPeace 21, 136, 149
roads police *see* traffic police
roadside surveys, drink drivers 80, 82
roadworthiness, testing 19
routine activity theory 54
Royal Society for the Prevention of Accidents (RoSPA) 184
rulemakers 6

safety culture, employers' lack of 195
safety hazards 19
safety measures 20
safety warnings, car advertisements 183
sanctions
drink-driving 94–6
speeding 121–5
SARTRE projects 80–1, 111
scrap metal prices 173, 174
secondary victimisation 151
security features 61
security measures 45
self control, and crime 9
self-esteem, showing off high-speed skills 58
self-help organisations 152
Self-Propelled Traffic Association 16

self-regulation, motor manufacturers 182–4
self reports
alcohol-impaired driving 81
drug-impaired driving 87
fatigue-impaired driving 91
joyriding 51
speeding 111–13
sensory impairment 73–4
sentencing deterrent strategies 65–6
short periods, speeding disqualifications 117–18
side-effects, medication 73, 101
single carriageways, speeding on 110t
situational prevention, vehicle theft 64–5
sleep disorders 97, 101
sleep-related crashes 92
smart speed limiters 121, 199
smell, early objections to 17
social construction, car crime 69
social control theories 9–10
bad driving 138–40
social factors, unlicensed driving 168
social harm, car culture 7
social history, car culture 193
social pressure, speeding 116–17
social theories 10–11
social utility, of cars 29
socio-economic factors, car crime 53
South Wales Police, scare tactics 63
speed
controlling the attraction and desirability of 124–5
engendering an attitude change 194–5
speed cameras
effects of, gender comparison 118–19
introduction of and reactions to 122–4
speed limit offences (1997–2000) 111
speed limits
abolishing of 19, 107
crash rates 105
debate about enforcement of 22

raising of 16, 17
vehicles travelling in excess of
(2000) 109–10
Speed Policy Review 22, 107–8
speed traps, resentment against 17
speeding 104–27
    crime control efforts 120–1
    decriminalisation of 18
    extent and trends in 109–18
    fatalities due to 27
    gender comparison 118–20
    historical and legal context of
        107–9
    police enforcement and sanctions
        121–5
standards of driving, variability
    between 75
statistics, occupational casualty
    figures 185
STATS 19
    crash statistics 118
    drink-driving 78, 79t
    sleep-related crashes 91
steering column locks 65
stereo equipment, theft of 48, 49, 50
strain theory 10, 169
structural-level theories 10–11
subcultural explanations, crime 168
support, for victims and bereaved
    151–2
survivors of crashes, psychological
    and physiological impacts 195
symbols, on medicines 97
sympathy, drink-drivers 72

taking a conveyance without the
    owner's consent (TWOC) 40
taking and driving away (TDA) 39,
    44
targeted vehicles 47–8
technological controls
    impaired driving 100
    speeding 120–1
    vehicle document and driving
        licence offences 198
technological distractions 145–6

telephones, theft of 49
temporary use, theft for 39, 45–6,
    50–9
testing, roadworthiness 19
Thatcherism, downgrading of car-
    related offending 32–3
theft see vehicle theft
Theft Act (1968) 39–40, 44, 45
theoretical perspectives, car crime
    8–11, 59
time changes, crashes due to 97–8,
    178
Tin Lizzie 18
tiredness
    as cause of crashes 6
    measuring 194
tracking technology 64
traffic congestion 2, 16, 21
traffic police
    antipathy towards enforcement
        activities 18
    numbers 26–7, 196–7
traffic volumes 1
traffic-calming installations 120
training, police drivers 149
tranquilisers 89
Transport 2000 22
Transport Act (1981) 76, 82
Transport Bill (1999) 21
transport policy, Labour 21–3
trap vehicles 63
TURAS project 66–7
TWOC see taking a conveyance
    without the owner's consent

undetected drink drivers 80
unfitness criterion, impaired driving
    77
unit fine system 107
United States
    car theft 47
    road rage 142
unlicensed driving 161–76
    abandoned and untaxed vehicles
        172–5
    crime control efforts 170–2

extent and trends in 164–70
historical and legal context 163
recognition of problem 195
unrecovered stolen vehicles 45–6
untaxed vehicles *see* abandoned and
untaxed vehicles
urban roads, speeding on 110t

VASCAR system 108
Vehicle (Crime) Act (2001) 174
Vehicle Crime Reduction Action
Team 62
vehicle defects, cover ups 6
vehicle forfeiture 170–1
vehicle interference and tampering 41
vehicle theft 3, 4, 37–70
for contents and parts 48–50
crime control efforts 62–8
extent and trends of 40–8
historical and legal context 39–40
international crime rings 193–4
for permanent deprivation 59–62
recognition of offences 19
scale of global problem 201
for temporary use 50–9
Victim Support 151–2
victimisation, risk of, vehicle theft
46–7
victims
perspectives, bad driving 149–53
of vehicle theft 37–8
Victims' Charter 152
violence, in car theft 61
Volkswagen Beetle 18
Volvo, product recall 181
vulnerability, to theft 47

warning labels, over-the-counter

medicines 90, 97, 178, 194
well-being, obligation to report
changes in 74
white man's crime, joyriding as 52
women
drink-driving 82
risk of victimisation, vehicle theft
46
see also female car thieves; female
drivers
work pressures, sleepy driving 93
work-related road risk
blame for crashes 184–5
driving as a dangerous occupation
184
problems with regulation
defective vehicles and
consumerist discourse 186–8
focus on immediate rather than
root causes 186
inadequate statistics 185
wrecked vehicles 173

young people
drift into offending 10–11, 55–6
drink-driving 83
expressions of masculinity, bad
driving 140
involvement in car crime 51, 52, 53
rise in positive breath tests 99
risk of victimisation, vehicle theft
46
speeding 113
unlicensed driving 165, 167
Young People and Crime survey
(YPAC) 165, 167, 168, 170

zero tolerance policy, speeding 107